The Yale Ben Jonson

GENERAL EDITORS: ALVIN B. KERNAN AND RICHARD B. YOUNG

Inigo Jones: A Whining, Ballading Lover from *Love's Triumph Through Callipolis*. Devonshire Collection, Chatsworth. All illustrations in this volume reproduced by permission of the trustees of the Chatsworth Settlement.

Ben Jonson: Selected Masques

EDITED BY STEPHEN ORGEL

NEW HAVEN AND LONDON:
YALE UNIVERSITY PRESS, 1970

TO JONAS A. BARISH

Contents

Contents

Preface of the General Editors

The Yale edition of the plays of Ben Jonson is intended to meet two fundamental requirements: first, the need of the modern reader for a readily intelligible text which will convey, as nearly as an edition can, the life and movement which invests the plays on the stage; second, the need of the critic and scholar for a readily available text which represents as accurately as possible, though it does not reproduce, the plays as Jonson printed them. These two requirements are not, we believe, incompatible, but the actual adjustment of one to the other has been determined by the judgment of the individual editors. In details of editorial practice, therefore, the individual volumes of the edition may vary, but in basic editorial principle they are consistent.

The texts are based primarily on the two folio volumes of Jonson's *Works*, the first published in 1616, the second in 1640. The 1616 volume was seen through the press by Jonson himself, and therefore represents to a degree unusual for dramatic texts of the period what the dramatist intended us to have. The 1640 volume presents more difficult textual problems; though Jonson himself began preparing individual plays for it as early as 1631, these were carelessly printed—a fact of which he was painfully aware—and the folio, under the editorship of the eccentric Sir Kenelm Digby, was not completed until after Jonson's death. The quarto editions have also been consulted, and where a quarto reading has been preferred by an editor the necessary information appears in the notes.

In editing Jonson for the modern reader, one of the central problems is that of annotation, a problem that is complicated rather than solved by providing a catalogue of Jonson's immense classical learning or of his contemporary lore. We have believed that annotation is most helpful not when it identifies or defines details but when it clarifies the context of the detail. Consequently, citation of sources, allusions, and analogues, whether classical or colloquial, has been controlled by and restricted to what is relevant in the judgment of the editors to a meaningful understanding of the dramatic and poetic values of the passage in question and of the play as a whole. For the same reason, all editorial apparatus—introductions, notes, and glosses—frequently and deliberately deal with critical and interpretative matters in order to reanimate the topical details and give substance to the imaginative world each play creates.

Where Jonson printed all verse in the metrical unit of the line, whether or not it represents the speech of one or more than one character, this edition divides the parts of such lines according to the speaker, and indicates the metrical unit by echeloning the parts of the line.

The original punctuation has been followed where its rhetorical effect has a dramatic value, but modern pointing has been used wherever necessary to clarify syntactical obscurities and to eliminate obvious errors or mere eccentricity. Spelling has been modernized except where orthographical change affects either meaning or meter. For example, where Jonson prints 'd to indicate an unstressed ending of a past participle, this edition prints -ed, and where Jonson printed -ed to indicate stress this edition prints -èd. Jonson's frequent elisions, e.g. th' or i', are retained, and all unusual accents are marked.

Foreword

The texts, commentary, and appendix for the masques in this selection are identical with those in the Yale edition of *The Complete Masques*. I have undertaken to include the best and most representative works from the range of Jonson's career. Naturally, I regret the necessary omission of some particular favorites—chiefly *Christmas His Masque* and *The Masque of Augurs*—and I wish that room could have been found for those two strange experiments, *Love Freed from Ignorance and Folly* and *Lovers Made Men*. Of the earliest masques, *Hymenaei* has been preferred to the more famous *Masques of Blackness and Beauty* because it seems to me, by any standards, to be more coherent and poetically superior; it is, moreover, the greatest Jonsonian example of the wedding masque.

Like every modern editor of Jonson, I owe an immense debt to the Oxford edition of C. H. Herford, Percy and Evelyn Simpson. Though it has proved impracticable to acknowledge every point adopted from their notes, the obligation is pervasive, and readers who use my edition in conjunction with theirs—the two are in some ways complementary—will be aware of it. Errors in the Oxford edition have been silently corrected, except in cases where our disagreement is so radical that to leave it unexplained would cause confusion.

Among colleagues and friends, it is a pleasure to acknowledge first the continuous assistance and advice of Jonas A. Barish. Christopher Ricks provided many elucidations, and one inspired emendation. I am indebted in various ways to Paul J. Alpers, Edward Berry, Philip Brett, Coppelia Kahn, David Kalstone, O. W. Neighbour, Allan Paulson, John H. Roberts, and Colin Timms. Lowell Edmunds and Richard S. Peterson did much of the groundwork for the appendix, and Nina Watkins was my guide through the murk of Jonson's Welsh. I owe a special debt to Professor D. J. Gordon, and to J. B. Trapp and the staff of the Warburg Institute of the University of London. A large part of the Introduction first appeared in *Renaissance Drama*, New Series I (1968).

I must conclude with a sadly final acknowledgment to the late Andrew Chiappe of Columbia University, who introduced me to the Jonsonian masque.

S. O.
London
25 January 1968

Introduction

It is an accident of time that to the modern reader the court masque appears a form of drama. For the most part, only the texts of these elaborate entertainments survive; but a masque to the contemporary spectator was not at all represented by its text. Where we possess a dozen pages of dialogue and verse, the seventeenth-century audience witnessed a production three hours in length, consisting largely of music, dancing, pageantry, and spectacular scenic effects. Historically, indeed, the relevance of drama to the masque appears only at the very end of a long tradition, and it is not until the time of James I that court entertainments begin regularly to be written by playwrights. The best and most characteristic Tudor and Elizabethan masques are the work of musicians and poets.

We might begin, then, by distinguishing the form from drama. A masque is as much a game as a show. The word was often used in the sixteenth century simply to mean masquerade, and the most common way the age had of defining the form was by its inclusion of masked or disguised courtiers. It involves its audience in ways that are impossible for the drama. Not only is it about the court it entertains, but its masquers are members of that audience, and almost always descend and join with it during the central dance, called the *revels*. The drama is properly a form of entertainment, and involves its audience vicariously. The masque is a form of play, and includes its audience directly.

The form was designed, then, both as a celebration of the court and as one in which the court could participate. Practical considerations aside, this was one characteristic that strongly attracted Ben Jonson to the writing of masques. For the Jacobean poet, the idealization of the virtue embodied in the king and aristocracy was in the highest sense a moral act. The democratic imagination thinks at once in terms of flattery, but the charge is misdirected. The Jonsonian masque must be seen in the light of poems like *To Penshurst* and the epistle *To Sir Robert Wroth*, which instruct through praise. Every masque concluded by merging spectator with masquer, in effect transforming the courtly audience into the idealized world of the poet's vision.

Yet Jonson was a special case among masque writers, because he treated the form seriously as literature. The reign of James I, for all its generosity to the creators of masques, came at an unpropitious moment in the history of taste. Objections to the form, whether those of aesthetic critics or Puritan moralists, were powerful and very new. For monarchs like Henry VIII and Lorenzo de' Medici, spectacular entertainments needed no defense; magnificence was the virtue of princes, liberality their obligation. But in 1625, Bacon could write in *Of Masques and Triumphs*, "these Things are but Toyes, to come amongst such Serious Observations. But yet, since Princes will have such Things, it is better, they should be Graced with Elegancy, than Daubed with Cost." And if it were not for Ben Jonson, the court masque would hardly find a place in the history of literature; indeed, from Bacon's essay one would not be aware that masques had texts at all. Instances primarily of royal prodigality and theatrical ingenuity, their poetry was, to the contemporary spectator, often enough a tedious brief scene, interrupting the spectacle and delaying or shortening the dancing.

But the form had a peculiar viability for Jonson's dramatic imagination. Its revels not only allowed the unmediated confrontation of actor and spectator, but demanded it; its metamorphoses provided a way of resolving and transcending the satiric vision that was in many ways the substance of Jonsonian drama. The masque, both as Jonson created it and as he received it from his Elizabethan predecessors, is always about the resolution of discord; antitheses, paradoxes, and the movement from disorder to order are central to its nature. We (like Bacon and many of his contemporaries) are accustomed to thinking of masques as the extravagant ephemera of a self-indulgent aristocracy: "They're tied," as Strabo says in *The Maid's Tragedy*, "to the rules of flattery." It is true that the masque did embody self-congratulation within conspicuous consumption on a massive scale. It was not uncommon for the king to spend £3000 (the equivalent of several hundred thousand dollars today) on a production that would be performed once or twice, and witnessed by a thousand people. Nevertheless, the form was not, for Jonson, ultimately spectacular, but didactic and moral, providing a logical concomitant to satiric comedy on the one hand and the poetry of praise on the other.

Jonson's first masque, *The Masque of Blackness*, was presented on Twelfth-night in the second year of the new king's reign, 1605. The previous year James's court had seen Samuel Daniel's *Vision of the Twelve Goddesses*, an allegorical procession with long explanatory speeches. This type of masque had been popular in England for almost a century; but something about it failed to please, and the royal commission went to Jonson the next year, and regularly thereafter until the end of the reign. So striking was the originality of Jonson's first production that contemporaries were uncertain whether it could even properly be called a masque. "At Night," wrote Sir Dudley Carleton, "we had the Queen's Maske in the Banquetting-House, or rather her Pagent."[1] The distinction is an important one. The primary qualities of the traditional English

---

1. Quoted by C. H. Herford, P. and E. Simpson, *Ben Jonson* [Works] (Oxford, 1925–52), X.448. In the Introduction, this edition is hereafter cited as *Jonson*. All texts have been normalized.

masque were music and dancing. Though the Elizabethans began to see the form in literary terms, on the whole the court entertainment was still the product of the musician, choreographer, and costumer, who employed dialogue only incidentally, if at all. But a "pageant" in 1605 had more specifically theatrical overtones. "The two main early senses," according to the Oxford English Dictionary, "were 'scene displayed on a stage,' and 'stage on which a scene is exhibited or acted,'" and the term came to be applied to any stage machinery or scenic device. Speeches, of course, are proper to the stage, though not to the dancing floor; but the trappings of theater were what most impressed the observer at Whitehall, quite overwhelming the subsequent dances proper to a masque.

Blackness appears to us staid and formal beside Jonson's later work. But it is not difficult to understand why contemporaries were startled by it. It was at once the most abstruse and the most spectacular masque England had ever seen. Its conceit relied heavily on hermetic emblems and symbolic poetry, and its production, devised by the great architect and stage designer Inigo Jones, brought the full resources of Italian theatrical machinery into use for the first time on an English stage. Moreover, the way the masque employed its noble participants was considered to border on the scandalous. The masquers' "Apparell was rich," wrote Carleton,

> but too light and Curtizan-like for such great ones. Instead of Vizzards, their Faces, and Arms up to the Elbows, were painted black, which was Disguise sufficient, for they were hard to be known; but it became them nothing so well as their red and white, and you cannot imagine a more ugly Sight, then a Troop of lean-cheek'd Moors.... [The Spanish ambassador danced with] the Queen, and forgot not to kiss her Hand, though there was Danger it would have left a Mark on his Lips.

And again, "Theyr black faces, and hands which were painted and bare up to the elbowes, was a very lothsome sight, and I am sory that strangers should see owr court so strangely disguised."[2]

---

2. *Jonson* X.448, 449.

4

It is the relationship between the reality and the symbol, the impersonators and the impersonation, that is of crucial importance for the seventeenth-century spectator. Although, as Jonson tells us, the masquers appeared in blackface by the queen's own command, Carleton cannot forget that however much they are the nymphs of the poet's fiction, they are also the queen and her ladies. Jonson would have to agree with the criticism, at least in principle: the first requirement of a masque was the creation of valid symbols for the court, parts that royalty could play without ceasing to be royal.

Thus the form was obliged to observe, in addition to the demands of its own structure, all the complex rules of court protocol and decorum. It was permissible for masquers to be dancers, because dancing is the prerogative of every lady and gentleman. But masked or not, they remained ladies and gentlemen: Queen Anne was at fault for forgetting that the etiquette of dancing involved the kissing of hands. Acting, however—playing a role other than one's own—was out of the question; hence all the speaking parts in masques were performed by professional actors.[3] In *Blackness* this was merely a matter of convenience, a way of satisfying the courtly proprieties. In the world of Jonson's first masque, the professionals are not distinguished either dramatically or morally from the courtiers; they are present simply to explain the action. But four years later, when Jonson adapted the traditional *antic-masque*, the grotesque or acrobatic entertainment, to his own purposes as an *antimasque*, "a foil or false masque" to *The Masque of Queens*, the world of the theater became firmly established within the ethical and dramatic structure of the form as well. This dramatic quality is the element of which we, as modern readers, are most aware. The contemporary audience's response, as we have observed, was quite different. What was most striking in Jacobean Whitehall, in fact, was everything

---

3. The single, obviously anomalous, exception is *The Gypsies Metamorphosed*, which caters to Buckingham's histrionic talents.

that we cannot experience at all—spectacle, music, dancing. To understand the development of the form, we must consider all its parts together and see the text in relation to its production. In particular, Inigo Jones's stagecraft is in its own way a statement about the nature and form of the masque, and is, moreover, in the most direct sense an interpretation of the poet's text. Jonson's continuing insistence that the masque was properly poetry must be weighed against his increasing reliance on the resources of the complex theater Jones provided for him. For in writing a masque, Jonson was dealing with two separate problems: the demands of the particular performance on Twelfth-night, and the transmutation of the ephemeral qualities of the moment into a work of literature.

Blackness was the beginning of a long and stormy collaboration between Jonson and Jones, productive and profoundly significant for the future of the English stage, but ultimately too tense and violent to survive. The course of the quarrel need not be recounted in detail here; it is sufficient to observe that the collaboration between poet and designer was divided just as the form itself was, between text and production, visions of permanence and immediate necessities.[4] The final break came only at the end of Jonson's masque-writing career, and was precipitated by the poet's placing his own name ahead of Jones's on the title page of *Love's Triumph Through Callipolis* (1631). Our sympathies tend to lie with Jonson, but it is not necessary to take sides. The issue of the quarrel is a real one, based on contradictions inherent in the form itself. The violence of the dispute is a measure of the seriousness with which each artist treated his work. More important for our purposes than the quarrel are the interaction between the poet's invention and that of the designer, and the resultant achievements of the collaboration.

---

4. The most detailed and useful study of the quarrel is that of D. J. Gordon, "Poet and Architect: The Intellectual Setting of the Quarrel Between Ben Jonson and Inigo Jones," *Journal of the Warburg and Courtauld Institutes*, XII (1949), 152–78.

In the earliest masques text and production tend to be curiously independent of each other. Jonson provides admiring descriptions of costumes and scenic devices in the masques of *Blackness* and *Beauty*, but these are effectively pauses in the text; the poet is simply giving the designer his due. In production, at these moments the stage became essentially a dramatic entity, which by itself provided the "action" of the masque:

> This throne, as the whole island moved forward on the water, had a circular motion of it own, imitating that which we call *motum mundi*, from the east to the west, or the right to the left side. The steps whereon the Cupids sat had a motion contrary, with analogy *ad motum planetarum*, from the west to the east; both which turned with their several lights. And with these three varied motions at once, the whole scene shot itself to the land.
>
> Above which, the moon was seen in a silver chariot, drawn by virgins, to ride in the clouds and hold them greater light, with the sign Scorpio, and the character, placed before her.
>
> (*Beauty*, 218ff.)[5]

In *Hymenaei*, what must have been the outstanding moment of the masque in production barely finds a place in Jonson's text: "Here out of a microcosm, or globe, figuring man, with a kind of contentious music, issued forth the first masque, of eight men." (98–99.)

This was a spectacular device, and would have commanded a good deal of the audience's attention. There is no point looking for jealousies in the curtness of Jonson's description; the effect simply is not part of the masque-as-poem. At this moment in the work what is important to Jonson is not that the scene was breathtaking, but that it represented a microcosm. Later the poet devotes over a hundred lines to summarizing the magnificence of the scenes and costumes, and here at last, out of context, the great globe-machine is described and praised:

---

5. Jones did not design *Beauty*, but it was produced in his style. Line numbers in parentheses refer to the Yale edition of *The Complete Masques*.

> No less to be admired for the grace and greatness was the whole machine of the spectacle, from whence they came, the first part of which was a *mikrokosmos*, or globe, filled with countries, and those gilded; where the sea was expressed, heightened with silver waves. This stood, or rather hung (for no axle was seen to support it), and turning softly, discovered the first masque (as we have before but too runningly declared), which was of the men, sitting in fair composition within a mine of several metals; to which the lights were so placed as no one was seen, but seemed as if only Reason with the splendor of her crown illumined the whole grot.
>
> (577ff.)

Clearly the poet's text and the architect's stage are different phenomena.

But both artists appear to have had a notion of unity in the form; and despite their quarrel, what they produce does imply an increasing ability to think in each other's terms. In *The Masque of Queens*, Jonson makes the stage machine genuinely integral to the dramatic structure of the masque. His antimasque figures are "hags or witches, sustaining the persons of Ignorance, Suspicion, Credulity, etc., the opposites to good Fame" (15–16)—they are devised, that is, as the abstract antitheses of the virtues represented by the queens of the main masque. So conceived, the worlds of antimasque and revels are mutually exclusive, and no confrontation between them is possible. The moral victory, the triumph of virtue, is therefore achieved not through drama, the ordinary means of the poet and playwright, but through Inigo Jones's machinery, which Jonson employs to make a symbolic statement about the world of his masque:

> In the heat of their dance on the sudden was heard a sound of loud music, as if many instruments had made one blast; with which not only the hags themselves but the hell into which they ran quite vanished, and the whole face of the scene altered, scarce suffering the memory of such a thing. But in the place of it appeared a glorious and magnificent building figuring the House of Fame . . .
>
> (334ff.)

The structure of the masque does not simply allow for this spectacu-lar machine; it requires it.

In such a structure as this, the transition from antimasque to masque is a metamorphosis, and the theatrical machine is crucial to its accomplishment. Symbolically the total disappearance of the hags and their hell demonstrates a basic assumption of the universe Jonson has created: the world of evil is not real. It exists at all only in relation to the world of ideals, which are the norms of the masque's universe. So the antimasque is physically ugly, threatening but in fact dramatically powerless, and ultimately—when the transition takes place—without status even as a concept, "scarce suffering the memory of such a thing." This last is, of course, a moral statement, not a literal description of the spectators' experience, but it illustrates the extent to which Jonson was willing to use the theatrical realities as the metaphors of his text. In fact, as the form takes on more con-sistency in the years after 1609, the stage and its devices appear less and less as separate phenomena, and more as integral parts of a unified whole. *Queens* is the last of the great spectacular masques, and both artists show a steady and deliberate movement away from the sorts of devices it embodies. Though the masques of the next decade are various enough to defy easy categorization, they all reveal a new attitude toward the function of the scene and its machinery, and more specifically, they reveal what we might call an anti-spectacular bias. The culmination of this movement is in the masques produced by Jonson and Jones between 1615 and 1618, *The Golden Age Restored, Mercury Vindicated from the Alchemists at Court, The Vision of Delight*, and *Pleasure Reconciled to Virtue*.

On the surface, the move away from spectacle in the masque, however justified by formal considerations, would appear to have been self-defeating: spectators during the second decade of the seventeenth century complain regularly of the poverty of both the scenic and poetic inventions. This should give us pause. Surely there is no genre in Renaissance literature more directly involved with the demands and expectations of its audience than the court masque. Traditional explanations for what happened to the Jonsonian form after 1610 observe this fact without really taking it into account. For example, Enid Welsford, writing on *The Vision of Delight* (1617), adduces as primary sources for its form a French ballet of 1606 and an Italian production of 1608.[6] For Miss Welsford, the combination of bright ideas from the continent and audiences' demands for foreign pleasures produces a viable theory about the genesis of *The Vision of Delight*:

> All . . . masques written at this time by writers other than Ben Jonson show the increasing popularity of the antimasque and the tendency to multiply the grotesque dances and to emulate the bizarre inconsequence of the French ballet-masquerade; they help us to realize how strenuously Ben Jonson was resisting popular pressure in his attempt to keep the antimasque in a subordinate position. Gradually, however, even Ben was forced to give way, and the masques prepared by him in the year 1617 mark a fresh stage in his submission to foreign influence. . . . The introduction of two antimasques in the *Vision* shows that Jonson was having to accommodate himself to the prevailing fashion, and compose his masques *à la mode de France*. He resented the necessity.[7]

The trouble with this is that after claiming that the masques were slavishly responsive to public taste, the theory has no way of accounting for their striking unpopularity. Miss Welsford is particularly hard on *The Vision*'s first antimasque, which is "obviously an imitation of the first part of the Ballet de la Foire St. Germain."[8] She notes that the masque was unpopular, concurs with contemporary court opinion, explaining that "the first antimasque is certainly rather unattractive and pointless," and concludes that "it must have

---

6. *The Court Masque* (Cambridge, Eng., 1927), p. 202.

7. Ibid., pp. 198–203.

8. Ibid., p. 202.

filled up quite a considerable part of the performance, and may perhaps have altered and marred the balance of the whole piece." [9]

All this illustrates the dangers of treating influences as explanations. Miss Welsford justifies her dissatisfaction with the antimasque she mentions by observing that it has been imported from a French source in deference to popular tastes. In the critic's own terms, this ought at the very least to rank as a startling miscalculation on Jonson's part, since what was allegedly designed solely to please the public is here being held solely responsible for its displeasure. Moreover, in the following year Jonson produced *Pleasure Reconciled to Virtue*, a masque with many of the same characteristics, and even more unpopular. But on the other hand, if one argues what seems to me to be the case, that the antimasque in question is by no means pointless but both beautifully apt and structurally necessary, it would follow that the form of the work was determined not by influences and demands—pressures outside Jonson—but by the force of the poet's own creative intelligence. For surely artists *select* their influences, which are, properly speaking, aspects of their invention; and the relation between an audience's expectations and the artist's creation is far more complex than Miss Welsford allows. It is too simple to think merely in terms of the tyranny of the spectators' demands. For it must also be true that Jonson is educating his audiences, and employing his knowledge of their expectations as he employed conventions and traditions: as the tools and devices of his art.

We must be equally concerned with Inigo Jones's development during this period, for contemporaries ascribed the faults of the productions to him as well as to Jonson. "Mr. Inigo Jones hath lost in his reputacion," wrote Sir Edward Sherburne after *Pleasure Reconciled to Virtue* in 1618, "in regard some extraordinary devise

9. Ibid., p. 254.

was looked for . . . and a poorer was never sene."[10] In this case, it was presumably the spectacular scenic effects of *Hymenaei* and *Queens* that the audiences missed; nevertheless, Jones throughout the period ignored the expectation. Again, traditional explanations for this are confused, but Jonson is usually held to be somehow liable. For example, Allardyce Nicoll observes that in the masques of this decade Jones introduced nothing new, and cites, approvingly, Sherburne's comment quoted above.[11] The difficulties of interpretation are compounded by lack of information, but here the poet's aged malice becomes the culprit:

> "The scene chang'd" in Jonson's *The Golden Age Restored*, but by this time the crabbed old author was being very parsimonious in his notices of scenic display.[12]

"The crabbed old author" was 42 in 1615; he is present only because Professor Nicoll assumes that there is something sinister about the lack of scenic detail in Jonson's text. Behind this is the assumption that more ought to have been going on in Jones's theater than we find there, and that perhaps something is even being concealed from us.

I see no reason to make any of these assumptions. My sense of what happens to the Jonsonian masque between 1610 and 1618 is that poet and architect are moving toward a significant redefinition of the form. The movement is somewhat tentative, and the two artists are not always in perfect accord, but throughout the period a central idea is always in view, and it is specifically a structural idea. Behind this claim are two assumptions of my own: that Jonson, unlike most of his contemporaries, took the masque seriously as a form; and that Inigo Jones's concept of theater was throughout his

---

10. Quoted by G. E. Bentley, *The Jacobean and Caroline Stage* (Oxford, 1941–56), IV.670.

11. *Stuart Masques and the Renaissance Stage* (London, 1937), pp. 82–4.

12. Ibid., p. 82.

career dynamic and coherent. Considering the texts with these assumptions in mind, we might reasonably infer that Jonson does not pause to describe scenery because the masque has become for him a unified form, and the text as he published it a work of literature. The machines and devices of the stage no longer constitute a separate entity, but have become an integral part of that form. If this is true, it is as much the architect's doing as the poet's.

The new structural idea involved primarily the relation of antimasque to masque, or to the revels. We have observed that from the very beginning the resolution of discord, and hence the concept of the antimasque, was a defining feature of the form for Jonson, though it was a feature that he was not always able to express through the dramatic action of the masque. The fact that his career opens with the antithetical and complementary worlds of *Blackness* and *Beauty* [13] is evidence enough that the antimasque idea was essentially abstract and philosophical to him, and only incidentally involved with the traditional grotesquerie of the "antic masque." Jonson's own description of the witches' scene in *Queens*, "a foil or false masque," is misleading if we place the emphasis on "foil," and therefore assume that it is structurally insignificant. Its falseness explains the truth of the revels, for through the antimasque we comprehend in what way the masque's ideal world is real. At the same time, the crucial action of the form, the actual transition from disorder to order—from blackness to beauty or vice to virtue—is one that is omitted entirely from Jonson's first masque and its sequel, and can only be indicated and described by the text of *Queens*. After 1609, Jonson begins to conceive of the antimasque not as a simple antithesis to the world of the revels, but essentially as another aspect of it, a world that can therefore ultimately be accommodated to and even included in the ideals of the main masque. The productions of the second decade, starting with *Oberon* (1611), begin to represent

---

13. *Beauty* was not produced, however, till 1608.

the transition less as a single moment of transformation than as a gradual process of refinement. This process, for the courtly audience, is an education in the meaning of the revels.

The brief antimasque of boys in *The Haddington Masque* is a rudimentary version of this concept. The boys, "most anticly attired . . . represented the sports and pretty lightnesses that accompany Love" (135–36). Though they disappear after their dance is over, the qualities they embody are not banished from the masque, but are summoned up and included in the final epithalamion:

> Love's common-wealth consists of toys;
> His council are those antic boys,
> Games, laughter, sports, delights,
> That triumph with him on these nights . . .
>
> (345–48)

Wedding masques can hardly reject the delights of love. Jonson's purpose is to place those delights in their proper perspective, to move them from the capriciousness of their first appearance to the larger order implied by words like "common-wealth" and "council."

In *Oberon*, Jonson first fully conceives of the transition from antimasque to revels as the ordering and redirecting of a vital energy that is both essential and good. The antimasque of satyrs is in every sense a part of the world of Oberon, and during the course of the masque the satyrs are converted from their games to the prince's service. All this is accomplished in what is dramatically the most completely realized masque Jonson composed. Its very coherence causes difficulties, chiefly at the moment when the action must break through the boundaries of the stage and move outward to include the king and court.[14] This crucial movement would naturally be less problematical in works with a less solid dramatic form, and

---

14. A detailed discussion will be found in my study *The Jonsonian Masque* (Cambridge, Mass., 1965), pp. 82ff.

Jonson, in the decade following, experiments significantly with non-dramatic masques, such as *The Golden Age Restored* and *The Vision of Delight*.

Let us consider what kind of theater Inigo Jones was providing for the masque.[15] In the early years it was heavily dependent on machinery, from simple devices like pageant cars (e.g. the floating island in *Blackness*) to wave and cloud machines, and the great *machina versatilis*, the turning machine, of *Hymenaei*, used again the following year in *The Haddington Masque*. This last device, combined with carefully planned lighting that was reflected as it turned, seems to have produced the most striking effects of the early productions. Late in Jones's career, he was to describe the masque as "nothing else but pictures with Light and Motion,"[16] and the combination of these elements is essential to his stage from the beginning. Control over lighting was, of course, minimal by modern standards, and the hall could not be darkened, but Jones made full use of mirrors and magnifiers, colored lamps, and metallic or sequined costumes. Bacon was describing the architect's practice when in 1625, in the essay *Of Masques and Triumphs*, he wrote, "Let the scenes abound with light, specially coloured and varied."

Jones's early stages were designed to operate as much on the vertical axis as on the horizontal. *Blackness* opens with a seascape, in which the realistic properties of perspective are clearly of much importance. But by the middle of the masque, the action has moved upward:

> ... the moon was discovered in the upper part of the house, triumphant in a silver throne ... and crowned with a luminary, or sphere of light ...

15. The most useful general discussions of the subject are Richard Southern, *Changeable Scenery* (London, 1952), pp. 1–106; Nicoll, *Stuart Masques*; and Lily B. Campbell, *Scenes and Machines on the English Stage* (Cambridge, Eng., 1923), pp. 164ff.

16. E. K. Chambers, ed., *Aurelian Townshend's Poems and Masks* (Oxford, 1912), p. 83.

> The heaven about her was vaulted with blue silk and set with stars of silver which had in them their several lights burning.
>
> (186ff.)

The seascape had included "an obscure and cloudy nightpiece," presumably painted on a curtain at the rear of the stage. When this was removed, the moon, the heavens, and a whole new dimension of action were revealed above.

The stages of the next few productions make little use of the realistic illusions of perspective, and almost abandon the horizontal assumptions of the normal stage entirely. In fact, what Jones provides for *Hymenaei* and *The Haddington Masque* are, properly speaking, not settings at all, but symbolic pageants; that is, they are not the scenes in which actions take place: they are themselves the actions. The scenery is concentrated on the center of the stage, forming, in *Hymenaei*, a series of theatrical emblems—an altar with a mystic inscription, which is interpreted by the characters; the microcosm; Juno on her throne surrounded by appropriate symbols. "The scene" for *The Haddington Masque* "was a high, steep, red cliff advancing itself into the clouds, figuring the place from whence . . . the honorable family of the Radcliffes first took their name" (20ff.). Onto this emblematic mountain Venus and the graces descend from above, and finally the mountain opens to reveal the turning machine, the great globe, surrounded by the masquers, each representing a sign of the zodiac. *The Masque of Beauty* a month earlier, though not designed by Jones, had exhibited the same notion of the function of settings through an even more elaborate *machina versatilis*. Jonson's description of the floating island bearing its symbolic throne forward with "three varied motions at once," has already been quoted.

After all this, what is striking about *Queens* is not its machinery, but how much better co-ordinated its symbolic stage is with Jonson's text; or, to put it another way, how much more significance the text has in the action of the masque. Again, there is little here that resembles a normal dramatic stage, either Jacobean or Italian; and

both texts and settings throughout this period serve to remind us
that the masque was providing a radically different sort of theatrical
experience from even the most elaborate private playhouses. The
axis of the stage is still as much vertical as horizontal, and the action
still tends to be grouped around a series of central symbols. The
witches enter from hell by rising through trap doors, and disappear
by the same route. For the antimasque, the symbolic setting is for
once the whole stage, rather than a single pavilion, or machine, or
pageant, and Jones uses fire and smoke as well as scenery to create his
hell. But with the transition to the main masque, we are back in the
theater of emblems:

> . . . in the place of it appeared a glorious and magnificent building figuring
> the House of Fame, in the top of which were discovered the twelve
> masquers sitting upon a throne triumphal erected in form of a pyramid
> and circled with all store of light.
>
> (337ff.)

The full metamorphosis is accomplished by the turning machine,
which by now has a relatively minor function in the spectacle:
"Here the throne wherein they sat, being *machina versatilis*, suddenly
changed, and in the place of it appeared *Fama bona*." (422ff.)

It is the movement toward drama in the development of the masque that should surprise us, not the move away from it. The solidly
realized world of *Oberon* is something new, and marks a turning
point for both poet and architect. Much of the action of the masques
before 1611 is concerned with elucidating the emblems of their
stages; but the action of *Oberon* is dramatic, and requires a different
kind of theater. Instead of pageant cars and the *machina versatilis*,
Jones began to devise settings that could serve as the media for
action of some complexity. It is a mistake to assume that this is
something Jonson has forced on the architect, or that Jones's settings
have suddenly become subservient to the poet's texts. Jonson from
the beginning was "the inventor," and Jones's machines were, at

least till the final years of the collaboration, realizations of Jonson's poetic symbols. What is new is that the machinery has become integrated with the action, and that thus *Oberon* has a new sort of unity.

For *Oberon*, Jones turned his attention to the *scena ductilis*, the "tractable scene," a device he had occasionally used before. Basically this was a series of flats set in grooves in the stage, which could be swiftly and quietly drawn aside into the wings to reveal the setting behind them. Since the number of scene changes with this device was limited only by the number of grooves the platform could contain, the flexibility of the masque stage became, through the *scena ductilis*, almost infinite. And while the *machina versatilis* could turn, say, a cave into a temple, only the *scena ductilis* could wholly transform the entire stage. This was presumably the device in *Queens* by which "the whole face of the scene altered, scarce suffering the memory of such a thing."

Oberon opens in a wilderness:

> The first face of the scene appeared all obscure, and nothing perceived but a dark rock with trees beyond it and all wildness that could be presented; till at one corner of the cliff, above the horizon, the moon began to show, and rising, a satyr was seen by her light to put forth his head and call.
>
> (1–4)

The satyrs are unruly but good-natured; their pleasures, indeed, are courtly ones: dancing and drinking. They are presided over by a silene, the exemplar of wisdom, and under his tutelage they are educated to the virtues of reason and decorum, and led to submit to Oberon, the fairy prince. This is accomplished in verse of wonderful delicacy and variety, which constantly controls and directs the energy of the antimasque.

Jones's designs for *Oberon* have been preserved,[17] and the setting

---

17. See P. Simpson and C. F. Bell, *Designs by Inigo Jones for Masques and Plays at Court* (Oxford, 1924), nos. 40–55.

he creates for this scene provides an interesting parallel.[18] Jonson's direction (or is it his description?) calls for "all wildness that could be presented," but in fact the rocky landscape, like the figures it contains, is clearly controlled by principles of decorum, balanced and symmetrical. This was presumably painted on one or more pairs of shutters. Halfway through the antimasque, Silenus observes the *scena ductilis* in action: "See, the rock begins to ope!"

> There the whole scene opened, and within was discovered the frontispiece of a bright and glorious palace whose gates and walls were transparent.
>
> (97–98)

The removal of the front panels has not only transformed the face of the scene; it has moved the action farther back on the stage and into the perspective. That is, the spectators' sense of the reality that the theatrical illusion is providing has been, literally, deepened. In Jones's design for the second scene,[19] the stage is now framed by high rocks—the outermost panels from the first scene have not been removed—and the palace itself is a curious combination of rustication and elegance, a medieval fortress with a Palladian balustrade and pediment, and surmounted by a very Italian dome. Here, as in the action of the masque, the ideal is classic order, attained (again literally) by gradual stages.

Like the opening landscape, the front of the palace must be a pair of flats set in grooves, constituting essentially a backdrop for the action of the second scene. But not entirely, because the "gates and walls were transparent," and this implies to a spectator that more is behind the scene, that the action extends somehow beyond the background. It is not until the next, and final, transformation that the full depth of the stage appears:

---

18. No. 40 in Simpson and Bell. Reproduced in *Jonson*, II.284–85.
19. No. 42 in Simpson and Bell. Reproduced in *Jonson*, II.286–87.

> There the whole palace opened, and the nation of fays were discovered,
> ... and within, afar off in perspective, the knights masquers sitting in
> their several sieges. At the further end of all, Oberon, in a chariot ...
> (213ff.)

What the spectator sees now is the inside of the palace. Jones's
drawing[20] shows only the central portion of the setting. It is a
pavilion from the emblematic theater of earlier masques, a Renaissance classical temple; but we see through it and beyond it down the
whole length of a perspective setting. It is from the depths of this
image of order, now fully realized, that Oberon's chariot comes "as
far forth as the face of the scene," and that the masquers at last move
out into the Renaissance classical world of the audience, the colum-
ned and galleried Banqueting House at Whitehall.

We may observe that what the stage presents in this masque is
radically different from anything Jones has conceived up to this
time. The axis of the stage is now entirely horizontal, with the
single exception of the appearance at the end of "Phosphorus, the
day star," presumably in the heavens. The setting is the medium for
action, and unlike the microcosm of *The Haddington Masque* or the
House of Fame in *Queens*, it has no independent existence. It is
wholly co-ordinated with Jonson's text, and indeed may be considered an aspect of it. More than this, the world it represents, however
idealized, is a version of the spectators' own world, and scenic realism
has become a prerequisite of symbolic glory. Visually the masque is
a triumph of elegance and taste; it is significantly less spectacular
than any of the Jonsonian productions preceding it.

The other Christmas masque for 1611 was *Love Freed from
Ignorance and Folly*, presented by the queen as *Oberon* had been by

---

20. I take Simpson and Bell's no. 45 (plate VIII) to be the design for this scene.
    It is probably related, however, not to the medieval palace, but to the
    alternative version of that scene (no. 44, plate VII), which it closely
    resembles.

Prince Henry. In view of the inventiveness of Jones's work on *Oberon*, it is especially unfortunate that we have no information about the later masque's production. Jonson's silence is usually ascribed to his vindictive malice toward his collaborator, but this can hardly be the explanation. The texts of both masques were prepared and published at the same time, and *Oberon* includes as much scenic detail as we could ask. The answer more probably lies in the special nature of the queen's masque. *Love Freed* is a curious experiment, the most thoroughly literary of all Jonson's court entertainments. Essentially allegorical, it depends on a running marginal commentary to explain its action, and Jonson might reasonably have felt that in a text addressed so completely to the reader, details of the staging were superfluous. One wonders what the contemporary audience could have made of it. Jonson, at least, seems to have found it unsatisfactory, for the experiment was not repeated.

The two artists did not work together again until *The Golden Age Restored*, in 1615. In 1612, when *Love Restored* was presented, Jones was employed on another project, the sumptuous production of Campion's *Lords' Masque* for the wedding of King James's daughter Elizabeth. And the next Christmas, when the court saw *A Challenge at Tilt* and *The Irish Masque*, Jones was in the midst of an eighteen-month stay in Italy. Jonson's three masques during these years are witty and lively, and rely for their effectiveness largely on the techniques of stage drama; indeed, they hardly appear to require any settings at all. But with *The Golden Age Restored*, the poet's invention is once again joined with the architect's, and whatever the intensity of their quarrel, it did not prevent them from entering upon the most fruitful period of their association. In this masque and those of the next three years, *Mercury Vindicated* (1616), *The Vision of Delight* (1617), and *Pleasure Reconciled to Virtue* (1618), we can see the form coming fully to maturity.

During this period what Jones appears to be creating is an efficient machine wholly integrated with the dramatic action. Like Jonson, that is, he sees the masque as essentially a unified form. And the properties of the stage that he is most interested in developing have only incidentally to do with spectacular effects. He is primarily concerned with the control of realistic visual illusions. The stage becomes a total picture, working inward and backward from a proscenium arch, and his devices now more and more involve the manipulation of shutters in grooves and flats on pivots (or *periaktoi*) for instantaneous changes of complex perspectives. It would be a mistake not to see this development as the joint responsibility of both poet and architect, and Jonson's relative silence about scenic effects may testify more than anything else to their efficiency.

Contemporary accounts, on the other hand, testify with remarkable unanimity to general dissatisfaction with the new developments. Of *The Golden Age Restored*, John Chamberlain reports that "neither in devise nor shew was there anything extraordinarie but only excellent dauncing."[21] Of *The Vision of Delight*, he writes, "I have heard no great speach nor commendations of the maske neither before nor since."[22] And Sir Edward Sherburne's observation that because of *Pleasure Reconciled to Virtue*, "Mr. Inigo Jones hath lost in his reputacion," is one of many in the same vein. It is evident that a radical transformation of the masque, at least to the contemporary spectator's eye, was in progress, and that the result was less than satisfactory. The complaints rarely cite anything more specific than lack of invention, or simply dullness. But one comment of Chamberlain's on Campion's *Lords' Masque* (1613) makes an interesting attempt at explaining the general displeasure. The effects that Jones created for this production comprise almost an anthology of scenic machinery of the time; reading Campion's descriptions, one would think the success of the spectacle would have been assured. Chamberlain reports, however, that he hears "no great commendation" of

---

21. Quoted in *Jonson*, X.553.
22. Ibid., 568.

the production, "save only for riches, their devices being long and tedious, and more like a play than a mask."[23] To a modern reader there is little about Campion's text that suggests drama, and "like a play" may only mean that Chamberlain finds the speeches too long; but it is worth noting that a masque in 1613 was not expected to be "like a play." Moreover, though "devices" can refer only to the dialogue, the spectacle of Inigo Jones's machinery falls under the general curse. At the very least, it is doing nothing to relieve the work from the onus of being like a play. Perhaps there is simply not enough of it in proportion to the speeches, or perhaps its very integration with action and speech is felt to be inappropriate.

Whatever Chamberlain meant by "like a play," it is apparent that from the time of *Oberon* on, and especially after Inigo Jones's return from Italy in 1614, masques began to look a good deal more like what we, at least, conceive plays to be. Perspective was the basic scenic device in the masques of the period, and all the action, until the crucial move off the stage and onto the dancing floor, was separated from the audience by a proscenium wall. This would not, of course, have been recognized by a contemporary English spectator as being like a play. On the contrary, dramatic stages that employed proscenia, perspective, and its attendant machinery did not appear until more than twenty years later, and then were imitating the masque.[24] Indeed, the physical embodiment of both masque and drama, the theater, was undergoing an important transformation in this era. The continuing charge that masques were dull implies not so much that Jones was introducing nothing new as that English audiences were not yet educated to appreciate what he *was* doing. Italian observers are much more alive to the ingenuity of the scenes. For example, *The Lords' Masque*, which for Chamberlain was too

---

23. Quoted by E. K. Chambers, *The Elizabethan Stage* (Oxford, 1923), III.243.
24. See Irwin Smith, *Shakespeare's Blackfriars Playhouse* (New York, 1964), pp. 269ff.

much like a play, was called "very beautiful" by the Venetian ambassador, who admired its three changes of setting, and particularly praised the way in which "certain stars danced in the heavens by a most ingenious device."[25] And at *Pleasure Reconciled to Virtue* (1618), another admiring Venetian observer is at some pains to account for the mechanics of the scenic effects:

> The mountain opened by the turning of two doors, and dawn was seen to break between small hills above a distant perspective, some false gilded columns being placed along the sides to make the distance seem greater.[26]

To an English audience this sort of theater was relatively unfamiliar, and unspectacular enough for the ingenuity of its devices to pass unnoticed. Glynne Wickham even argues that in 1606 the average London theater-goer "would not have been aware of many material differences between the stage conventions that met his gaze" at court masques and at public and private playhouses, and that this would still have been true over twenty years later.[27] It is difficult to see why this should have been so, but the point must be granted on documentary evidence alone: insofar as contemporary English observers took note of the new devices at all, they did so merely to declare their lack of interest in them. Yet Jones was starting to conceive the stage as a unified machine, not as a series of individual effects; this was a revolutionary idea in the English theater, and the Italian visitors recognized it as worthy of comment.

Moreover, Inigo Jones's masque settings were making the most far-reaching statements about the nature of the theatrical illusion; for a realistic scene implies that seeing—not hearing, or understanding—is believing. Jonson's famous *Expostulation with Inigo Jones* shows the process fairly well completed in 1631:

---

25. *Calendar of State Papers (Venetian)*, XII (1610–13), ed. H. F. Brown (London, 1905), p. 499.
26. Quoted in Italian in *Jonson*, X.582.
27. *Early English Stages*, II, Part 1 (London, 1963), pp. 7–8.

> O shows! Shows! Mighty shows!
> The eloquence of masques! What need of prose,
> Or verse, or sense t'express immortal you?
> You are the spectacles of state!...
> You ask no more than certain politic eyes,
> Eyes that can pierce into the mysteries
> Of many colors!
>
> (39–47)[28]

We shall consider the implications of this development presently. Here, it is sufficient to remark that the integration of setting with text in the masques of the second decade of the century is amply indicated by the fact that descriptions of the stage, however desirable they may be for the theatrical historian, are no longer *necessary* for the masque to express its meaning. But ironically, this is also the first step toward the poet's becoming superfluous. We may find a curious correspondence between the beginning and end of Jonson's and Jones's collaboration. In 1605, the court saw the emblems of *Blackness*, crystallizations of pure meaning requiring Jonson's prose for explication; in 1631, it saw the perspectives of *Love's Triumph Through Callipolis*, in which sight has so overwhelmed sense that Jonson must prefix to it an essay entitled "To Make the Spectators Understanders." In both cases, though in very different ways, the meaning is somewhere outside the courtly entertainment, available finally not to an audience but only to a reader. It is the particular triumph of a few works from this uneasy coalition that spirit and body did, for a time, unite.

The Golden Age Restored is, in most regards, a wholly new departure, abandoning the drama of *Oberon* for an essentially lyric and musical mode. But drama had proved a dubious virtue in the masque, both for playwright and for spectator, and here it is poetry that dictates the form of the work and establishes its values. *The*

---

28. In both this and subsequent citations, the text of the poem has been modernized.

Introduction

Golden Age is a series of lyric poems. There is no way of knowing how much of it was set to music, but Jonson's preference in it for stanzaic verse rather than declamation, and the use of duets, a quartet, and a choir, strongly suggest that music played a large part. Its plot —the banishment of the Iron Age by Pallas, and the return to earth of Astraea and the Golden Age—is roughly that of *The Masque of Queens*, but the difference in the handling of the antimasque and in the realization of the ideal world shows us that the Jonsonian form has entered a new phase. To begin with, this antimasque is presided over by Pallas: as in *Oberon*, wisdom opens the masque and pervades it. James's pacifism is celebrated in verse whose clarity and order establish from the outset the controlling principles of this world:

> Look, look! rejoice and wonder!
>   That you offending mortals are,
>   For all your crimes, so much the care
> Of him that bears the thunder!
>
> Jove can endure no longer,
>   Your great ones should your less invade,
>   Or that your weak, though bad, be made
> A prey unto the stronger;
>
> And therefore means to settle
>   Astraea in her seat again,
>   And let down in his golden chain
> The age of better metal.
>
> (3–14)

As the Iron Age and his antimasquers appear, Pallas withdraws, not because wisdom is threatened, but in order to establish a moral point:

> Hide me, soft cloud, from their profaner eyes,
>   Till insolent rebellion take the field,
> And as their spirits with their counsels rise,
>   I frustrate all with showing but my shield.
>
> (28–31)

Still later, routing the antimasque, she points the moral further:

> 'Twas time t'appear, and let their follies see
> 'Gainst whom they fought, and with what destiny.
>
> (75–76)

The antimasque itself has much in common with that of *Queens*; but given the new context, its effect is quite different. The antimasquers, like the witches of 1609, personify all the evils of a fallen world—Avarice, Fraud, Slander, and so forth. But here they are summoned up in an invocation of only thirty-five lines, and their function in the masque is limited to their dance, accompanied, to strengthen the point, by "a confusion of martial music." The moment analogous to the sudden blast of many instruments that overthrew the hags in *Queens* is here provided by Pallas showing her shield; and Jonson's remark about the transformation of hell "scarce suffering the memory of such a thing" now becomes explicitly part of the moral and dramatic structure of the masque, enunciated by Pallas as a concomitant to her action:

> So change and perish scarcely knowing how,
> That 'gainst the gods do take so vain a vow . . .
>
> (71–72)

The resolution is accomplished and the Golden Age established literally by poetry: Chaucer, Gower, Lydgate, and Spenser are summoned, "the scene of light discovered" (136), the darkness of night and the cold of winter are banished, and Astraea returns to earth.

Stage directions for this production are extremely brief and, for the most part, marginal. They tell us nothing of the masque's physical appearance, and doubtless it was ungracious of Jonson not to give Jones more credit. Nevertheless, what the three sets represented is amply indicated in the text. Pallas descends in her chariot, perceives a "tumult from yond' cave" (24), and hides behind a cloud (28).

Then "the scene changed," and shortly afterward she is indicating "yonder souls, set far within the shade,/And in Elysian bowers" (124–25). For the third setting, "the scene of light [is] discovered" (136). There is quite enough information here to show that the stage of *The Golden Age Restored* is very much that of *Oberon*, with the addition of machines for descending and ascending—Pallas, the Golden Age, Astraea, and the poets all descend to enter, though only Pallas reascends, leaving the rest in a world of Elysian bowers and light.

Such a conclusion is, on the whole, justified by the realities of Jacobean history: the king has, after all, banished war from the realm and given poetry a real place at his court. The sort of reality that Inigo Jones's settings provide for the truths of Jonson's fiction is worth considering. Perspective stages establish their particular kind of reality by depending on a set of assumptions that the English spectator was not, on the whole, used to exercising in the theater. These assumptions are not moral ones, such as that beauty is better than blackness or that man is a microcosm, but empirical ones, involving not what we believe but how we perceive our world. Actions on such a stage begin necessarily to take on the quality of empirical data: the abstract vices and virtues of *Queens* gradually become the exemplary figures of *Pleasure Reconciled to Virtue*; and in part, the increasing appearance of dramatic characters in the masque, rather than symbolic figures, is an aspect of this movement. The transition obviously was neither immediate nor self-conscious, and nothing in *The Golden Age Restored* suggests that Jonson was aware of the implications of his collaborator's stage. But the very lack of commentary in the text reflects the character of the new theater: symbols must be explained, but facts are self-evident. Surely this bears also on the movement of the later antimasques toward comedy, with its empirical assumptions and basic, worldly realities. This is an organic movement, part of the joint development of poet and architect. It grows directly and logically out of the new stage and Jonson's response to its nature and possibilities. It can hardly be seen as an instance of the tyranny of the audience's tastes.

With these considerations in mind, we may re-examine the general modern critical attitude toward Jonson's later productions with their comic antimasques. "The elaboration of the antimasque begins with this piece," the Oxford editors write of *For the Honor of Wales*; "it leads in the later masques to a lack of balance, but it suited the taste of the Court for which the dances alone were important and a comic induction was tolerable."[29] Presumably the texts, comic or otherwise, were more than tolerable to somebody, because Jonson received steady employment from the court for twenty years. But for our purposes, the significant assumption has to do with comic antimasques producing a "lack of balance." "The element of comedy," Herford and Simpson observe again, "at this period encroaches more and more on the antimasque."[30] Comedy, then (we are asked to believe), is inappropriate to antimasques, and the proportionate relation between antimasque and masque is a fixed one which, when violated, results in a lack of balance. What norms these assumptions derive from are never stated; needless to say, they are not Jonson's norms. The nature of the antimasque and its relation to the main masque are continually changing throughout Jonson's career, and both elements are essential from the beginning. It would be strange to find the author of *Volpone* and *Bartholomew Fair* disapproving of comedy, and writing it only because he is forced to do so by the low tastes of his courtly employers: obviously the notion that comedy has no place in the masque is not Jonson's. All claims that the poet's true interests lay with the main masque must contend with the evident and pervasive vitality and inventiveness of the antimasque, whether grotesque, comic, or satiric. The great achievement of the last period is *The Gypsies Metamorphosed*, that

---

29. *Jonson*, X.590.
30. Ibid., 635.

vast triumph of vulgarity and wit, crudity and finesse, tastelessness and grace. It was the king's favorite masque, and the court's. It is difficult to believe that it was not Jonson's favorite as well.

But far from dictating the tone or structure of the masques, the audience at best followed the inventors' lead, and often enough lagged very far behind. "Neither in devise nor shew was there anything extraordinarie," reported John Chamberlain on *The Golden Age Restored*. Chamberlain did not like being made to *listen* to a masque—Campion's had been too like a play—and moreover was not interested in what he saw. There was, however, "excellent dauncing"; his pleasure derived from the courtly realities.[31] In fact, the first masque for which we have evidence of any more general approbation was not produced until three years later. It is *For the Honor of Wales*, the revised version of the most unpopular *Pleasure Reconciled to Virtue*. The nature of the revision is worth considering carefully, since this is the only instance in Jonson's entire career of his rewriting an unpopular masque. The complaints are, as usual, about dullness, but there are two that make more specific charges. The first has to do with what Jonson had called, in *The Masque of Queens*, "the nobility of the invention." Edward Sherburne writes that "some extraordinary devise was looked for (it being the Prince [Charles] his first Mask) and a poorer was never sene."[32] The second is even more pertinent, being King James's own reaction to the performance. An Italian observer reports that the king, finding the dances too brief, angrily shouted, "Why don't they dance? What did you make me come here for? The devil take all of you, dance!"[33] Now if Jonson were really concerned with his audience's demands,

---

31. Perhaps Jonson is alluding to such attitudes when, in *Christmas His Masque*, Christmas, disgusted with Cupid's botched recitation, exclaims, "This it is to have speeches!" (line 249).

32. *Jonson*, X.576.

33. Ibid., 583. For a fuller discussion of the incident and its implications, see my book *The Jonsonian Masque*, pp. 70–71, 183.

the masque's second version would surely be an instance to demonstrate the fact. But *For the Honor of Wales* does not undertake to meet either objection. Its comic Welshmen and goats hardly make the masque more appropriate for the prince's debut; and if the production included more dancing than *Pleasure Reconciled to Virtue*, the additions find no place in Jonson's text.

Moreover, even with the revision Chamberlain was unimpressed: ". . . the Princes mask for twelf-night was represented again with some few alterations and additions, but little bettered." But another correspondent writes that "it was much better liked then twelveth-night; by reason of the newe Conceites and ante maskes and pleasant merry speeches made to the kinge, by such as Counterfeyted welsmen." A third is less approving, but nevertheless responsive to the work: "The princes maske was shewed againe . . . with som few additions of Goats and welshe speeches sufficient to make an English man laugh and a welsh-man cholerique, without deserving so great honour as to be sent to your Lordship."[34] Leaving questions of taste aside, we may observe that this appears to be the first masque in many years to which the court responded with interest of any kind. Its success must in part be due to the crudeness of its humor—dialect jokes have always been good for a laugh—but the real point of the joke lies in its attack on *Pleasure Reconciled to Virtue*. The Welshmen complain that the masque was irrelevant and inept: ". . . there was neither poetries nor architectures nor designs in that belly-god, nor a note of musics about him" (182–83). This is a parody of court opinion—indeed, of the court opinion of the last five years—and its wit lies in the way it makes dramatic capital out of the failure of the Twelfth-night production. *For the Honor of Wales* was a Jacobean in-group joke, and it shows Jonson using in a new way the realities of court life as part of the substance of his invention.

---

34. All are quoted in *Jonson*, X.576–77.

For the Honor of Wales establishes a norm for the late Jonsonian masque. From this time till the death of King James in 1625, the antimasque was a scene from comedy, unified and dramatic. The 1618 production carries the logic of the realistic stage to an extreme, dispensing entirely with scenic illusions and in effect denying that it is theater. Jonson had used this kind of antimasque only once before, in *The Irish Masque* of 1613, but he was to employ it again in four of the eight remaining masques presented before King James. Apparently a new departure, this was in fact only an extension of a very familiar idea: for Jonson, one of the most compelling aspects of Jones's theater was the way it could make the stage's illusion merge with the court's reality, and we may view the group of works between *The Golden Age Restored* and *For the Honor of Wales* as studies in the potentialities of this idea.

All masques are, of course, about the court, and conclude by uniting spectator and masquer; but these masques often seem to be about masques themselves, about the function of poetry and the uses of art in the world of the court. We have seen how poetry in the persons of Chaucer, Gower, Lydgate, and Spenser is essential to the establishment of James's golden age. *Mercury Vindicated from the Alchemists at Court*, in the next year, is about false and true artists, and the proper use to which Mercury—wit and learning—may be put. *The Vision of Delight* is almost an anatomy of the devices and conventions of masques, and undertakes to define the true nature of their courtly pleasures. And *Pleasure Reconciled to Virtue* considers the whole concept of revelry, banishing the riots of Comus in favor of the art of Daedalus, through whom poetry, song, and dance become the means by which princes are educated to virtue. *For the Honor of Wales*, with its ironic critique of *Pleasure Reconciled to Virtue*, is an appropriate end to the sequence.

Relating these texts to their stages reveals something interesting about the progress of the masque-idea. For *The Golden Age Restored* we have seen that Inigo Jones employed a stage that was essentially that of *Oberon*, with the addition of some machinery. *Mercury Vindicated* undertakes something quite new to masques. The scene opens in "a laboratory, or alchemist's workhouse"; Vulcan is "looking to the registers," a Cyclops is "tending to the fire." When Mercury appears, he does so "thrusting out his head and afterward his body at the tunnel of the middle furnace." The last phrase suggests at least two more furnaces, one on either side, and the amount of elaboration and particularity in this setting reveals how far Jones has come from the emblems of *Hymenaei* on the one hand and the generalized façades and landscapes of *Oberon* on the other. The antimasque of *Mercury Vindicated* is conceived as a tiny comic drama. Jonson's earlier experiments with the same device—in *Love Restored* (1612) and *The Irish Masque at Court* (1613)—appear to have employed no settings at all; and even *Oberon* had required essentially only a series of backdrops. But *Mercury Vindicated* opens on something we would recognize as a full dramatic stage. Its very consistency and realism would have been part of the masque's point for the audience at Whitehall: the alchemists are practicing below stairs at court. The transformation, when it comes, is from naturalism to Nature:

> At which the whole scene changed to a glorious bower wherein Nature was placed with Prometheus at her feet, and the twelve masquers standing about them.
>
> (172ff.)

The transformation of a "middle furnace" to a central bower sounds like the work of the *machina versatilis*, here combined with the side flats of the *scena ductilis*, which completed the change. This sophistication of an old device is an ingenious solution to the problems of a new kind of text, and suggests the extent to which Jones and Jonson were genuinely responsive to each other's ideas.

Mercury Vindicated is conceived around the relatively simple antithesis of artifice and nature, the worlds of Vulcan and Prometheus.

Introduction

The Vision of Delight, in the following year, is structurally quite different, presenting a series of scenes and a gradual progression from antimasque to revels. It is perhaps Jonson's most eclectic masque, and its continental aspects would have been apparent at once to the spectator. The scene opens on a formal theatrical prospect, "a street in perspective of fair building discovered." Into this Serlian setting [35] "Delight is seen to come as afar off"; she announces the masque's subject at once:

> Let us play and dance and sing,
>   Let us now turn every sort
> O' the pleasures of the spring
>   To the graces of a court,
> From air, from cloud, from dreams, from toys,
>   To sounds, to sense, to love, to joys . . .
>
> (5–10)

The masque is to find suitable devices for celebrating the court, and to define the proper nature of courtly pleasures. What follows is a series of presentations, visions summoned by Delight, that increase in substance, relevance, and rationality. First appears "a she-monster delivered of six burratines that dance with six pantaloons" (17–18). The masque's pleasures begin on a pre-verbal level as a grotesque comic figure gives birth, appropriately enough in the conventional Italian comic scene, to stock characters from the *commedia dell' arte*. This is the "antic masque" in its purest and most traditional form. But then under the tutelage of Delight, the antimasque moves beyond the familiar world of grotesque comedy; the daytime setting dissolves; Night and the moon are summoned, and in their turn they call up Fantasy. "The scene here changed to cloud, and

---

35. The prototypes for the Renaissance comic, tragic, and satiric scenes were designed by Sebastiano Serlio (1475–1554), Italian painter and architect. His study of perspective in the theater, Book II of his general treatise on architecture, appeared in 1545.

Fant'sy breaking forth spake" (48). The delusively rational "perspective of fair building" disappears, and the antimasque now offers a new vision of delight. In a cloudy setting, Fantasy brilliantly puts forth the claims of gluttony and lechery, describing a series of surrealistic emblems conceived in the manner of Brueghel or Bosch. These are then realized in a second antimasque of phantasms.

But the dreams of Fantasy, too, pass as the night proceeds, and when "the gold-haired Hour" descends, "the whole scene changed to the bower of Zephyrus" (117–18). Delight is finally established within the world of nature and an idealized court. Even winter is banished on this Twelfth-night, "the bower opens, and the masquers discovered as the glories of the spring" (160–61), with King James identified as the god who makes the idealization possible. As the revels conclude, Aurora appears, and the masque leads into a new day.

Inigo Jones's stage for *The Vision of Delight* is far more flexible than that for *Mercury Vindicated*, and its settings are clearly an important part of the masque's meaning. The scene moves from a perspective street to a cloudy dream world to a pastoral bower; from afternoon to night to dawn; from winter to spring. Part of this is accomplished illusionistically, part (such as the change from night to morning) symbolically. Jones was able to use the conventions of both emblematic and realistic theaters without feeling a sense of strain. By contrast, when a month later Lord Hay presented Jonson's *Lovers Made Men* for the entertainment of the French ambassador, the setting conceived by Nicholas Lanier was a single and unchanging perspective landscape.

The masque for 1618 was *Pleasure Reconciled to Virtue*. In Jonson's moral fable, Hercules is the courtly hero; he banishes the pleasures of Comus—gluttony, drunkenness, riot—in favor of the rational delights of song and formal dancing.[36] For this production, Jones

---

36. For a detailed study of the work, see *The Jonsonian Masque*, pp. 150–85.

provides a central symbol, Mount Atlas, the embodiment of wisdom. This device commands the scene throughout the performance. Jonson describes the mountain, "his top ending in the figure of an old man, his head and beard all hoary and frost as if his shoulders were covered with snow" (1–3). English observers were as usual unimpressed; however, our Venetian correspondent was delighted with the setting, and adds the information that it "rolled its eyes and moved itself with wonderful cunning."[37] The action begins in an ivy grove at the foot of the mountain; when Comus is banished, "the whole grove vanished, and the whole music was discovered, sitting at the foot of the mountain, with Pleasure and Virtue seated above them" (106–08). Presently the masquers are called forth from the lap of the mountain (the Italian visitor's description of the opening of the device has already been quoted). It then remains open during the dances and revels, and finally, to conclude the masque, the performers "returned into the scene, which closed and was a mountain again as before" (318–19).

There is nothing particularly spectacular about this setting, but (as the Venetian observer realized) it is a beautiful machine; moreover, it is designed to supply a principle of coherence for a work whose action tends to be diffuse. Everything in the masque proceeds from the mountain or disappears into it. Always in view, it serves as both symbol and locale, and provides both unity of place and unity of action. There are few masques in which the imagination of the architect is so thoroughly in touch with the nature and special requirements of the poet's text.

The attenuation of structure in *The Vision of Delight* and *Pleasure Reconciled to Virtue* is unusual only according to Jonson's own practice. Other productions of the period (e.g. Campion's Somerset masque of 1614) are far more shapeless, and all the problems that had become central for Jonson, involving the unification of the

---

37. Quoted in Italian in *Jonson*, X.582.

form and its transformation into literature, hardly exist for any of his contemporaries. *For the Honor of Wales*, the revised masque of 1618, will seem less of a radical departure if we remember that Jonson was constantly experimenting with a form that was, in large measure, his to define. Its conventions were those of its function— the adulation of the king, the inclusion of disguised courtiers, the accommodation of a great deal of dancing. By contrast, its form was and had always been infinitely mutable; indeed in the masque, novelty and variety were in themselves virtues. This means that we must be wary of treating any of these works as normative, and that we can speak of their "development" (at least once the basic problems have been solved) only in a limited sense. To conceive the development of Elizabethan drama is relatively easy, for powerful though possibly specious reasons: Shakespeare is so clearly its greatest playwright that we tend, whether rightly or wrongly, to see every play from *Gorboduc* forward in terms of the way it leads toward Shakespearean drama. But the masque requires a different sort of critical perspective. The crucial problem for Jonson was the unity and integrity of the form, and his solution was to treat the form fully as literature, to give moral and poetic life to its occasional elements, just as to its symbols and action. One might, then, be persuaded that a masque like *Lovers Made Men* is "better" than *The Masque of Queens* because it is more integrated, and thus more successful by Jonson's own standards, but nevertheless continue to prefer *Queens* on less exclusive grounds, such as that its poetry is better.

Any solution to the problems of so dynamic a form was necessarily a temporary one, and Jones was developing his own ideas about what was essential to a court masque. If allegory, myth, metaphor, and drama were central qualities of the masque-as-poem, it was nevertheless natural that the designer should have conceived these qualities in terms of spectacle and machinery, not of language. By the time of the Caroline masque, as the title pages of *Love's*

Triumph and *Chloridia* proclaim, the architect has at last firmly taken his place beside the poet as inventor. Jonson's *Expostulation*, however, makes clear that his own sense of the form is no longer the operative one:

> I have met with those
> That do cry up the machine, and the shows;
> The majesty of Juno in the clouds,
> And peering forth of Iris in the shrouds;
> Th'ascent of Lady Fame which none could spy,
> Not they that sided her; Dame Poetry,
> Dame History, Dame Architecture too,
> And Goody Sculpture, brought with much ado
> To hold her up.
>
> (31–39)

These are the goddesses that had appeared in *Chloridia*; for Jonson the masque's allegorical figures are no longer poetry but stagecraft:

> O, to make boards to speak! There is a task!
> Painting and carpentry are the soul of masque.
>
> (49–50)

This will seem less prejudicial to Jones if we recall that they were about to become the soul of drama too. Here is Antony à Wood's account of the production of William Strode's play *The Floating Island* before the king and queen at Oxford in 1636:

It was acted on a goodly stage reaching from the upper end of the Hall almost to the hearth place, and had on it three or four openings on each side thereof, and partitions between them, much resembling the desks or studies in a Library, out of which the Actors issued forth. The said partitions they could draw in and out at their pleasure upon a sudden, and thrust out new in their places according to the nature of the Screen, whereon were represented Churches, Dwelling-houses, Palaces, etc. which for its variety bred very great admiration. Over all was delicate painting, resembling the Sky, Clouds, etc. At the upper end a great fair shut [i.e. shutter] of two leaves that opened and shut without any visible help.

Within which was set forth the emblem of the whole Play in a mysterious manner. Therein was the perfect resemblance of the billows of the Sea rolling, and an artificial Island, with Churches and Houses waving up and down and floating, as also rocks, trees and hills. Many other fine pieces of work and Landscapes did also appear at sundry openings· thereof, and a Chair was also seen to come gliding on the Stage without any visible help. All these representations, being the first . . . that were used on the English stage.[38]

Jonson might have observed, vindictively, that Wood scarcely sees the play for the scenery. But for us, at least, the old collaborators cannot be so easily dissociated. Wood's description represents the end product of a unique coalition in the history of the English stage, which in great measure determined the course of English drama for the next three hundred years. Its triumph, though Jonson would probably be loath to acknowledge it, properly belongs as much to him as to the architect.

---

38. Quoted in *Jonson*, X.410–11.

A Note on the Text

This selection contains works included in the Masque sections of the Jonson folios of 1616 and 1640. Since Jonson prepared his own text for the publication of the 1616 folio, and saw the volume through the press, it clearly represents his final revised copy, and any edition of the masques through *The Golden Age Restored* and *Mercury Vindicated* (the masques of 1615 and 1616, printed in reverse order by Jonson) must be based upon it. (The Oxford editors' confusing statement that the copy for the first folio went to the printer in 1612 "or at latest 1613" [IX.14] is frequently, understandably, and erroneously taken to mean that the folio contains nothing written after 1612.) The case of the second volume of the 1640 folio, containing the masques after 1616, is more problematical; it was badly edited by Sir Kenelm Digby, and haphazardly proofread. Nevertheless, it contains emendations that can only have been made by Jonson, and I have therefore assumed that it too represents, however inadequately, Jonson's final text. Aside from the correction of obvious errors, all changes adopted from manuscripts or quartos have been indicated in the textual notes. The special problems of *The Gypsies Metamorphosed* are discussed at the beginning of the notes to that masque.

Jonson's stage directions tend to be skimpy; in a few instances they have been editorially supplied, and are enclosed in brackets. In the case of speech and song headings Jonson was extremely erratic;

where these have been added, they too are enclosed in brackets, but in the interests of clarity, I have not always retained the exact form Jonson used, and have deleted occasional unnecessary duplications; in these instances it has been felt unnecessary to indicate an editorial emendation. At the same time, to impose consistency on Jonson's practice would be both difficult and misleading, and I have not attempted it. Textual information is given at the beginning of the notes to each masque. There and in the textual notes the following symbols have been used:

MS   a manuscript contemporary with the masque's performance, whether a holograph or not.

Q   a quarto published at the time of the performance.

F^1 the 1616 folio, prepared for the press by Jonson.

F^2 the 1640 reprint of F^1, published as the first volume of Jonson's works.

F^3 the second volume of the 1640 folio, prepared for the press from Jonson's papers by Sir Kenelm Digby.

During the course of printing, a number of pages of F^1 were reset, either because the type had been disturbed, or more probably because after the type had been distributed it was found that too few of certain sheets had been printed for the size of the edition. The resettings are therefore not revisions; indeed, rather than correcting errors, they tend to introduce them. Their variants have not been included in the textual notes, with the single exception of the conclusion of *The Golden Age Restored*, revised by Jonson while the folio was in the press.

A reading that differs from those of all texts cited for a particular masque is an editorial emendation; those which are not based on the precedent of some later edition are explained in the notes. Obvious errors have been silently corrected, and only the most significant variants have been recorded.

Modernization

Modernization has been undertaken in a fashion perhaps best described as gingerly. No old spellings have been retained simply for their picturesque qualities (hence *poulder* has, regrettably, become *powder*), but to sacrifice *inginer* to *engineer* is to sacrifice as well the rhythm of the lines of verse in which it appears, and in such cases the old spelling has, for consistency's sake, been retained in prose passages also. Similarly, spellings that indicate radically different syllabifications from ours (e.g. *heroës, commandement*) have been retained; but the pronunciation of modern English is as a whole so unlike that of Jonson's time that it has seemed pointless to attempt to retain old spellings merely because they appear to record contemporary pronunciations. The pun on *Albion* in *Love Freed,* "all by one," will not work for a modern reader no matter what orthography is used; and I have not thought it necessary to remind American readers that standard English has always said *clark* for *clerk* and *Darby* for *Derby.* On the other hand, to change the strictly analogous *Tibbal's* and *Bever* to *Theobald's* and *Belvoir* would clearly be perverse. *Verdingale* has always become *farthingale*: Jonson used both forms, and the two spellings must have represented the same pronunciation. But where modern English has replaced an Elizabethan word with a genuinely alternative form, and not simply with a different spelling, I have kept the original: hence *tralucent* has not become *translucent,* and *tyranne* in its various spellings has been normalized to *tyran,* not *tyrant.* In general, I have let common sense be my guide, to the detriment of absolute consistency.

Jonson's etymologizing spellings (e.g. *windore* for *window*) have been abandoned, though this has sometimes meant a weakening of meaning (e.g. *holiday* for *holy-day*); but such spellings have been retained in a few cases where the modern meaning really is not intended: e.g., "Love's common-wealth consists of toys" means not Love's republic but its shared possessions. And I have tried to preserve certain Jonsonian distinctions—for example, between the general term *prospective* (any scene, whether painted or not) and the more technical *perspective*; between *subtile* (complex, cunning) and *subtle*, etc.

These are relatively minor matters: except for the odd pun, a word is the same no matter how it is spelled. The problem of punctuation, however, is more vexed, and no method of modernizing can be wholly satisfactory. I have lightened punctuation, and clarified syntax wherever possible. But Elizabethan syntax was vastly different from ours, and included devices for which there is no modern equivalent—for example, the extraordinary *apo koinu* in *Hymenaei* (lines 741–42). More generally, our rules for the subordination of clauses are largely eighteenth-century, and to attempt to reduce Jonson's practice to ours is as impossible as it is misguided. It is not at all uncommon in Jonsonian prose to find a series of clauses, both independent and dependent, seemingly arbitrarily connected by semicolons and colons, concluding with a period, and then followed by a dependent clause introduced by a relative pronoun. To the modern reader, who is used to having his clauses arranged in neater piles, such passages are almost unreadable; and I have attempted to break them up into more manageable segments wherever possible. This is purely a visual aid, however; the resulting syntax is rarely any less peculiar by modern standards. Some sense of the nature of the problem may be quickly gained by any reader who cares to look, in *The Complete Masques*, at *Blackness*, lines 113–29, and undertakes to find the verb. It is important to realize that Jonson is not being careless here, nor is Elizabethan syntax sloppy. Jonson writes admirable Elizabethan English; and the burden of historical awareness is on us.

A Note on the Appendix

The appendix includes all of Jonson's marginal glosses, which deal for the most part with background and source material. Since the glosses were designed strictly for use, I have considered the convenience of the modern reader to be of primary importance in preparing my text. Hence both Jonson's Latin and Greek notes and all quotations are given in translation, and citations appear in their normal modern form. (Passages other than quotations appearing in Latin or Greek in Jonson's text are italicized.) Information that has been editorially supplied is enclosed in brackets, but obvious errors of Jonson's have been silently emended, and the numbering system used in references to classical texts is in all cases the standard modern one, and, wherever possible, that of the Loeb Library. Where this differs from the numbering of Jonson's references, it has been thought unnecessary to note that an emendation has been made. In cases where no modern text exists, every effort has been made to avoid requiring the reader to have access to any particular edition, and references are thus for the most part given only to book and chapter or section numbers. Fortunately, Renaissance chapters tended to be short. Particular editions have been cited by page or folio numbers only when the numbering system of a work varies from edition to edition, or when individual sections are unusually long, or when a book exists in only one edition.

Occasionally Jonson's glosses are quoted or adapted from contemporary handbooks, usually without acknowledgment. The reader interested in the sources of Jonson's sources should consult the Oxford editors' notes. On the glosses to *The Masque of Queens*, W. Todd Furniss' article "The Annotation of Ben Jonson's *Masque of Queens*," *Review of English Studies*, V (1954), pp. 344–60, is useful, though badly obscured by a number of confusions and errors.

Hymenaei,
or the Solemnities of Masque and Barriers at a Marriage

It is a noble and just advantage that the things subjected to understanding have of those which are objected to sense that the one sort are but momentary and merely taking, the other impressing and lasting. Else the glory of all these solemnities had perished like a blaze and gone out in the beholders' eyes. So short lived 5 are the bodies of all things in comparison of their souls. And, though bodies ofttimes have the ill luck to be sensually preferred, they find afterwards the good fortune, when souls live, to be utterly forgotten. This it is hath made the most royal princes and greatest persons, who are commonly the personators of these 10 actions, not only studious of riches and magnificence in the outward celebration or show, which rightly becomes them, but curious after the most high and hearty inventions to furnish the inward

Note: Jonson's text includes an extensive commentary dealing largely with Roman marriage customs. These notes are indicated by asterisks and will be found in the appendix.
Title BARRIERS *entertainment at which knights fought a joust across a bar in the center of the hall.* MARRIAGE N.
1 SUBJECTED TO *inherent in.*
2 OBJECTED *exposed.* SENSE *the senses.*
3 TAKING *charming.*
10 PERSONATORS *performers.*

parts, and those grounded upon antiquity and solid learnings;
15   which, though their voice be taught to sound to present occasions,
their sense or doth or should always lay hold on more removed
mysteries. And howsoever some may squeamishly cry out that all
endeavor of learning and sharpness in these transitory devices,
especially where it steps beyond their little or (let me not wrong
20   'em) no brain at all, is superfluous, I am contented these fastidious
stomachs should leave my full tables and enjoy at home their clean
empty trenchers, fittest for such airy tastes, where perhaps a few
Italian herbs picked up and made into a salad may find sweeter
acceptance than all the most nourishing and sound meats of the
25   world.

For these men's palates let me not answer, O muses. It is not my
fault if I fill them out nectar and they run to metheglin.

Vaticana bibant, si delectentur.

All the courtesy I can do them is to cry again,

30   *Praetereant, si quid non facit ad stomachum.*

As I will, from the thought of them to my better subject.

On the night of the masques (which were two, one of men, the other of
women) the scene being drawn, there was first discovered an altar, upon
which was inscribed in letters of gold,

35   ★   IONI. OIMAE. MIMAE.

UNIONI

SACR.

18–9 devices, especially] *so* F²; devices especially, Q, F¹.

17 SOME . . . OUT N.

27 METHEGLIN *a Welsh spiced honey-liquor.*

28 VATICANA . . . *They may drink bad wine if they like.*

30 PRAETEREANT . . . *They may proceed, if it does not upset their stomachs.* (*Adapted from Martial, X.xlv.5–6.*)

33 SCENE *curtain.*

35 IONI. OIMAE. MIMAE *for* Iunoni Optimae Maximae, *to best and greatest Juno. Juno presided over marriages.*

36–7 UNIONI SACR. *for* Sacra, *sacred to marriage.*

*To this altar entered five pages attired in white, bearing five tapers of
*virgin wax; behind them, one representing a bridegroom, his hair short and
   bound with particolored ribbons and gold twist, his garments purple and   40
                                        white.

On the other hand entered Hymen, the god of marriage, in a saffron
colored robe, his under vestures white, his socks yellow, a yellow veil of
*silk on his left arm, his head crowned with roses and marjoram, in his right
                      hand a torch of pine tree.   45

*After him a youth attired in white bearing another light of white thorn;
under his arm a little wicker flasket, shut; behind him two others in white,
the one bearing a distaff, the other a spindle. Betwixt these a personated
bride, supported, her hair flowing and loose, sprinkled with grey; on her
head a garland of roses like a turret; her garments white, and on her back a   50
wether's fleece hanging down; her zone, or girdle about her waist, of white
             wool, fastened with the Herculean knot.

*In the midst went the auspices; after them, two that sung, in several-
colored silks; of which one bore the water, the other the fire; last of all the
*musicians, diversly attired, all crowned with roses, and with this song began.   55

SONG

         Bid all profane away;
         None here may stay
         To view our mysteries
         But who themselves have been,   60
         Or will in time be seen
         The self same sacrifice.
         For Union, mistress of these rites
         Will be observed with eyes
         As simple as her nights.   65

47 FLASKET *shallow basket.*

51 WETHER *ram.*

52 HERCULEAN KNOT *See Jonson's note to line 175.*

53 AUSPICES *sponsors of the marriage. See Jonson's note.*

Chorus.   Fly then, all profane, away,
          Fly far off, as hath the day;
          Night her curtain doth display,
          And this is Hymen's holiday.

70   *The song being ended, Hymen presented himself foremost, and after some*
          sign of admiration began to speak.

Hymen.   What more than usual light,
          Throughout the place extended,
          Makes Juno's fane so bright!
75   Is there some greater deity descended?

          Or reign on earth those powers
So rich, as with their beams
          Grace Union more than ours,
And bound her influence in their happier streams?

80   'Tis so: this same is he,
The king, and priest of peace!
          And that his empress, she
That sits so crownèd with her own increase!

          O you, whose better blisses
85   Have proved the strict embrace
          Of Union with chaste kisses,
And seen it flow so in your happy race;

          That know how well it binds
The fighting seeds of things,
90   Wins natures, sexes, minds,
And every discord in true music brings:

          Sit now propitious aides
To rites so duly prized,

71 ADMIRATION *wonder.*
81 PEACE *James's pacifism is a continual refrain in Jonson's masques.*
85 PROVED *experienced.*

And view two noble maids
Of different sex to Union sacrificed,   95
In honor of that blessed estate
Which all good minds should celebrate.

*Here out of a microcosm, or globe, figuring man, with a kind of contentious
music, issued forth the first masque, of eight men.*

★ *These represented the four humors and four affections, all gloriously attired,* 100
distinguished only by their several ensigns and colors, and dancing out on
the stage, in their return at the end of their dance drew all their swords,
offered to encompass the altar and disturb the ceremonies. At which Hymen,
troubled, spake:

Hymen. Save, save the virgins; keep your hallowed lights   105
Untouched, and with their flame defend our rites.
The four untempered humors are broke out,
And with their wild affections go about
To ravish all religion. If there be
A power like reason left in that huge body,   110
Or little world of man, from whence these came,
★   Look forth, and with thy bright and numerous flame
Instruct their darkness, make them know and see,
In wronging these, they have rebelled 'gainst thee.

Hereat Reason, seated in the top of the globe (as in the brain, or highest 115
part of man), figured in a venerable personage, her hair white and trailing

99 N.

---

94 MAIDS *i.e. both are chaste. Maid, like virgin, could be used of a man.*

98 MICROCOSM *literally, little world. See line 111.*

99 EIGHT MEN N.

100 FOUR . . . AFFECTIONS *The humors are the bodily fluids whose mixture controls*
the non-rational personality; the affections are the passions produced by
the imbalance of the humors.

101 ENSIGNS *insignia.*

107 UNTEMPERED *improperly mixed (hence* intemperate).

112 NUMEROUS *harmonious. See Jonson's note.*

to her waist, crowned with lights, her garments blue and semined with stars,
girded unto her with a white bend filled with arithmetical figures, in one
hand bearing a lamp, in the other a bright sword, descended and spake:

120 Reason. Forbear your rude attempt! What ignorance
        Could yield you so profane as to advance
        One thought in act against these mysteries?
     ★   Are Union's orgies of so slender price?
        She that makes souls with bodies mix in love,
125   Contracts the world in one, and therein Jove,
     ★   Is spring and end of all things: yet, most strange!
        Her self nor suffers spring nor end nor change.
        No wonder they were you that were so bold;
        For none but humors and affections would
130   Have dared so rash a venture. You will say
        It was your zeal that gave your powers the sway,
        And urge the maskèd and disguised pretense
        Of saving blood and succ'ring innocence?
        So want of knowledge still begetteth jars
135   When humorous earthlings will control the stars.
        Inform yourselves with safer reverence
        To these mysterious rites, whose mystic sense
        Reason, which all things but itself confounds,
        Shall clear unto you from th' authentic grounds.

140 *At this the humors and affections sheathed their swords and retired amazed*
to the sides of the stage, while Hymen began to rank the persons and order
the ceremonies. And Reason proceeded to speak.

117 SEMINED *seeded.*
118 BEND *band.*
123 ORGIES *celebrations.*
125 THEREIN JOVE *i.e. god is a part of the marriage.*
133 SAVING BLOOD *from the "sacrifice" of line 95.*
135 HUMOROUS *controlled by humors, irrational.*
139 CLEAR *explain.*

Reason. The pair which do each other side,
　　　　Though yet some space doth them divide,
　　　　This happy night must both make one　　　　145
　　　　Blest sacrifice to Union.
　　　　Nor is this altar but a sign
　　　　Of one more soft and more divine,
 ★ 　　The genial bed, where Hymen keeps
　　　　The solemn orgies, void of sleeps;　　　　150
　　　　And wildest Cupid, waking, hovers
　　　　With adoration twixt the lovers.
　　　　The tede of white and blooming thorn
　　　　In token of increase is borne,
 ★ 　　As also with the ominous light　　　　155
　　　　To fright all malice from the night.
 ★ 　　Like are the fire and water set,
　　　　That, even as moisture mixed with heat
　　　　Helps every natural birth to life,
　　　　So, for their race, join man and wife.　　　　160
 ★ 　　The blushing veil shows shamefastness
　　　　The ingenuous virgin should profess
 ★ 　　At meeting with the man. Her hair,
　　　　That flows so liberal and so fair,
　　　　Is shed with grey, to intimate　　　　165
　　　　She ent'reth to a matron's state,
 ★ 　　For which those utensils are borne.
　　　　And that she should not labor scorn,

162 ingenuous] ingenious Ff.

---

143 SIDE *stand side by side.*
149 GENIAL *nuptial.*
153 TEDE *torch.*
155 OMINOUS *presaging good fortune.*

★   Herself a snowy fleece doth wear,
170 ★   And these her rock and spindle bear,
          To show that nothing which is good
          Gives check unto the highest blood.
★   The zone of wool about her waist,
          Which, in contrary circles cast,
175 ★   Doth meet in one strong knot that binds,
          Tells you, so should all married minds.
          And lastly, these five waxen lights
          Imply perfection in the rites,
★   For five the special number is
180   Whence hallowed Union claims her bliss,
          As being all the sum that grows
          From the united strengths of those
★   Which male and female numbers we
          Do style, and are first two, and three;
185   Which joinèd thus you cannot sever
          In equal parts, but one will ever
          Remain as common: so we see
          The binding force of unity;
          For which alone the peaceful gods
190   In number always love the odds,
          And even parts as much despise,
          Since out of them all discords rise.

*Here the upper part of the scene, which was all of clouds and made
artificially to swell and ride like the rack, began to open, and, the air*
195 *clearing, in the top thereof was discovered Juno sitting in a throne supported*
    by two beautiful peacocks; her attire rich and like a queen, a white diadem

170 ROCK *distaff on which the fiber was held for spinning.*
172 GIVES . . . BLOOD *causes nobility to balk.*
173 ZONE *belt.*
179–92 FIVE . . . RISE N.
194 RACK *a mass of clouds driven by wind.*

*on her head from whence descended a veil, and that bound with a fascia of
several-colored silks, set with all sorts of jewels and raised in the top with
*lilies and roses; in her right hand she held a scepter, in the other a timbrel;
*at her golden feet the hide of a lion was placed; round about her sat the   200
spirits of the air, in several colors, making music. Above her the region of
fire with a continual motion was seen to whirl circularly, and Jupiter
standing in the top, figuring the heaven, brandishing his thunder; beneath
her the rainbow, Iris, and on the two sides, eight ladies, attired richly and
alike in the most celestial colors, who represented her powers (as she is the   205
*governess of marriage), and made the second masque. All which, upon the
discovery, Reason made narration of.

Reason. And see where Juno, whose great name
          Is Unio, in the anagram,
          Displays her glistering state and chair,   210
          As she enlightened all the air!
          Hark how the charming tunes do beat
          In sacred concords 'bout her seat!
          And lo! to grace what these intend,
          Eight of her noblest powers descend,   215
*   Which are enstyled her faculties
          That govern nuptial mysteries,
          And wear those masks before their faces,
          Lest, dazzling mortals with their graces
          As they approach them, all mankind   220
          Should be, like Cupid, strooken blind.
          These Order waits for on the ground,
          To keep that you should not confound
          Their measured steps, which only move
          About th' harmonious sphere of love.   225

197 FASCIA *headband.*
206–07 UPON . . . DISCOVERY *when it was revealed.*
223 TO . . . CONFOUND *to keep you from confusing.*

Their descent was made in two great clouds that put forth themselves severally and, with one measure of time, were seen to stoop and fall gently down upon the earth. The manner of their habits came after some statues of Juno, no less airy than glorious. The dressings of their heads, rare; so like-
230 *wise of their feet; and all full of splendor, sovereignty and riches. Whilst they were descending this song was sung at the altar.*

SONG

These, these are they
Whom humor and affection must obey;
235   Who come to deck the genial bower,
And bring with them the grateful hour
That crowns such meetings and excites
The married pair to fresh delights,
As courtings, kissings, coyings, oaths and vows,
240   Soft whisperings, embracements, all the joys
And melting toys
That chaster love allows.
Chorus. Haste, haste, for Hesperus his head down bows.

The song ended, they danced forth in pairs, and each pair with a varied and
245 *noble grace, to a rare and full music of twelve lutes, led on by Order, the servant of Reason, who was there rather a person of ceremony than use. His undergarment was blue, his upper white and painted full of arithmetical and geometrical figures; his hair and beard long, a star on his forehead, and in his hand a geometrical staff. To whom, after the dance, Reason spake.*

250 *Reason.* Convey them, Order, to their places,
And rank them so, in several traces,
As they may set their mixèd powers
Unto the music of the hours;

243 HESPERUS *the evening star.*
251 TRACES *rows.*

And these, by joining with them, know
In better temper how to flow;   255
Whilst I, from their abstracted names
Report the virtues of the dames.
★ First *Curis* comes to deck the bride's fair tress.
★ Care of the ointments *Unxia* doth profess.
★ *Juga*, her office to make one of twain;   260
★ *Gamelia* sees that they should so remain.
★ Fair *Iterduca* leads the bride her way,
★ And *Domiduca* home her steps doth stay;
★ *Cinxia* the maid, quit of her zone, defends;
★ *Telia*, for Hymen, perfects all, and ends.   265

By this time the ladies were paired with the men, and the whole sixteen
ranked forth, in order, to dance, and were with this song provoked.

SONG

Now, now begin to set
Your spirits in active heat,   270
And since your hands are met,
Instruct your nimble feet
In motions swift and meet,
The happy ground to beat:

254 THESE *the humors and affections.*
255 IN ... TEMPER *i.e. the dance will correct the disproportion of the humors'*
mixture, and they will cease to be intemperate.
258 CURIS *a spear. See Jonson's notes on this and the following names, all aspects*
of Juno as patroness of marriage.
259 UNXIA *anointer.*
260 JUGA *yoke.*
261 GAMELIA *nuptial goddess.*
262 ITERDUCA *the journey's guide.*
263 DOMIDUCA *the guide home.*
264 CINXIA *girdle.* ZONE *girdle, belt.*
265 TELIA *perfected.*
267 PROVOKED *called forth.*

275 *Chorus.*   Whilst all this roof doth ring,
                          And each discording string
                          With every varied voice
                          In union doth rejoice.

Here they danced forth a most neat and curious measure, full of subtlety
280 *and device, which was so excellently performed as it seemed to take away*
that spirit from the invention which the invention gave to it, and left it
doubtful whether the forms flowed more perfectly from the author's brain or
their feet. The strains were all notably different, some of them formed into
letters very signifying to the name of the bridegroom, and ended in manner
285   *of a chain, linking hands. To which this was spoken.*

    ★Reason. Such was the golden chain let down from heaven,
                          And not those links more even
                      Than these, so sweetly tempered, so combined
                          By Union, and refined.
290   Here no contention, envy, grief, deceit,
                          Fear, jealousy have weight,
                    But all is peace and love and faith and bliss:
                          What harmony like this?
                    The gall behind the altar quite is thrown;
295   This sacrifice hath none.
                    Now no affections rage nor humors swell,
                          But all composèd dwell.
                    O Juno, Hymen, Hymen, Juno! who
                          Can merit with you two?
300   Without your presence Venus can do nought,
                          Save what with shame is bought;
                    No father can himself a parent show,
                    Nor any house with prosp'rous issue grow.

280 DEVICE *inventiveness.*
286 GOLDEN CHAIN *reaching from earth to the throne of god.*
294 GALL *See Jonson's note on line 261.*

O then! what deities will dare
With Hymen or with Juno to compare? 305

*The speech being ended, they dissolved, and all took forth other persons,
men and women, to dance other measures, galliards and corantos, the whilst
this song importuned them to a fit remembrance of the time.*

SONG

Think yet how night doth waste, 310
How much of time is past,
What more than wingèd haste
Yourselves would take
If you were but to taste
The joy the night doth cast 315
(O might it ever last)
On this bright virgin, and her happy make.

Their dances yet lasting, they were the second time importuned by speech.

★Reason. See, see! the bright Idalian star
That lighteth lovers to their war 320
Complains that you her influence lose
While thus the night-sports you abuse.
★Hymen. The longing bridegroom in the porch
Shows you again the bated torch,
★ And thrice hath Juno mixed her air 325
With fire to summon your repair.
Reason. See, now she clean withdraws her light,
And, as you should, gives place to night
That spreads her broad and blackest wing
Upon the world, and comes to bring 330

307 MEASURES *slow dances.* GALLIARDS *quick dances.* CORANTOS *dances with a
running or gliding step.*
317 MAKE *mate.*
319 IDALIAN STAR *Venus.*
324 BATED *diminished.*

*   A thousand several-colored loves,
                 Some like sparrows, some like doves
                 That hop about the nuptial room,
                 And flutt'ring there, against you come,
335*   Warm the chaste bower, which Cypria strows
                 With many a lily, many a rose.
   Hymen. Haste therefore, haste, and call away;
                 The gentle night is pressed to pay
                 The usury of long delights
340   She owes to these protracted rites.

At this (the whole scene being drawn again, and all covered with clouds, as a night) they left off their intermixed dances and returned to their first places, where as they were but beginning to move, this song the third time urged them.

345   SONG

                 O know to end, as to begin;
                 A minute's loss in love is sin.
                 These humors will the night outwear
                 In their own pastimes here;
350   You do our rites much wrong
                 In seeking to prolong
                 These outward pleasures:
                 The night hath other treasures
                 Than these, though long concealed,
355   Ere day to be revealed.
                 Then know to end, as to begin;
                 A minute's loss in love is sin.

Here they danced their last dances, full of excellent delight and change, and in their latter strain fell into a fair orb or circle, Reason standing in the
360   *midst and speaking.*

334 AGAINST . . . COME *in preparation for your coming.*
335 CYPRIA *Venus.*
341 SCENE . . . AGAIN *curtain being closed.*
346 KNOW *know how.*

Reason. Here stay, and let your sports be crowned:
  The perfect'st figure is the round.
  Nor fell you in it by adventure,
  When Reason was your guide and center.
  This, this that beauteous Ceston is   365
  Of lovers' many-colored bliss.
  Come Hymen, make an inner ring
  And let the sacrificers sing;
  Cheer up the faint and trembling bride
  That quakes to touch her bridegroom's side; 370
  Tell her, what Juno is to Jove,
  The same shall she be to her love:
  His wife, which we do rather measure
  A name of dignity than pleasure.
  Up youths, hold up your lights in air,   375
  And shake abroad their flaming hair.
  Now move united and in gait,
  As you in pairs do front the state,
  With grateful honors thank his grace
  That hath so glorified the place,   380
  And as in circle you depart
  Linked hand in hand, so heart in heart
  May all those bodies still remain
  Whom he, with so much sacred pain,
  No less hath bound within his realms 385
  Than they are with the ocean's streams.
  Long may his union find increase
  As he to ours hath deigned his peace.

With this, to a soft strain of music, they paced once about in their ring,

363 ADVENTURE *chance.*
365 CESTON *the girdle of Venus.*
378 FRONT . . . STATE *stand before the king's throne.*

390 *every pair making their honors as they came before the state; and then*
dissolving, went down in couples led on by Hymen, the bride and auspices
following, as to the nuptial bower. After them, the musicians with this song,
of which then only one staff was sung; but because I made it both in form
★*and matter to emulate that kind of poem which was called* epithalamium,
395 *and by the ancients used to be sung when the bride was led into her*
chamber, I have here set it down whole, and do heartily forgive their
ignorance whom it chanceth not to please, hoping that nemo doctus me
iubeat thalassionem verbis dicere non thalassionis.

EPITHALAMION

400   Glad time is at his point arrived
             For which love's hopes were so long-lived.
                    Lead, Hymen, lead away;
                    And let no object stay,
                    Nor banquets (but sweet kisses),
405   The turtles from their blisses.
★   'Tis Cupid calls to arm,
                    And this his last alarm.
             Shrink not, soft virgin, you will love
             Anon what you so fear to prove.
410   This is no killing war
                    To which you pressèd are,
                    But fair and gentle strife
                    Which lovers call their life.
                    'Tis Cupid cries to arm,
415   And this his last alarm.

393 STAFF *stanza.*
397–98 NEMO . . . *No learned man will order me to write a wedding song in words*
      not suited to weddings. (Adapted from Martial, I.xxxv.6–7.)
403 STAY *keep.*
405 TURTLES *doves.*
409 PROVE *experience.*

Help, youths and virgins, help to sing
The prize which Hymen here doth bring,
  And did so lately rap
  From forth the mother's lap
  To place her by that side   420
  Where she must long abide.
  On Hymen, Hymen call;
  This night is Hymen's all.
See, Hesperus is yet in view!
What star can so deserve of you?   425
  Whose light doth still adorn
  Your bride, that, ere the morn,
  Shall far more perfect be,
  And rise as bright as he,
  When, like to him, her name   430
  Is changed, but not her flame.
Haste, tender lady, and adventure;
The covetous house would have you enter
  That it might wealthy be,
  And you her mistress see: 435
  Haste your own good to meet,
  And lift your golden feet
  Above the threshold high
  With prosperous augury.
Now, youths, let go your pretty arms; 440
The place within chants other charms.
  Whole showers of roses flow,
  And violets seem to grow,

418 RAP *ravish. See Jonson's note.*
424 HESPERUS *the evening star.*
432 ADVENTURE *venture.*

63

Strewed in the chamber there,
445 As Venus' mead it were.
On Hymen, Hymen call,
This night is Hymen's all.
Good matrons, that so well are known
To agèd husbands of your own,
450 Place you our bride tonight,
★ And snatch away the light,
★ That she not hide it dead
Beneath her spouse's bed,
★ Nor he reserve the same
455 To help the funeral flame.
So, now you may admit him in;
The act he covets is no sin,
But chaste and holy love,
Which Hymen doth approve,
460 Without whose hallowing fires
All aims are base desires.
On Hymen, Hymen call,
This night is Hymen's all.
Now free from vulgar spite or noise,
465 May you enjoy your mutual joys;
Now you no fear controls,
But lips may mingle souls,
And soft embraces bind
To each the other's mind,
470 Which may no power untie
Till one or both must die.
And look, before you yield to slumber,
That your delights be drawn past number:
Joys got with strife increase.
475 Affect no sleepy peace,

445 MEAD *meadow.*

64

But keep the bride's fair eyes
Awake with her own cries,
Which are but maiden fears,
And kisses dry such tears.
Then coin them 'twixt your lips so sweet,   480
And let no cockles closer meet,
        Nor may your murmuring loves
★   Be drowned by Cypris' doves;
        Let ivy not so bind
        As when your arms are twined,   485
        That you may both ere day
        Rise perfect every way.
And Juno, whose great powers protect
The marriage bed, with good effect
        The labor of this night   490
        Bless thou for future light;
        And thou, thy happy charge,
★   Glad Genius, enlarge,
        That they may both ere day
        Rise perfect every way.   495
★   And Venus, thou, with timely seed
    (Which may their after-comforts breed)
        Inform the gentle womb,
        Nor let it prove a tomb,
        But ere ten moons be wasted,   500
        The birth, by Cynthia hasted.
        So may they both ere day
        Rise perfect every way.
    And when the babe to light is shown,
    Let it be like each parent known;   505

483 CYPRIS *Venus.*
493 GENIUS *god of begetting children. See Jonson's note.*
501 CYNTHIA *Diana as the moon, connected with childbirth.*

Much of the father's face,
More of the mother's grace,
And either grandsire's spirit
And fame let it inherit,
510 That men may bless th'embraces
That joinèd two such races.
Cease youths and virgins, you have done;
Shut fast the door: and as they soon
To their perfection haste,
515 So may their ardors last;
So either's strength outlive
All loss that age can give,
And though full years be told,
Their forms grow slowly old.

520 Hitherto extended the first night's solemnity, whose grace in the execution left not where to add unto it with wishing; I mean (nor do I court them) in those that sustained the nobler parts. Such was the exquisite performance, as (beside the pomp, splendor, or what we may call apparelling of such presentments) that alone, had all else been absent, was of power to surprise with delight, and steal away the spectators from themselves. Nor was there wanting whatsoever might give to the furniture or complement, either in riches, or strangeness of the habits, delicacy of dances, magnificence of the scene, or divine rapture of music. Only the envy was that it lasted not still, or, now it is past, cannot by imagination, much less description, be recovered to a part of that spirit it had in the gliding by.

Yet that I may not utterly defraud the reader of his hope, I am drawn to give it those brief touches which may leave behind some shadow of what it was: and first of the attires.

521 WHERE *anywhere.*
527 FURNITURE *details of the performance; the "production."*
528 HABITS *costumes.*

   That of the lords had part of it (for the fashion) taken from the antique Greek statue, mixed with some modern additions, which made it both graceful and strange. On their heads they wore Persic crowns that were with scrolls of gold plate turned outward, and wreathed about with a carnation and silver net lawn, the one end 540 of which hung carelessly on the left shoulder, the other was tricked up before in several degrees of folds between the plates, and set with rich jewels and great pearl. Their bodies were of carnation cloth of silver, richly wrought, and cut to express the naked, in manner of the Greek thorax, girt under the breasts with a broad 545 belt of cloth of gold embroidered and fastened before with jewels. Their labels were of white cloth of silver, laced and wrought curiously between, suitable to the upper half of their sleeves, whose nether parts, with their bases, were of watchet cloth of silver chevronned all over with lace. Their mantles were of 550 several-colored silks, distinguishing their qualities, as they were coupled in pairs; the first, sky color; the second, pearl color; the third, flame color; the fourth, tawny; and these cut in leaves which were subtly tacked up and embroidered with oos, and between every rank of leaves, a broad silver lace. They were fastened on the 555 right shoulder and fell compass down the back in gracious folds, and were again tied with a round knot to the fastening of their swords. Upon their legs they wore silver greaves, answering in work to their labels; and these were their accoutrements.

538 PERSIC *Persian.*
540 LAWN *fine linen.*
541–42 TRICKED . . . BEFORE *elaborately arranged in front.*
547 LABELS *the vertical bands on the short sleeves and skirts of the Greek military costume.*
549 WATCHET *light blue.*
554 OOS *metal eyelets used as decoration.*
556 COMPASS *curving.*
558 GREAVES *leg armor.*
558–59 ANSWERING . . . TO *with the same design as.*

560   The ladies' attire was wholly new, for the invention, and full of glory, as having in it the most true impression of a celestial figure: the upper part of white cloth of silver wrought with Juno's birds and fruits; a loose undergarment, full gathered, of carnation, striped with silver and parted with a golden zone; beneath that 565   another flowing garment of watchet cloth of silver, laced with gold; through all which, though they were round and swelling, there yet appeared some touch of their delicate lineaments, preserving the sweetness of proportion and expressing itself beyond expression. The attire of their heads did answer, if not 570   exceed; their hair being carelessly (but yet with more art than if more affected) bound under the circle of a rare and rich coronet adorned with all variety and choice of jewels, from the top of which flowed a transparent veil down to the ground, whose verge, returning up, was fastened to either side in most sprightly manner. 575   Their shoes were azure and gold set with rubies and diamonds; so were all their garments, and every part abounding in ornament.

      No less to be admired for the grace and greatness was the whole machine of the spectacle, from whence they came, the first part of which was a *mikrokosmos*, or globe, filled with countries, and those 580   gilded; where the sea was expressed, heightened with silver waves. This stood, or rather hung (for no axle was seen to support it), and turning softly, discovered the first masque (as we have before but too runningly declared), which was of the men, sitting in fair composition within a mine of several metals; to which the lights 585   were so placed as no one was seen, but seemed as if only Reason with the splendor of her crown illumined the whole grot.

562 JUNO'S BIRDS *peacocks*.
564 ZONE *belt*.
569 ANSWER *equal*.
571 AFFECTED *elaborate*.
573 VERGE *edge*.
579 MIKROKOSMOS *literally, little world*.

On the sides of this (which began the other part) were placed two great statues feigned of gold, one of Atlas, the other of Hercules, in varied postures, bearing up the clouds, which were of *relève*, embossed, and tralucent, as naturals. To these a curtain of painted 590 clouds joined, which reached to the upmost roof of the hall, and suddenly opening, revealed the three regions of air; in the highest of which sat Juno in a glorious throne of gold, circled with comets and fiery meteors engendered in that hot and dry region, her feet reaching to the lowest, where was made a rainbow, and within it, 595 musicians seated, figuring airy spirits, their habits various, and resembling the several colors caused in that part of the air by reflection. The midst was all of dark and condensed clouds, as being the proper place where rain, hail and other watery meteors are made; out of which, two concave clouds from the rest thrust 600 forth themselves (in nature of those *nimbi* wherein by Homer, Virgil, etc. the gods are feigned to descend) and these carried the eight ladies over the heads of the two terms, who (as the engine moved) seemed also to bow themselves (by virtue of their shadows) and discharge their shoulders of their glorious burden; 605 when, having set them on the earth, both they and the clouds gathered themselves up again, with some rapture of the beholders.

But that which (as above in place, so in the beauty) was most taking in the spectacle was the sphere of fire, in the top of all, encompassing the air, and imitated with such art and industry as 610 the spectators might discern the motion, all the time the shows lasted, without any mover; and that so swift as no eye could distinguish any color of the light, but might form to itself five hundred several hues out of the tralucent body of the air objected betwixt it and them. 615

588 FEIGNED *fashioned.*
589 OF RELÈVE *in relief.*
590 TRALUCENT *translucent.* AS NATURALS *like real clouds.*
603 TERMS *statues:* "*Atlas and Hercules, the figures mentioned before.*" (J)
614 OBJECTED *interposed.*

And this was crowned with a statue of Jupiter the Thunderer.

*On the next night, whose solemnity was of barriers (all mention of the
former being utterly removed and taken away) there appeared at the lower
end of the hall a mist made of delicate perfumes, out of which, a battle being*
620 *sounded under the stage, did seem to break forth two ladies, the one
representing Truth, the other Opinion, but both so alike attired as they
could by no note be distinguished. The color of their garments were blue,
their socks white; they were crowned with wreaths of palm, and in their
hands each of them sustained a palm bough. These, after the mist was*
625 *vanished, began to examine each other curiously with their eyes, and
approaching the state, the one expostulated the other in this manner.*

Truth. Who art thou thus that imitat'st my grace
    In steps, in habit and resembled face?
*Opinion. Grave time and industry my parents are;
630   My name is Truth, who through these sounds of war
    (Which figure the wise mind's discursive fight)
    In mists by nature wrapped, salute the light.
Truth. I am that Truth, thou some illusive sprite
    Whom to my likeness the black sorceress Night
635   Hath of these dry and empty fumes created.
Opinion. Best herald of thine own birth, well related:
    Put me and mine to proof of words and facts
    In any question this fair hour exacts.
Truth. I challenge thee, and fit this time of love
640   With this position, which Truth comes to prove:
    That the most honored state of man and wife
    Doth far exceed th'insociate virgin life.

616 N.
617 BARRIERS *joust over a bar in the center of the hall.*
626 STATE *throne.*
642 INSOCIATE *solitary.*

Opinion. I take the adverse part; and she that best
      Defends her side, be Truth by all confessed.
Truth.   It is confirmed. With what an equal brow   645
★   To Truth Opinion's confident! and how
      Like Truth her habit shows to sensual eyes!
      But whosoe'er thou be in this disguise,
      Clear Truth anon shall strip thee to the heart,
      And show how mere fantastical thou art.   650
        Know then the first production of things
      Required two; from mere one nothing springs:
      Without that knot, the theme thou gloriest in
      (Th'unprofitable virgin) had not been.
      The golden tree of marriage began   655
      In paradise, and bore the fruit of man,
      On whose sweet branches angels sat and sung,
      And from whose firm root all society sprung.
      Love (whose strong virtue wrapped heav'n's soul in earth,
      And made a woman glory in his birth)   660
      In marriage opens his inflamèd breast;
      And lest in him nature should stifled rest,
      His genial fire about the world he darts,
      Which lips with lips combines, and hearts with hearts.
      Marriage Love's object is, at whose bright eyes   665
      He lights his torches, and calls them his skies.
      For her he wings his shoulders, and doth fly
      To her white bosom, as his sanctuary,
      In which no lustful finger can profane him,
      Nor any earth with black eclipses wane him.   670
      She makes him smile in sorrows, and doth stand
      'Twixt him and all wants with her silver hand.

647 SHOWS *appears.*
659 HEAV'N'S SOUL *Christ, to whom "his" in the next line also refers.*
663 GENIAL *nuptial.*

In her soft locks his tender feet are tied,
And in his fetters he takes worthy pride.
675 And as geometricians have approved
That lines and superficies are not moved
By their own forces, but do follow still
Their bodies' motions, so the self-loved will
Of man or woman should not rule in them,
680 But each with other wear the anadem.
Mirrors, though decked with diamonds, are nought worth
If the like forms of things they set not forth;
So men or women are worth nothing neither
If either's eyes and hearts present not either.
685 *Opinion.* Untouched virginity, laugh out to see
Freedom in fetters placed, and urged 'gainst thee.
What griefs lie groaning on the nuptial bed?
What dull satiety? In what sheets of lead
Tumble and toss the restless married pair,
690 Each oft offended with the other's air?
From whence springs all-devouring avarice
But from the cares which out of wedlock rise?
And where there is in life's best-tempered fires
An end set in itself to all desires,
695 A settled quiet, freedom never checked;
How far are married lives from this effect?
★ Euripus, that bears ships in all their pride
'Gainst roughest winds, with violence of his tide,

688 satiety] society Ff.

---

675 APPROVED *demonstrated.*
676 SUPERFICIES *surfaces.*
677 STILL *always.*
680 ANADEM *wreath.*
693 WHERE *whereas.*
697 EURIPUS *a narrow strait between the island of Euboea and the Greek mainland.*

And ebbs and flows seven times in every day,
Toils not more turbulent or fierce than they.   700
And then, what rules husbands prescribe their wives!
In their eyes' circles they must bound their lives.
The moon when farthest from the sun she shines
Is most refulgent; nearest, most declines:
But your poor wives far off must never roam,   705
But waste their beauties near their lords at home;
And when their lords range out, at home must hide
(Like to begged monopòlies) all their pride.
When their lords list to feed a serious fit,
They must be serious; when to show their wit   710
In jests and laughter, they must laugh and jest;
When they wake, wake; and when they rest, must rest.
And to their wives men give such narrow scopes,
As if they meant to make them walk on ropes:
No tumblers bide more peril of their necks   715
In all their tricks than wives in husbands' checks;
Where virgins in their sweet and peaceful state
Have all things perfect, spin their own free fate,
Depend on no proud second, are their own
Center and circle, now and always one.   720
To whose example we do still hear named
One god, one nature, and but one world framed,
One sun, one moon, one element of fire,
So, of the rest; one king that doth inspire
Soul to all bodies in this royal sphere—   725

725 this] their Ff.

---

708 BEGGED MONOPÒLIES *corporations petitioning the state for the right of monopoly.*
   Jonson regularly accented monopoly on the third syllable.
709 LIST TO FEED *feel like indulging in.*
716 CHECKS *rebukes.*
717 WHERE *whereas.*

Truth.		And where is marriage more declared than there?
		Is there a band more strict than that doth tie
		The soul and body in such unity?
		Subjects to sovereigns? Doth one mind display
730		In th'one's obedience and the other's sway?
		Believe it, marriage suffers no compare
		When both estates are valued as they are.
		The virgin were a strange and stubborn thing
		Would longer stay a virgin than to bring
735		Herself fit use and profit in a make.
Opinion.		How she doth err! and the whole heav'n mistake!
		Look how a flower that close in closes grows,
		Hid from rude cattle, bruisèd with no plows,
		Which th'air doth stroke, sun strengthen, showers shoot
		higher,
740		It many youths and many maids desire;
		The same when cropped by cruel hand is withered,
		No youths at all, no maidens have desired:
		So a virgin, while untouched she doth remain,
		Is dear to hers; but when with body's stain
745		Her chaster flower is lost, she leaves to appear
		Or sweet to young men, or to maidens dear.
		That conquest then may crown me in this war,
		Virgins, O virgins, fly from Hymen far.
Truth.		Virgins, O virgins, to sweet Hymen yield,
750		For as a lone vine in a naked field
		Never extols her branches, never bears

734 WOULD LONGER *who would rather.*
735 MAKE *mate.*
736 THE . . . HEAV'N *totally.*
741 THE . . . WITHERED N.
746 OR . . . OR *either . . . or.*
751 EXTOLS *raises.*

Ripe grapes, but with a headlong heaviness wears
Her tender body, and her highest sprout
Is quickly levelled with her fading root;
By whom no husbandmen, no youths will dwell;   755
But if by fortune she be married well
To th'elm, her husband, many husbandmen
And many youths inhabit by her then:
So whilst a virgin doth, untouched, abide
All unmanured, she grows old with her pride;   760
But when to equal wedlock in fit time
Her fortune and endeavor lets her climb,
Dear to her love and parents she is held.
Virgins, O virgins, to sweet Hymen yield.

Opinion. These are but words; hast thou a knight will try   765
    By stroke of arms the simple verity?
Truth.   To that high proof I would have darèd thee.
    I'll straight fetch champions for the bride and me.
Opinion. The like will I do for Virginity.

Here they both descended the hall, where at the lower end, a march being   770
sounded with drums and fifes, there entered (led forth by the Earl of
Nottingham, who was Lord High Constable for that night, and the Earl
of Worcester, Earl Marshal) sixteen knights armed with pikes and swords,
their plumes and colors carnation and white, all richly accoutred; and
making their honors to the state as they marched by in pairs, were all ranked   775
on one side of the hall. They placed, sixteen others like accoutred for riches
and arms, only that their colors were varied to watchet and white, were by
the same earls led up, and passing in like manner by the state, placed on the
opposite side.

779 N.

---

760 UNMANURED *literally, uncultivated.*
775 STATE *throne.*
776 THEY PLACED *when they were placed.*
779 N.

780   *By this time the bar being brought up, Truth proceeded.*

Truth.   Now join; and if this varied trial fail
            To make my truth in wedlock's praise prevail,
            I will retire, and in more power appear,
            To cease this strife and make our question clear.

785   *Whereat Opinion, insulting, followed her with this speech.*

Opinion. Aye, do; it were not safe thou shouldst abide:
            This speaks thy name, with shame to quit thy side.

Here the champions on both sides addressed themselves for fight, first
single, after three to three; and performed it with that alacrity and vigor as
790 *if Mars himself had been to triumph before Venus and invented a new*
music. When on a sudden (the last six having scarcely ended) a striking
light seemed to fill all the hall, and out of it an angel or messenger of glory
                           appearing.

Angel.   Princes, attend a tale of height and wonder.
795   Truth is descended in a second thunder,
            And now will greet you with judicial state
            To grace the nuptial part in this debate
            And end with reconcilèd hands these wars.
               Upon her head she wears a crown of stars
800   Through which her orient hair waves to her waist,
            By which believing mortals hold her fast,
            And in those golden cords are carried even,
            Till with her breath she blows them up to heaven.
            She wears a robe enchased with eagles' eyes
805   To signify her sight in mysteries;

791 music] masque Ff.

---

780 BAR *at which the barriers were to be fought.*
800 ORIENT *lustrous.*

Upon each shoulder sits a milk-white dove,
And at her feet do witty serpents move;
Her spacious arms do reach from east to west,
And you may see her heart shine through her breast.
Her right hand holds a sun with burning rays,   810
Her left a curious bunch of golden keys,
With which heaven gates she locketh and displays.
A crystal mirror hangeth at her breast,
By which men's consciences are searched and dressed;
On her coach wheels Hypocrisy lies racked;   815
And squint-eyed Slander, with Vainglory backed,
Her bright eyes burn to dust, in which shines fate.
An angel ushers her triumphant gait,
Whilst with her fingers fans of stars she twists
And with them beats back Error, clad in mists.   820
Eternal Unity behind her shines,
That fire and water, earth and air combines.
Her voice is like a trumpet, loud and shrill,
Which bids all sounds in earth and heav'n be still.
And see! descended from her chariot now,   825
In this related pomp she visits you.

Truth.   Honor to all that honor nuptials,
To whose fair lot in justice now it falls
That this my counterfeit be here disclosed,
Who for virginity hath herself opposed.   830
Nor, though my brightness do undo her charms,
Let these her knights think that their equal arms
Are wronged therein: *for valor wins applause*
That dares but to maintain the weaker cause.

807 WITTY *wise.*
812 DISPLAYS *opens.*
814 DRESSED *guided.*
826 RELATED *just described.*

835 And princes, see, 'tis mere Opinion,
That in Truth's forcèd robe for Truth hath gone!
Her gaudy colors, pieced with many folds,
Show what uncertainties she ever holds:
Vanish, adult'rate Truth, and never dare
840 With proud maids' praise to press where nuptials are.
And champions, since you see the truth I held,
To sacred Hymen, reconcilèd, yield;
Nor so to yield think it the least despite:
It is a conquest to submit to right.
845   This royal judge of our contention
Will prop, I know, what I have undergone;
To whose right sacred highness I resign
Low, at his feet, this starry crown of mine,
To show his rule and judgment is divine;
850 These doves to him I consecrate withal
To note his innocence, without spot or gall;
These serpents, for his wisdom, and these rays
To show his piercing splendor; these bright keys
Designing power to ope the ported skies,
855 And speak their glories to his subjects' eyes.
   Lastly this heart, with which all hearts be true:
And truth in him make treason ever rue.

*With this they were led forth hand in hand, reconciled, as in triumph; and
thus the solemnities ended.*

860   *Vivite concordes, et nostrum discite munus.*

---

854 PORTED *having gates.*
860 VIVITE . . . *Live in harmony, and learn to perform our duty.* (*Claudian,* Carmina
Minora *XXV.130.*)

Prince Henry as *Oberon*.

The Masque of Queens

Celebrated from the House of Fame, by the queen of Great Britain
with her ladies. At Whitehall, February 2, 1609.

It increasing now to the third time of my being used in these
services to her majesty's personal presentations, with the ladies
whom she pleaseth to honor, it was my first and special regard to
see that the nobility of the invention should be answerable to the
dignity of their persons. For which reason I chose the argument to
be a celebration of honorable and true fame bred out of virtue,
observing that rule of the best artist, to suffer no object of delight
to pass without his mixture of profit and example. And because
her majesty (best knowing that a principal part of life in these
spectacles lay in their variety) had commanded me to think on
some dance or show that might precede hers and have the place of
a foil or false masque, I was careful to decline not only from others',

1 *N.*

Note: *Jonson's glosses, mainly on the sources of his demonology, are indicated by
asterisks and will be found in the appendix. A few included in the notes are
identified by (J).*

1 N.
7 BEST ARTIST *Horace, in* Ars Poetica. (J)
12 CAREFUL . . . DECLINE *afraid to vary.*

but mine own steps in that kind, since the last year I had an antimasque of boys; and therefore now devised that twelve women in
the habit of hags or witches, sustaining the persons of Ignorance,   15
Suspicion, Credulity, etc., the opposites to good Fame, should fill
that part, not as a masque but a spectacle of strangeness, producing
multiplicity of gesture, and not unaptly sorting with the current
and whole fall of the device.

His majesty, then, being set, and the whole company in full expectation,   20
the part of the scene which first presented itself was an ugly hell, which
flaming beneath, smoked unto the top of the roof. And in respect all evils
are, morally, said to come from hell, as also from that observation of
Torrentius upon Horace his Canidia, quae tot instructa venenis, ex Orci
*faucibus profecta videri possit, *these witches, with a kind of hollow and*   25
infernal music, came forth from thence. First one, then two, and three, and
more, till their number increased to eleven, all differently attired: some with
rats on their head, some on their shoulders; others with ointment pots at
their girdles; all with spindles, timbrels, rattles or other venefical instru-
ments, making a confused noise, with strange gestures. The device of their   30
attire was Master Jones his, with the invention and architecture of the
whole scene and machine. Only I prescribed them their properties of vipers,
snakes, bones, herbs, roots and other ensigns of their magic, out of the
authority of ancient and late writers, wherein the faults are mine, if there
be any found, and for that cause I confess them.   35

**These eleven witches beginning to dance (which is an usual ceremony at*
their convents, or meetings, where sometimes also they are vizarded and
masked) on the sudden one of them missed their chief, and interrupted the
rest with this speech.

13–14 ANTIMASQUE . . . BOYS *in the masque at my Lord Haddington's wedding.* (J)
24–25 QUAE . . . POSSIT *who, equipped with so many poisons, might seem to have*
      come from the mouth of hell.
29 VENEFICAL *associated with witchcraft.*
31 MASTER JONES *Inigo Jones.*
37 CONVENTS *gatherings.*

40 ★ Sisters, stay, we want our Dame;
  Call upon her by her name,
  And the charm we use to say,
★ That she quickly anoint, and come away.

CHARM I

45 Dame, Dame, the watch is set:
  Quickly come, we all are met.
★ From the lakes and from the fens,
  From the rocks and from the dens,
  From the woods and from the caves,
50 From the churchyards, from the graves,
  From the dungeon, from the tree
  That they die on, here are we.
    Comes she not yet?
    Strike another heat.

55 ### CHARM 2

  The weather is fair, the wind is good;
★ Up, Dame, o' your horse of wood;
  Or else tuck up your gray frock,
★ And saddle your goat or your green cock,
60 And make his bridle a bottom of thread
  To roll up how many miles you have rid.
  Quickly come away,
  For we all stay.
    Nor yet? Nay, then,
65   We'll try her again.

CHARM 3

  The owl is abroad, the bat and the toad,
  And so is the cat-a-mountain;

54 STRIKE . . . HEAT *give another try.*
60 BOTTOM *spool.*
68 CAT-A-MOUNTAIN *wild cat.*

The ant and the mole fit both in a hole,
    And frog peeps out o' the fountain;   70
The dogs they do bay, and the timbrels play,
    The spindle is now a-turning;
The moon it is red and the stars are fled,
    But all the sky is a-burning;
The ditch is made, and our nails the spade,   75
With pictures full, of wax and of wool;
Their livers I stick with needles quick;
There lacks but the blood to make up the flood.
    Quickly Dame, then, bring your part in,
    Spur, spur upon little Martin,   80
    Merrily, merrily make him sail,
    A worm in his mouth and a thorn in's tail,
    Fire above, and fire below,
    With a whip i' your hand to make him go.
    O, now she's come!   85
    Let all be dumb.

At this the Dame entered to them, naked armed, barefooted, her frock tucked, her hair knotted and folded with vipers; in her hand a torch made of a dead man's arm, lighted; girded with a snake. To whom they all did reverence, and she spake, uttering by way of question the end wherefore 90 they came: which, if it had been done either before or otherwise, had not been so natural. For to have made themselves their own decipherers, and each one to have told upon their entrance what they were and whether they would, had been a most piteous hearing, and utterly unworthy any quality of a poem, wherein a writer should always trust somewhat to the capacity 95 of the spectator, especially at these spectacles, where men, beside inquiring eyes, are understood to bring quick ears, and not those sluggish ones of porters and mechanics that must be bored through at every act with narrations.

93–94 WHETHER . . . WOULD *what they wished.*

100 [*Dame.*] Well done, my hags. And come we fraught with spite
　　　　　To overthrow the glory of this night?
　　　　　Holds our great purpose?

Hag.　　　　　　　　　　　　Yes.

Dame.　　　　　　　　　　　　　But wants there none
　　　　　Of our just number?

Hag.　　　　　　　　　Call us one by one,
　　　　　And then our Dame shall see.

　Dame.　　　　　　　　　　　First, then, advance,
105　　　My drowsy servant, stupid Ignorance,
　　　　　Known by thy scaly vesture, and bring on
　　　　　Thy fearful sister, wild Suspicion,
　　　　　Whose eyes do never sleep; let her knit hands
　　　　　With quick Credulity, that next her stands,
110　　　Who hath but one ear, and that always ope;
　　　　　Two-facèd Falsehood follow in the rope;
　　　　　And lead on Murmur, with the cheeks deep hung;
　　　　　She Malice, whetting of her forkèd tongue;
　　　　　And Malice Impudence, whose forehead's lost;
115　　　Let Impudence lead Slander on, to boast
　　　　　Her oblique look; and to her subtle side,
　　　　　Thou, black-mouthed Execration, stand applied;
　　　　　Draw to thee Bitterness, whose pores sweat gall;
　　　　　She flame-eyed Rage; Rage, Mischief.

Hag.　　　　　　　　　　　　Here we are all.

120*Dame.* Join now our hearts, we faithful opposites
　　　　　To Fame and Glory. Let not these bright nights
　　　　　Of honor blaze thus to offend our eyes;
　　　　　Show ourselves truly envious, and let rise
　　　　　Our wonted rages; do what may beseem
125　　　Such names and natures: Virtue else will deem

102 WANTS *lacks.*

Our powers decreased, and think us banished earth,
No less than heaven. All her antique birth,
As Justice, Faith, she will restore, and, bold
Upon our sloth, retrieve her Age of Gold.
We must not let our native manners thus   130
Corrupt with ease. Ill lives not but in us.
I hate to see these fruits of a soft peace,
And curse the piety gives it such increase.
*   Let us disturb it then, and blast the light;
Mix hell with heaven, and make Nature fight   135
Within herself; loose the whole hinge of things,
And cause the ends run back into their springs.

Hag.   What our Dame bids us do
        We are ready for.
Dame.   Then fall to.
*   But first relate me what you have sought,   140
Where you have been, and what you have brought.

**1st Hag.*   I have been all day looking after
       A raven feeding upon a quarter,
       And soon as she turned her beak to the south,
       I snatched this morsel out of her mouth.   145

**2nd Hag.*   I have been gathering wolves' hairs,
       The mad dogs' foam and the adders' ears,
       The spurging of a dead man's eyes,
       And all since the evening star did rise.

**3rd Hag.*   I last night lay all alone   150
       O' the ground to hear the mandrake groan,
       And plucked him up, though he grew full low,
       And as I had done, the cock did crow.

---

132 PEACE *James was a pacifist.*
143 QUARTER *dismembered carcase.*
148 SPURGING *excretion.*

*4th Hag.	And I ha' been choosing out this skull
155	From charnel houses that were full,
	From private grots and public pits,
	And frighted a sexton out of his wits.
*5th Hag.	Under a cradle I did creep
	By day, and when the child was asleep
160	At night I sucked the breath, and rose
	And plucked the nodding nurse by the nose.
*6th Hag.	I had a dagger: what did I with that?
	Killed an infant to have his fat.
	A piper it got at a church-ale,
165	I bade him again blow wind i' the tail.
*7th Hag.	A murderer yonder was hung in chains,
	The sun and the wind had shrunk his veins;
	I bit off a sinew, I clipped his hair,
	I brought off his rags that danced i' the air.
170 *8th Hag.	The scritch-owl's eggs and the feathers black,
	The blood of the frog and the bone in his back
	I have been getting, and made of his skin
	A purset to keep Sir Cranion in.
*9th Hag.	And I ha' been plucking, plants among,
175	Hemlock, henbane, adder's tongue,
	Nightshade, moonwort, libbard's bane,
	And twice by the dogs was like to be ta'en.
*10th Hag.	I from the jaws of a gardener's bitch
	Did snatch these bones, and then leaped the ditch;
180	Yet went I back to the house again,
	Killed the black cat, and here's the brain.

163 FAT N.
164 PIPER *bagpiper, i.e. lecher.* GOT *begot.* CHURCH-ALE *church fair at which ale was sold; the practice was widely condemned.*
165 BLOW . . . TAIL *The pun is both anal and phallic. (Cf. Othello, III.i.6–10.)*
173 SIR CRANION *a fly. See Jonson's note on line 170.*
176 LIBBARD'S BANE *leopard's bane.*

11th Hag.	I went to the toad breeds under the wall,
	I charmed him out and he came at my call;
	I scratched out the eyes of the owl before,
	I tore the bat's wing; what would you have more? 185
Dame.	Yes, I have brought, to help our vows,
	Hornèd poppy, cypress boughs,
	The fig-tree wild that grows on tombs,
	And juice that from the larch tree comes,
	The basilisk's blood and the viper's skin: 190
	And now, our orgies let's begin.

Here the Dame put herself in the midst of them and began her following invocation, wherein she took occasion to boast all the power attributed to witches by the ancients, of which every poet (or the most) do give some: Homer to Circe, in the Odyssey; *Theocritus to Simatha, in* Pharma-   195 ceutria; *Virgil to Alphesiboeus in his; Ovid to Dipsas, in* Amores; *to Medea and Circe, in* Metamorphoses; *Tibullus to* saga; *Horace to Canidia, Sagana, Veia, Folia; Seneca to Medea, and the Nurse, in* Hercules Oetacus; *Petronius Arbiter to his* saga, *in* Fragmenta; *and Claudian to Megaera,* liber I, In Rufinum, *who takes the habit of a witch,*   200 *as these do, and supplies that historical part in the poem, beside her moral person of a fury, confirming the same drift in ours.*

*	You fiends and furies, if yet any be
	Worse than ourselves, you that have quaked to see
*	These knots untied, and shrunk when we have charmed, 205
	You that to arm us have yourselves disarmed,
	And to our powers resigned your whips and brands
	When we went forth, the scourge of men and lands;
	You that have seen me ride when Hecatè
	Durst not take chariot, when the boisterous sea 210

195–200 N.
197, 199 SAGA *sorceress.*

Without a breath of wind hath knocked the sky,
And that hath thundered, Jove not knowing why;
When we have set the elements at wars,
Made midnight see the sun, and day the stars;
215 When the winged lightning in the course hath stayed,
And swiftest rivers have run back, afraid
To see the corn remove, the groves to range,
Whole places alter, and the seasons change;
When the pale moon at the first voice down fell
220 Poisoned, and durst not stay the second spell;
You that have oft been conscious of these sights,
★ And thou three-formèd star, that on these nights
Art only powerful, to whose triple name
Thus we incline, once, twice and thrice the same:
225 If now with rites profane and foul enough
We do invoke thee, darken all this roof
With present fogs. Exhale earth's rott'nest vapors,
And strike a blindness through these blazing tapers.
Come, let a murmuring charm resound
230 ★ The whilst we bury all i' the ground.
★ But first see every foot be bare,
And every knee.
Hag.   Yes, Dame, they are.

CHARM 4

★ Deep, O deep, we lay thee to sleep;
235 We leave thee drink by, if thou chance to be dry,
Both milk and blood, the dew and the flood.
We breathe in thy bed, at the foot and the head;
We cover thee warm, that thou take no harm;

---

222 THREE-FORMÈD STAR *Hecate. See Jonson's note.*
227 PRESENT *immediate.*

And when thou dost wake,
    Dame earth shall quake,   240
    And the houses shake,
    And her belly shall ache
    As her back were brake
    Such a birth to make
    As is the blue drake,   245
    Whose form thou shalt take.

Dame.   Never a star yet shot?
       Where be the ashes?

Hag.   Here i' the pot.

*Dame.   Cast them up, and the flintstone
     Over the left shoulder bone   250
     Into the west.

Hag.   It will be best.

CHARM 5

The sticks are a-cross, there can be no loss,
The sage is rotten, the sulfur is gotten
Up to the sky that was i' the ground.   255
Follow it then with our rattles, round,
Under the bramble, over the briar;
A little more heat will set it on fire;
Put it in mind to do it kind,
Flow water, and blow wind.   260
Rouncy is over, Robble is under,
A flash of light and a clap of thunder,
A storm of rain, another of hail.
We all must home i' the egg shell sail;

243 BRAKE *broken.*
245 BLUE *"the color of plagues and things hurtful"* (OED). DRAKE *dragon.*
253 A-CROSS *crossed.*
259 DO . . . KIND *do its kind, obey its nature.*
261 ROUNCY, ROBBLE *onomatopoeia for thunder.*

265 The mast is made of a great pin,
The tackle of cobweb, the sail as thin,
And if we go through and not fall in—
*Dame. Stay! All our charms do nothing win
Upon the night; our labor dies!
270 Our magic feature will not rise,
Nor yet the storm! We must repeat
More direful voices far, and beat
The ground with vipers till it sweat.

CHARM 6

275 Bark dogs, wolves howl,
Sea roar, woods roll,
Clouds crack, all be black
But the light our charms do make.
Dame. Not yet? My rage begins to swell;
280 Darkness, devils, night and hell,
Do not thus delay my spell!
I call you once and I call you twice,
I beat you again if you stay my thrice;
Through these crannies where I peep
285★ I'll let in the light to see your sleep,
And all the secrets of your sway
Shall lie as open to the day
As unto me. Still are you deaf?
★ Reach me a bough that ne'er bare leaf
290★ To strike the air, and aconite
To hurl upon this glaring light;
★ A rusty knife to wound mine arm,
And as it drops I'll speak a charm
Shall cleave the ground as low as lies
295 Old shrunk-up Chaos, and let rise
Once more his dark and reeking head

To strike the world and nature dead
Until my magic birth be bred.

CHARM 7

Black go in, and blacker come out;   300
At thy going down we give thee a shout.
       Hoo!
At thy rising again thou shalt have two,
And if thou dost what we would have thee do,
Thou shalt have three, thou shalt have four,   305
Thou shalt have ten, thou shalt have a score.
     Hoo! Har! Har! Hoo!

CHARM 8

A cloud of pitch, a spur and a switch
To haste him away, and a whirlwind play   310
Before and after, with thunder for laughter
And storms for joy of the roaring boy,
His head of a drake, his tail of a snake.

CHARM 9

About, about and about,   315
Till the mist arise and the lights fly out;
The images neither be seen nor felt;
The woolen burn and the waxen melt;
Sprinkle your liquors upon the ground
And into the air, around, around.   320
    Around, around,
    Around, around,
    Till a music sound
    And the pace be found
    To which we may dance   325
    And our charms advance.

313 DRAKE *dragon*.

At which, with a strange and sudden music they fell into a magical
dance full of preposterous change and gesticulation, but most applying to
their property, who at their meetings do all things contrary to the custom
330 *of men, dancing back to back and hip to hip, their hands joined, and making*
their circles backward, to the left hand, with strange fantastic motions of
their heads and bodies. All which were excellently imitated by the maker of
the dance, Master Hierome Herne, whose right it is here to be named.

In the heat of their dance on the sudden was heard a sound of loud music, as
335 *if many instruments had made one blast; with which not only the hags*
themselves but the hell into which they ran quite vanished, and the whole
face of the scene altered, scarce suffering the memory of such a thing. But in
the place of it appeared a glorious and magnificent building figuring the
House of Fame, in the top of which were discovered the twelve masquers
340 *sitting upon a throne triumphal erected in form of a pyramid and circled*
with all store of light. From whom a person, by this time descended, in the
furniture of Perseus, and expressing heroic and masculine virtue, began to
speak.

Heroic Virtue. So should, at Fame's loud sound and Virtue's sight,
345   All dark and envious witchcraft fly the light.
     ★   I did not borrow Hermes' wings, nor ask
            His crooked sword, nor put on Pluto's casque,
            Nor on my arm advanced wise Pallas' shield
            (By which, my face aversed, in open field

---

345 dark] poor MS.

---

328 PREPOSTEROUS *literally, having in front what should come behind.*
333 HIEROME HERNE *a court musician and dancing master.*
342 FURNITURE *trappings.*
346–50 I . . . GORGON N.
347 CROOKED *curved.* CASQUE *helmet.*
348 PALLAS *Athena.*
349 AVERSED *turned aside.*

I slew the Gorgon) for an empty name. 350
When Virtue cut off Terror, he gat Fame.
And if when Fame was gotten Terror died,
What black *Erinyes* or more hellish pride
Durst arm these hags now she is grown and great,
To think they could her glories once defeat? 355
I was her parent, and I am her strength.
Heroic Virtue sinks not under length
Of years or ages, but is still the same
While he preserves, as when he got good Fame.
My daughter, then, whose glorious house you see 360
Built of all-sounding brass, whose columns be
Men-making poets, and those well made men
Whose strife it was to have the happiest pen
Renown them to an after-life, and not
With pride to scorn the muse and die forgot; 365
She that inquireth into all the world,
And hath about her vaulted palace hurled
All rumors and reports, or true, or vain,
What utmost lands or deepest seas contain,
But only hangs great actions on her file; 370
She to this lesser world and greatest isle
Tonight sounds Honor, which she would have seen
In yond' bright bevy, each of them a queen.
Eleven of them are of times long gone.
Penthesilea, the brave Amazon, 375

351 GAT *begat*.
353 ERINYES *furies*.
370 FILE *"a string . . . on which papers are placed for preservation and reference"*
(OED).
371 LESSER . . . ISLE *England. Cf. Fortunate Isles, line 298 and note.*
373 YOND . . . BEVY *the masquers: the queen and her ladies.*

Swift-foot Camilla, queen of Volscia,
Victorious Thomyris of Scythia,
Chaste Artemisia, the Carian dame,
And fair-haired Berenicè, Egypt's fame,
380   Hypsicratea, glory of Asia,
Candacè, pride of Ethiopia,
The Britain honor, Voadicea,
The virtuous Palmyrene, Zenobia,
The wise and warlike Goth, Amalasunta,
385   And bold Valasca of Bohemia;
These in their lives, as fortunes, crowned the choice
Of womankind, and 'gainst all opposite voice,
Made good to time, had after death the claim
To live eternised in the House of Fame.
390   Where hourly hearing (as, what there is old?)
The glories of Bel-Anna so well told,
Queen of the ocean; how that she alone
Possessed all virtues, for which one by one
They were so famed; and wanting then a head
395   To form that sweet and gracious pyramid
Wherein they sit, it being the sovereign place
Of all that palace, and reserved to grace
The worthiest queen; these without envy on her,
In life desired that honor to confer,
400   Which with their death no other should enjoy.
She this embracing with a virtuous joy,
Far from self-love, as humbling all her worth
To him that gave it, hath again brought forth
Their names to memory; and means this night
405   To make them once more visible to light,
And to that light from whence her truth of spirit
Confesseth all the luster of her merit:

391 BEL-ANNA *Jonson's coinage for Queen Anne.*

To you, most royal and most happy king,
Of whom Fame's house in every part doth ring
For every virtue, but can give no increase,   410
Not through her loudest trumpet blaze your peace;
To you, that cherish every great example
Contracted in yourself, and being so ample
A field of honor, cannot but embrace
A spectacle so full of love and grace   415
Unto your court, where every princely dame
Contends to be as bounteous of her fame
To others as her life was good to her.
For by their lives they only did confer
Good on themselves, but by their fame, to yours,   420
And every age the benefit endures.

Here the throne wherein they sat, being machina versatilis, *suddenly
changed, and in the place of it appeared* Fama bona, *as she is described (in*
Iconologia di Cesare Ripa), *attired in white, with white wings, having
a collar of gold about her neck and a heart hanging at it, which Orus Apollo*   425
in his Hieroglyphica *interprets the note of a good Fame. In her right hand
she bore a trumpet, in her left an olive branch; and for her state, it was as
Virgil describes her, at the full, her feet on the ground and her head in the
clouds. She, after the music had done, which waited on the turning of the
machine, called from thence to Virtue, and spake this following speech.*   430

Fame. Virtue, my father and my honor, thou
          That mad'st me good, as great, and dar'st avow
          No fame for thine but what is perfect, aid
          Tonight the triumphs of thy white-winged maid.

---

422 MACHINA VERSATILIS *a revolving scene.*
423 FAMA BONA *good Fame.*
424 ICONOLOGIA . . . RIPA N.
425 ORUS APOLLO N.
428 VIRGIL Aeneid *IV* [*176–77*]. (J)

435   Do those renownèd queens all utmost rites
                 Their states can ask. This is a night of nights.
                 In mine own chariots let them crownèd ride,
                 And mine own birds and beasts in gears applied
                 To draw them forth. Unto the first car tie
440   Far-sighted eagles, to note Fame's sharp eye.
                 Unto the second, griffins, that design
                 Swiftness and strength, two other gifts of mine.
                 Unto the last, our lions, that imply
                 The top of graces, state and majesty.
445   And let those hags be led as captives, bound
                 Before their wheels whilst I my trumpet sound.

At which the loud music sounded as before, to give the masquers time of descending. And here we cannot but take the opportunity to make some ★*more particular description of their scene . . . which was the House of Fame.*
450 *The structure and ornament of which (as is professed before) was entirely Master Jones his invention and design. First, for the lower columns, he chose the statues of the most excellent poets, as Homer, Virgil, Lucan, etc., as being the substantial supporters of Fame. For the upper, Achilles, Aeneas, Caesar, and those great heroes which these poets had celebrated.*
455 *All which stood as in massy gold. Between the pillars, underneath, were figured land battles, sea fights, triumphs, loves, sacrifices, and all magnificent subjects of honor, in brass, and heightened with silver. In which he professed to follow that noble description made by Chaucer of the place. Above were sited the masquers, over whose heads he devised two eminent*
460 *figures of Honor and Virtue for the arch. The friezes both below and above were filled with several-colored lights like emeralds, rubies, sapphires,*

438 GEARS *harness.*
449 *Jonson's discussion of the sources for his queens has been removed to the appendix.* N.
458 CHAUCER Hous of Fame, *lines 1184ff.*
459 SITED *placed.*

carbuncles, etc., the reflex of which, with other lights placed in the concave, upon the masquers' habits, was full of glory. These habits had in them the excellency of all device and riches, and were worthily varied by his invention to the nations whereof they were queens. Nor are these alone his due, but 465 *divers other accessions to the strangeness and beauty of the spectacle, as the hell, the going about of the chariots, the binding the witches, the turning machine with the presentation of Fame. All which I willingly acknowledge for him, since it is a virtue planted in good natures that what respects they wish to obtain fruitfully from others they will give ingenuously themselves.* 470

By this time imagine the masquers descended, and again mounted into three triumphant chariots ready to come forth. The first four were drawn with eagles (whereof I gave the reason, as of the rest, in Fame's speech), their four torch-bearers attending on the chariot sides, and four of the hags bound before them. Then followed the second, drawn by griffins, with their 475 *torch-bearers and four other hags. Then the last, which was drawn by lions, and more eminent, wherein her majesty was, and had six torch-bearers more, peculiar to her, with the like number of hags. After which a full triumphant music, singing this song while they rode in state about the stage:*

SONG 480

Help, help all tongues to celebrate this wonder:
The voice of Fame should be as loud as thunder.
Her house is all of echo made
Where never dies the sound,
And as her brows the clouds invade,
Her feet do strike the ground.
Sing then good Fame that's out of Virtue born,
For who doth Fame neglect doth Virtue scorn.

485

Here they lighted from their chariots and danced forth their first dance; then a second, immediately following it; both right curious and full of subtile and 490 *excellent changes, and seemed performed with no less spirits than of those*

462 REFLEX *reflection.*
490 CURIOUS *complicated.*

they personated. The first was to the cornets, the second to the violins. After
which they took out the men and danced the measures, entertaining the
time almost to the space of an hour with singular variety; when, to give
495 *them rest, from the music which attended the chariots, by that most excellent*
tenor voice and exact singer her majesty's servant Master John Allin, this
ditty was sung.

SONG

When all the ages of the earth
500   Were crowned but in this famous birth,
And that, when they would boast their store
Of worthy queens, they knew no more,
How happier is that age, can give
A queen in whom all they do live!

505 *After it, succeeded their third dance, than which a more numerous composi-*
tion could not be seen, graphically disposed into letters, and honoring the
name of the most sweet and ingenious prince, Charles, Duke of York;
wherein, beside that principal grace of perspicuity, the motions were so even
and apt and their expression so just, as if mathematicians had lost proportion
510 *they might there have found it. The author was Master Thomas Giles.*
After this, they danced galliards and corantos, and then their last dance, no
less elegant in the place than the rest; with which they took their chariots
again, and triumphing about the stage had their return to the House of Fame
celebrated with this last song, whose notes, as the former, were the work and
515   *honor of my excellent friend Alfonso Ferrabosco.*

SONG

Who, Virtue, can thy power forget
That sees these live and triumph yet?

493 MEASURES *slow dances.*
505 NUMEROUS *consisting of numbers, or rhythmical units; hence rhythmical.*
508 PERSPICUITY *clarity.*
510 GILES *Prince Henry's dancing master.*
511 GALLIARDS *quick dances.* CORANTOS *dances with a running or gliding step.*

Th'Assyrian pomp, the Persian pride,
Greeks' glory, and the Romans', died;   520
   And who yet imitate
Their noises, tarry the same fate.
   Force greatness all the glorious ways
     You can, it soon decays,
   But so good Fame shall never: 525
Her triumphs, as their causes, are forever.

To conclude which, I know no worthier way of epilogue than the celebration
of who were the celebrators.

The queen's majesty	Countess of Montgomery
Countess of Arundel	Viscountess Cranborne
Countess of Derby	Lady Elizabeth Guildford
Countess of Huntington	Lady Anne Winter
Countess of Bedford	Lady Windsor
Countess of Essex	Lady Anne Clifford

530

Oberon
The Fairy Prince

A Masque of Prince Henry's

*The first face of the scene appeared all obscure, and nothing perceived but a
dark rock with trees beyond it and all wildness that could be presented; till
at one corner of the cliff, above the horizon, the moon began to show, and
rising, a satyr was seen by her light to put forth his head and call.*

1st Satyr. Chromis! Mnasil! None appear?   5
          See you not who riseth here?
*   You saw Silenus late, I fear!
          I'll prove if this can reach your ear.

*He wound his cornet and thought himself answered, but was deceived by
the echo.*   10

          O, you wake then! Come away,
          Times be short, are made for play;

*Note: Jonson's notes, indicated by asterisks, will be found in the appendix. A few
    included in the glosses are identified by (J).*
Title PRINCE HENRY *He danced the title role.*
5 CHROMIS, MNASIL *The names are from Virgil's sixth eclogue.*
7 YOU . . . LATE *i.e. you were up late drinking.*
8 PROVE *try.*
12 ARE *that are.*

The hum'rous moon too will not stay:
What doth make you thus delay?
15 ★ Hath his tankard touched your brain?
Sure, they're fall'n asleep again;
Or I doubt it was the vain
Echo did me entertain.
Prove again—

He wound the second time and found it.

                    I thought 'twas she!
20   Idle nymph, I pray thee, be
          Modest, and not follow me;
          I nor love myself nor thee.

Here he wound the third time and was answered by another satyr, who likewise showed himself. To which he spoke:

25   Aye, this sound I better know:
          List! I would I could hear mo.

At this they came running forth severally from divers parts of the rock, leaping and making antic action and gestures, to the number of ten, some of them speaking, some admiring; and amongst them a silene, who is ever
30 *the prefect of the satyrs, and so presented in all their chori and meetings.*

2nd Satyr. Thank us, and you shall do so.
3rd Satyr. Aye, our number soon will grow.
★*2nd Satyr.* See Silenus!
3rd Satyr.   Cercops too!

13 HUM'ROUS *capricious.*
17 DOUBT *suspect.*
22 I . . . MYSELF *Respecting that known fable of Echo's following Narcissus, and his self-love.* (J)
26 MO *more.*
30 CHORI *groups.*
33 CERCOPS *mischievous apelike creatures who appear in the legends of Hercules.*

4th Satyr.	Yes. What is there now to do?
5th Satyr.	Are there any nymphs to woo?	35
★*4th Satyr.*	If there be, let me have two.
★*Silenus.*	Chaster language! These are nights
	Solemn to the shining rites
	Of the fairy prince and knights,
	While the moon their orgies lights.	40
2nd Satyr.	Will they come abroad anon?
3rd Satyr.	Shall we see young Oberon?
4th Satyr.	Is he such a princely one
	As you spake him long agone?
Silenus.	Satyrs, he doth fill with grace	45
	Every season, every place;
	Beauty dwells but in his face:
★	He's the height of all our race.
★	Our Pan's father, god of tongue,
	Bacchus, though he still be young,	50
★	Phœbus, when he crownèd sung,
★	Nor Mars when first his armor rung
	Might with him be named that day.
	He is lovelier than in May
	Is the spring, and there can stay	55
	As little as he can decay.
Chorus.	O that he would come away!
★*3rd Satyr.*	Grandsire, we shall leave to play
★	With Lyæus now, and serve

40 ORGIES *celebrations. See Jonson's note to* Hymenaei, *line 123.*

49 PAN'S FATHER *Mercury. See Jonson's note.* GOD . . . TONGUE *Mercury, as messenger of the gods, was patron of eloquence.*

50 BACCHUS *god not only of wine, but also of theater and ecstatic music and poetry.*

51 PHOEBUS *Apollo. See Jonson's note.*

55–6 CAN . . . DECAY *i.e. he continually improves and cannot deteriorate.*

59 LYAEUS *Bacchus.*

		Only Ob'ron?
60	*Silenus.*	He'll deserve
		All you can, and more, my boys.
	4th Satyr.	Will he give us pretty toys
		To beguile the girls withal?
	3rd Satyr.	And to make 'em quickly fall?
65	*Silenus.*	Peace, my wantons; he will do
		More than you can aim unto.
	4th Satyr.	Will he build us larger caves?
	Silenus.	Yes, and give you ivory staves
		When you hunt, and better wine—
70	*1st Satyr.*	Than the master of the vine?
	2nd Satyr.	And rich prizes to be won
		When we leap or when we run?
	1st Satyr.	Aye, and gild our cloven feet?
	3rd Satyr.	Strew our heads with powders sweet?
75	*1st Satyr.*	Bind our crooked legs in hoops
		Made of shells with silver loops?
	2nd Satyr.	Tie about our tawny wrists
		Bracelets of the fairy twists?
	4th Satyr.	And to spite the coy nymphs' scorns,
80		Hang upon our stubbèd horns
		Garlands, ribands and fine posies—
	3rd Satyr.	Fresh as when the flower discloses?
	1st Satyr.	Yes, and stick our pricking ears
		With the pearl that Tethys wears.
85	*2nd Satyr.*	And to answer all things else,
		Trap our shaggy thighs with bells,
		That as we do strike a time
		In our dance shall make a chime—

61 CAN *are capable of.*
70 MASTER . . . VINE *Bacchus.*
84 TETHYS *a sea goddess, wife of Oceanus.*

3rd Satyr. Louder than the rattling pipes
          Of the wood-gods—

1st Satyr.   Or the stripes   90

*   Of the tabor when we carry

          Bacchus up, his pomp to vary.

Chorus.   O that he so long doth tarry!

Silenus. See, the rock begins to ope!

          Now you shall enjoy your hope;   95

          'Tis about the hour, I know.

There the whole scene opened, and within was discovered the frontispiece
of a bright and glorious palace whose gates and walls were transparent.
Before the gates lay two sylvans, armed with their clubs and dressed in
    leaves, asleep. At this, the satyrs wondering, Silenus proceeds: 100

          Look! does not his palace show
          Like another sky of lights?
          Yonder with him live the knights
          Once the noblest of the earth,
          Quickened by a second birth,   105
          Who for prowess and for truth
          There are crowned with lasting youth,
          And do hold, by Fate's command,
          Seats of bliss in fairyland.
          But their guards, methinks, do sleep!   110
          Let us wake 'em. Sirs, you keep
          Proper watch, that thus do lie
          Drowned in sloth!

1st Satyr.   They ha' ne'er an eye
      To wake withal.

2nd Satyr.   Nor sense, I fear;
      For they sleep in either ear.   115

91 TABOR *drum.*
115 IN . . . EAR *soundly; a Latinism.*

3rd Satyr. Holla, sylvans! Sure they're caves
              Of sleep, these, or else they're graves!

4th Satyr. Hear you, friends, who keeps the keepers?

1st Satyr. They're the eighth and ninth sleepers!

2nd Satyr. Shall we cramp 'em?

120 *Silenus.*   Satyrs, no.

3rd Satyr. Would we'd Boreas here to blow
              Off their leavy coats and strip 'em.

4th Satyr. Aye, aye, aye; that we might whip 'em!

3rd Satyr. Or that we'd a wasp or two
              For their nostrils!

125 *1st Satyr.*   Hairs will do
              Even as well: take my tail.

2nd Satyr. What d' you say t'a good nail
              Through their temples?

3rd Satyr.   Or an eel
              In their guts, to make 'em feel?

130 *4th Satyr.* Shall we steal away their beards?

3rd Satyr. For Pan's goat, that leads the herds?

2nd Satyr. Or try whether is more dead,
              His club, or th' other's head?

Silenus. Wags, no more; you grow too bold.

135 *1st Satyr.* I would fain now see 'em rolled
              Down a hill, or from a bridge
              Headlong cast, to break their ridge-
              Bones; or to some river take 'em,

---

119 SLEEPERS *The Seven Sleepers of Ephesus were Christian youths who were walled in a cave during the persecution of Decius* (A.D. *250*), *and miraculously were still alive when they were discovered almost two centuries later.*

121 BOREAS *the north wind.*

122 LEAVY *leafy.*

132 WHETHER *which.*

137–38 RIDGE-BONES *spines.*

Plump, and see if that would wake 'em.
2nd Satyr. There no motion yet appears.   140
Silenus. Strike a charm into their ears.

  At which the satyrs fell suddenly into this catch.

   Buzz, quoth the blue fly,
    Hum, quoth the bee;
   Buzz and hum they cry, 145
    And so do we.
   In his ear, in his nose,
    Thus, do you see?
   He ate the dormouse,
    Else it was he. 150

The two sylvans starting up amazed and betaking themselves to their arms
were thus questioned by Silenus.

Silenus. How now, sylvans! can you wake?
   I commend the care you take
   I' your watch. Is this your guise, 155
   To have both your ears and eyes
   Sealed so fast as these mine elves
   Might have stol'n you from yourselves?
3rd Satyr. We had thought we must have got
   Stakes, and heated 'em red-hot, 160
   And have bored you through the eyes,
   With the Cyclops, ere you'd rise.
2nd Satyr. Or have fetched some trees to heave
   Up your bulks, that so did cleave
   To the ground there.
4th Satyr.   Are you free 165

149, 150 HE, HE *i.e. either one sylvan or the other.* DORMOUSE *traditionally, a*
 sleepy animal.
155 GUISE *habit.*

Yet of sleep, and can you see
Who is yonder up aloof?

1st Satyr.	Be your eyes yet moon-proof?
Sylvan.	Satyrs, leave your petulance,

170 And go frisk about and dance,
Or else rail upon the moon;
Your expectance is too soon.
For before the second cock
Crow, the gates will not unlock;
175 And till then we know we keep
Guard enough, although we sleep.

1st Satyr. Say you so? then let us fall
To a song or to a brawl.
Shall we, grandsire? Let us sport,
180 And make expectation short.

Silenus. Do, my wantons, what you please.
I'll lie down and take mine ease.

1st Satyr. Brothers, sing then, and upbraid,
As we use, yond' seeming maid.

185

SONG

Now, my cunning lady, moon,
Can you leave the side so soon
   Of the boy you keep so hid?
Midwife Juno sure will say
190 This is not the proper way

---

167 ALOOF *far off.*
178 BRAWL *dance.*
180 EXPECTATION *waiting.*
188 BOY *Endymion, a shepherd loved by the moon, who made him sleep forever so that she could always enjoy his beauty.*
189 MIDWIFE JUNO *Juno presided over marriages.*
190–95 THIS . . . MAID N.

Of your paleness to be rid.
But perhaps it is your grace
To wear sickness i' your face,
    That there might be wagers laid
    Still, by fools, you are a maid.   195

Come, your changes overthrow
What your look would carry so;
    Moon, confess then what you are.
And be wise, and free to use
Pleasures that you now do lose: 200
    Let us satyrs have a share.
Though our forms be rough and rude,
Yet our acts may be endued
    With more virtue: everyone
    Cannot be Endymion.   205

The song ended, they fell suddenly into an antic dance full of gesture and swift motion, and continued it till the crowing of the cock, at which they were interrupted by Silenus.

Silenus. Stay, the cheerful chanticleer
    Tells you that the time is near.   210
    See, the gates already spread!
    Every satyr bow his head.

There the whole palace opened, and the nation of fays were discovered, some with instruments, some bearing lights, others singing; and within, afar off in perspective, the knights masquers sitting in their several sieges. 215 At the further end of all, Oberon, in a chariot, which to a loud triumphant

195 MAID *virgin.*
200 CHANGES *The moon is notorious for inconstancy.*
204 VIRTUE *with an equivocation on "value."*
209 CHANTICLEER *rooster.*
215 SIEGES *seats.*

music began to move forward, drawn by two white bears, and on either side guarded by three sylvans, with one going in front.

SONG

220   Melt earth to sea, sea flow to air,
       And air fly into fire,
    Whilst we in tunes to Arthur's chair
       Bear Oberon's desire,
       Than which there nothing can be higher,
225   Save James, to whom it flies:
    But he the wonder is of tongues, of ears, of eyes.

    Who hath not heard, who hath not seen,
       Who hath not sung his name?
    The soul that hath not, hath not been;
230   But is the very same
       With buried sloth, and knows not fame,
    Which doth him best comprise:
    For he the wonder is of tongues, of ears, of eyes.

By this time the chariot was come as far forth as the face of the scene; and
235 *the satyrs beginning to leap and express their joy for the unused state and solemnity, the foremost sylvan began to speak.*

Sylvan. Give place and silence; you were rude too late.
    This is a night of greatness and of state,
    Not to be mixed with light and skipping sport:
240   A night of homage to the British court,
    And ceremony due to Arthur's chair,

220–21 EARTH . . . FIRE *the four elements ascending to higher and purer forms.*
222 ARTHUR'S CHAIR *the hereditary throne of British monarchs.* N.
234 FACE *façade.*
235 UNUSED *unusual.*

From our bright master, Oberon the fair;
Who with these knights, attendants, here preserved
In fairyland, for good they have deserved
Of yond' high throne, are come of right to pay   245
Their annual vows; and all their glories lay
At feet, and tender to this only great
True majesty, restorèd in this seat;
To whose sole power and magic they do give
The honor of their being, that they live   250
Sustained in form, fame and felicity,
From rage of fortune or the fear to die.
Silenus. And may they well. For this indeed is he,
My boys, whom you must quake at when you see.
He is above your reach, and neither doth   255
Nor can he think within a satyr's tooth.
Before his presence you must fall or fly.
He is the matter of virtue, and placed high.
His meditations to his height are even,
And all their issue is akin to heaven.   260
He is a god o'er kings, yet stoops he then
Nearest a man when he doth govern men,
To teach them by the sweetness of his sway,
And not by force. He's such a king as they
Who're tyrans' subjects, or ne'er tasted peace,   265
Would, in their wishes, form for their release.
'Tis he that stays the time from turning old,
And keeps the age up in a head of gold;
That in his own true circle still doth run,
And holds his course as certain as the sun.   270
He makes it ever day and ever spring

256 TOOTH *taste, style.*
258 MATTER *both essence and theme.*
265 TYRANS' *tyrants'.*

Where he doth shine, and quickens everything
Like a new nature; so that true to call
Him by his title is to say, he's all.

275 *Sylvan.* I thank the wise Silenus for this praise.
Stand forth, bright fays and elves, and tune your lays
Unto his name; then let your nimble feet
Tread subtle circles that may always meet
In point to him, and figures to express

280 The grace of him and his great empress;
That all that shall tonight behold the rites
Performed by princely Oberon and these knights,
May without stop point out the proper heir
Designed so long to Arthur's crowns and chair.

285 *The* SONG, *by two fays.*

1st Fay. Seek you majesty, to strike?
Bid the world produce his like.
2nd Fay. Seek you glory, to amaze?
Here let all eyes stand at gaze.
290 *Both.* Seek you wisdom, to inspire?
Touch then at no other's fire.
1st Fay. Seek you knowledge, to direct?
Trust to his without suspect.
2nd Fay. Seek you piety, to lead?
295 In his footsteps only tread.

272 QUICKENS *brings to life.*
274 ALL *in Greek,* Pan, *the name of the pastoral god.*
278 SUBTLE *artful.*
279 FIGURES *dance formations.*
284 DESIGNED . . . TO *intended . . . for.* CROWNS *of England and Scotland, two separate kingdoms until the eighteenth century, and of Wales.*
289 STAND . . . GAZE *marvel.*
293 SUSPECT *suspicion.*

Chorus.   Every virtue of a king,
                And of all in him we sing.

*Then the lesser fays dance forth their dance; which ended, a full song
follows by all the voices.*

SONG   300

    The solemn rites are well begun,
        And though but lighted by the moon,
    They show as rich as if the sun
      Had made this night his noon.
    But may none wonder that they are so bright;   305
    The moon now borrows from a greater light.
        Then, princely Oberon,
        Go on,
    This is not every night.

*There Oberon and the knights dance out the first masque dance, which was   310
followed with this song.*

SONG

    Nay, nay,
    You must not stay,
    Nor be weary yet;   315
    This's no time to cast away,
    Or for fays so to forget
    The virtue of their feet.
    Knotty legs and plants of clay
    Seek for ease, or love delay,   320
    But with you it still should fare
    As with the air of which you are.

314 STAY *stop.*
319 PLANTS *feet.*

*After which they danced forth their second masque dance, and were again
excited by a song.*

325   SONG

1st Fay. Nor yet, nor yet, O you in this night blessed,
          Must you have will or hope to rest.
2nd Fay.   If you use the smallest stay,
               You'll be overta'en by day.
330 *1st Fay.* And these beauties will suspect
          That their forms you do neglect
          If you do not call them forth.
2nd Fay.   Or that you have no more worth
               Than the coarse and country fairy
335   That doth haunt the hearth or dairy.

*Then followed the measures, corantos, galliards, etc., till Phosphorus, the
day star, appeared and called them away; but first they were invited home
by one of the sylvans with this song.*

                                       SONG

340   Gentle knights,
             Know some measure of your nights.
             Tell the high-graced Oberon
             It is time that we were gone.
                 Here be forms so bright and airy,
345   And their motions so they vary
                 As they will enchant the fairy,
                 If you longer here should tarry.

324 EXCITED *summoned.*
330 THESE BEAUTIES *the ladies in the audience.*
332 CALL . . . FORTH *to dance in the revels.*
336 MEASURES *slow dances.* CORANTOS *dances with running or gliding steps.*
     GALLIARDS *quick dances.*

Phosphorus. To rest, to rest! the herald of the day,
  Bright Phosphorus, commands you hence; obey.
  The moon is pale and spent, and wingèd night   350
  Makes headlong haste to fly the morning's sight,
  Who now is rising from her blushing wars,
  And with her rosy hand puts back the stars;
  Of which myself the last, her harbinger,
  But stay to warn you that you not defer   355
  Your parting longer. Then do I give way,
  As night hath done, and so must you, to day.

*After this they danced their last dance into the work; and with a full song,
  the star vanished, and the whole machine closed.*

SONG   360

  O yet how early, and before her time,
  The envious morning up doth climb,
      Though she not love her bed!
  What haste the jealous sun doth make
  His fiery horses up to take,   365
      And once more show his head!
  Lest, taken with the brightness of this night,
  The world should wish it last, and never miss his light.

Love Restored

In a Masque at Court, by Gentlemen, the King's Servants.

Masquerado. I would I could make 'em a show myself. In troth,
ladies, I pity you all. You are here in expectation of a device
tonight, and I am afraid you can do little else but expect it.
Though I dare not show my face, I can speak truth under a
5   vizard. Good faith, an 't please your majesty, your masquers
are all at a stand; I cannot think your majesty will see any show
tonight, at least worth your patience. Some two hours since,
we were in that forwardness, our dances learned, our masquing
attire on and attired. A pretty fine speech was taken up o' the
10   poet too, which if he never be paid for now, it's no matter; his
wit costs him nothing. Unless we should come in like a morris-
dance, and whistle our ballad ourselves, I know not what we

Title BY . . . SERVANTS *performed by the theatrical company The King's Men.*
1 MASQUERADO *masked man.*
2 DEVICE *masque.*
5 AN *if.*
6 STAND *standstill.*
7 SINCE *ago.*
8 IN . . . FORWARDNESS *getting prepared.*
9 ATTIRED *adorned.*
11–12 MORRIS-DANCE *"A grotesque dance performed by persons in fancy costume,
      usually representing characters from the Robin Hood legend. Hence, any
      similar mumming performance."* (OED)

should do: we ha' no other musician to play our tunes but the wild music here, and the rogue play-boy that acts Cupid is got so hoarse, your majesty cannot hear him half the breadth o' 15 your chair. [*Enter Plutus disguised as Cupid.*] See, they ha' thrust him out at adventure. We humbly beseech your majesty to bear with us. We had both hope and purpose it should have been better; howsoever, we are lost in it.

Plutus. What makes this light, feathered vanity here? Away, 20 impertinent folly! Infect not this assembly.

Masquerado. How, boy!

Plutus. Thou common corruption of all manners and places that admit thee!

Masquerado. Ha' you recovered your voice to rail at me? 25

Plutus. No, vizarded impudence. I am neither player nor masquer, but the god himself whose deity is here profaned by thee. Thou and thy like think yourselves authorized in this place to all license of surquidry. But you shall find custom hath not so grafted you here but you may be rent up and thrown out as 30 unprofitable evils. I tell thee, I will have no more masquing; I will not buy a false and fleeting delight so dear. The merry madness of one hour shall not cost me the repentance of an age.

[*Enter Robin Goodfellow.*]

Robin Goodfellow. How! no masque, no masque? I pray you say, are 35 you sure on't? no masque indeed? What do I here then? Can you tell?

Masquerado. No, faith.

Robin Goodfellow. 'Slight, I'll be gone again an there be no masque. There's a jest. Pray you resolve me. Is there any? or no? a 40 masque?

13 no other] neither Ff.

17 AT ADVENTURE *recklessly.*
29 SURQUIDRY *presumption.*

Plutus. Who are you?

Robin Goodfellow. Nay, I'll tell you that when I can. Does anybody
know themselves here, think you? I would fain know if there
45   be a masque or no.

Plutus. There is none, nor shall be, sir. Does that satisfy you?

Robin Goodfellow. 'Slight, a fine trick! a piece of *England's Joy*, this.
Are these your court sports! Would I had kept me to my
gambols o' the country still, selling of fish, short service, shoe-
50   ing the wild mare, or roasting of robin redbreast. These were
better than after all this time no masque: you look at me. I
have recovered myself now for you. I am the honest plain
country spirit and harmless, Robin Goodfellow, he that
sweeps the hearth and the house clean (riddles for the country
55   maids) and does all their other drudgery while they are at hot
cockles; one that has discoursed with your court spirits ere now,
but was fain tonight to run a thousand hazards to arrive at this
place: never poor goblin was so put to his shifts to get in to see
nothing. So many thorny difficulties as I have passed deserved
60   the best masque, the whole shop of the revels. I would you
would admit some of my feats, but I ha' little hope o' that,
i'faith; you let me in so hardly.

Plutus. Sir, here's no place for them, nor you. Your rude good
fellowship must seek some other sphere for your admitty.

65 *Robin Goodfellow.* Nay, so your stiff-necked porter told me at the
gate, but not in so good words. His staff spoke somewhat to
that boisterous sense. I am sure he concluded all in a non-entry,

47 ENGLAND'S JOY N.

49 SHORT SERVICE *being a domestic servant for short periods.*

55–6 HOT COCKLES *"A rustic game in which one player lay face downwards, or
knelt down with his eyes covered, and being struck on the back by the others
in turn, guessed who struck him."* (OED)

62 HARDLY *unwillingly.*

64 ADMITTY *admittance: a Jonsonian coinage. The Oxford editors believe it is a
misprint for "activity."*

which made me e'en climb over the wall and in by the wood-yard, so to the terrace, where when I came, I found the oaks of the guard more unmoved, and one of 'em, upon whose arm I 70 hung, shoved me off o' the ladder and dropped me down like an acorn. 'Twas well there was not a sow in the verge; I had been eaten up else. Then I heard some talk o' the carpenters' way, and I attempted that; but there the wooden rogues let a huge trap door fall o' my head. If I had not been a spirit, I had 75 been mazarded. Though I confess I am none of those subtle ones that can creep through at a keyhole or the cracked pane of a window. I must come in at a door, which made me once think of a trunk, but that I would not imitate so catholic a cockscomb as Coryat, and make a case o' catsos. Therefore I 80 took another course. I watched what kind of persons the door most opened to, and one of their shapes I would belie to get in with. First I came with authority and said I was an engineer and belonged to the motions. They asked me if I were the fighting bear of last year, and laughed me out of that, and said 85 the motions were ceased. Then I took another figure, of an old tirewoman, but tired under that too, for none of the masquers

80 case o'catsos] case: vses F¹; F² *om. all after* Coryat. N.

68–9 WOOD-YARD *a yard just outside the palace of Whitehall, otherwise known as Scotland Yard.*

69–70 OAKS . . . GUARD *guardsmen standing like oaks.*

72 VERGE *precincts of the court.*

76 MAZARDED *knocked on the head.*

79 CATHOLIC *universal.*

80 COCKSCOMB *rogue.* CORYAT *Thomas Coryat (1577?–1617), famous traveler, had himself smuggled into a court masque in a trunk.* CASE *pair, with a quibble on trunk.* CATSOS *rogues.* N.

82 BELIE *fake.*

84 MOTIONS (1) *stage machinery.* (2) *show. Robin means the former, but the guards take him to mean the latter.*

87 TIREWOMAN *woman who helps the masquers dress.*

would take note of me; the mark was out of my mouth. Then
I pretended to be a musician; marry, I could not show mine
90   instrument, and that bred a discord. Now there was nothing
left for me that I could presently think on but a feather-maker
of Blackfriars, and in that shape I told 'em, "Surely I must
come in, let it be opened unto me"; but they all made as light
of me as of my feathers, and wondered how I could be a
95   Puritan, being of so vain a vocation. I answered, "We all are
masquers sometimes"; with which they knocked hypocrisy o'
the pate, and made room for a bombard-man that brought
bouge for a country lady or two that fainted, he said, with
fasting for the fine sight since seven o'clock i' the morning. O
100   how it grieved me that I was prevented o' that shape, and had
not touched on it in time. It liked me so well. But I thought
I would offer at it yet. Marry, before I could procure my
properties, alarum came that some o' the whimlens had too
much; and one showed how fruitfully they had watered his
105   head as he stood under the grices; and another came out

88 MARK . . . MOUTH *i.e. I was too old. The metaphor relates to marks on horses'
      teeth determining their age.*
91–2 FEATHER-MAKER . . . BLACKFRIARS *Blackfriars was the Puritan center of
      London, and making feathers for court costumes was a common trade in the
      district. The supposed moral anomaly was a frequent butt of satire.*
93 LET . . . ME *Puritan rhetoric.*
97 BOMBARD-MAN *man with a large leather wine-sack.*
98 BOUGE *provisions.*
100 PREVENTED O' *anticipated by.*
101 LIKED *suited.*
102 OFFER AT *try.*
103–04 WHIMLENS *miserable creatures.* TOO MUCH *i.e. to drink.*
104–07 ONE . . . STARGAZING *The women who have had too much to drink have
      been standing on the steps leading to the masquing hall waiting to be admitted.
      The two observers who complain that they have been "watered" have been
      standing underneath the steps looking up.*
105 GRICES *steps.*

complaining of a cataract shot into his eyes by a planet as he was stargazing. There was that device defeated! By this time I saw a fine citizen's wife or two let in, and that figure provoked me exceedingly to take it, which I had no sooner done but one o' the blackguard had his hand in my vestry and was groping of 110 me as nimbly as the Christmas cutpurse. He thought he might be bold with me because I had not a husband in sight to squeak to. I was glad to forgo my form, to be rid of his hot steaming affection; it so smelt o' the boiling-house. Forty other devices I had, of wiremen, and the chandry, and I know not what else; 115 but all succeeded alike. I offered money too, but that could not be done so privately as it durst be taken, for the danger of an example. At last a troop of strangers came to the door, with whom I made myself sure to enter; but before I could mix, they were all let in, and I left alone without, for want of an 120 interpreter. Which, when I was fain to be to myself, a colossus o' the company told me I had English enough to carry me to bed, with which all the other statues of flesh laughed. Never till then did I know the want of a hook and a piece of beef, to have baited three or four o' those goodly widemouths with. In 125 this despair, when all invention—and translation too—failed me, I e'en went back and stuck to this shape you see me in, of mine own, with my broom and my candles, and came on confidently, giving out I was a part o' the device. At which,

106 CATARACT *waterfall, with a quibble on the eye disease.*
110 BLACKGUARD *scullions.* VESTRY *dress.*
111 CHRISTMAS CUTPURSE *one John Selman, caught picking pockets in the royal chapel during the Christmas service, and executed on January 7, 1612, the day after the masque.*
115 WIREMEN *wire workers.* CHANDRY *men who provided candles for the royal household.*
118 STRANGERS *foreigners.*
128 BROOM . . . CANDLES *Robin was a household sprite.*
129 DEVICE *masque.*

130 though they had little to do with wit, yet because some on't
might be used here tonight contrary to their knowledge, they
thought it fit way should be made for me; and as it falls
out, to small purpose.

Plutus. Just as much as you are fit for. Away, idle spirit; and thou,
135 the idle cause of his advent'ring hither, vanish with him. 'Tis
thou that art not only the sower of vanities in these high places,
but the call of all other light follies to fall and feed on them. I
will endure thy prodigality nor riots no more; they are the
ruin of states. Nor shall the tyranny of these nights hereafter
140 impose a necessity upon me of entertaining thee. Let 'em embrace more frugal pastimes! Why should not the thrifty and
right worshipful game of post and pair content 'em? Or the
witty invention of noddy, for counters? or God make them
rich, at the tables? But masquing and revelling? Were not
145 these ladies and their gentlewomen more housewifely employed, a dozen of 'em to a light, or twenty—the more the
merrier—to save charges, i' their chambers at home, and their
old nightgowns, at draw-gloves, riddles, dreams, and other
pretty purposes, rather than to wake here, in their flaunting
150 wires and tires, laced gowns, embroidered petticoats and other
taken-up braveries? Away; I will no more of these superfluous
excesses. They are these make me hear so ill, both in town and

130 ON'T *of it.*

137–39 I . . . STATES N.

142–44 POST AND PAIR, NODDY *card games.* GOD . . . RICH *a form of backgammon.*

148 DRAW-GLOVES *a parlor game: the object was to see who could remove her
gloves most quickly at a given signal.* DREAMS *amateur interpretation of
dreams, another popular parlor game.*

149 WAKE *stay up late.*

150 WIRES *used to make ruffs stand up.* TIRES *fine clothes.*

151 TAKEN-UP BRAVERIES *fancy clothes bought on credit.*

152 HEAR . . . ILL *so ill spoken of.*

country, as I do; which if they continue, I shall be the first shall leave 'em.

Masquerado. Either I am very stupid, or this a reformed Cupid.   155

Robin Goodfellow. How? Does any take this for Cupid, the Love-in-Court?

Masquerado. Yes, is't not he?

Robin Goodfellow. Nay then, we spirits I see are subtler yet, and somewhat better discoverers. No; it is not he, nor his brother   160
Anti-Cupid, the Love of Virtue, though he pretend to it with his phrase and face. 'Tis that impostor Plutus, the god of money, who has stol'n Love's ensigns, and in his belied figure reigns i' the world, making friendships, contracts, marriages and almost religion; begetting, breeding and holding the   165
nearest respects of mankind, and usurping all those offices in this age of gold which Love himself performed in the Golden Age. 'Tis he that pretends to tie kingdoms, maintain commerce, dispose of honors, make all places and dignities arbitrary from him, even to the very country, where Love's name   170
cannot be rased out, he has yet gained there upon him, by a proverb insinuating his preëminence: *Not for love or money.* There Love lives confined by his tyranny to a cold region, wrapped up in furs like a Muscovite and almost frozen to death, while he, in his enforced shape and with his ravished   175
arms, walks as if he were to set bounds and give laws to destiny. 'Tis you, mortals, that are fools, and worthy to be such, that worship him; for if you had wisdom, he had no godhead. He

---

161 ANTI-CUPID *or Anteros. Cupid and he represent single and mutual love respectively. See Jonson's* A Challenge at Tilt, *lines 177ff.*

166 NEAREST . . . OF *closest relationships to.*

169–70 ARBITRARY . . . HIM *dependent on his whim.*

170 COUNTRY *i.e. the natural world, as opposed to the court and city.*

171 RASED *erased.*

175–76 HIS . . . ARMS *the weapons he has pillaged.*

should stink in the grave with those wretches whose slave he
180 was. Contemn him and he is one. Come, follow me. I'll bring
you where you shall find Love, and by the virtue of this
majesty, who projecteth so powerful beams of light and heat
through this hemisphere, thaw his icy fetters and scatter the
darkness that obscures him. Then, in despite of this insolent
185 and barbarous Mammon, your sports may proceed, and the
solemnities of the night be complete without depending on so
earthy an idol.

Plutus. Aye, do; attempt it! 'Tis like to find most necessary and
fortunate event, whatsoever is enterprised without my aids.
190 Alas! how bitterly the spirit of poverty spouts itself against my
weal and felicity! But I feel it not. I cherish and make much of
myself, flow forth in ease and delicacy, while that murmurs
and starves.

Enter Cupid in his chariot, guarded with the masquers.

195 SONG

O how came Love, that is himself a fire,
To be so cold!
Yes, tyran money quencheth all desire,
Or makes it old.
200 But here are beauties will revive
Love's youth and keep his heat alive:
As often as his torch here dies,
He needs but light it at fresh eyes.
Joy, joy the more; for in all courts
205 If Love be cold, so are his sports.

Cupid. I have my spirits again, and feel my limbs.
Away with this cold cloud that dims

189 EVENT *outcome.*
198 TYRAN *tyrant.*

124

My light! Lie there, my furs and charms;
Love feels a heat that inward warms,
And guards him naked in these places,   210
As at his birth, or 'mongst the Graces.
Impostor Mammon, come, resign
This bow and quiver; they are mine.
Thou hast too long usurped my rites;
I now am lord of mine own nights.   215
Begone, whilst yet I give thee leave!
When thus the world thou wilt deceive,
Thou canst in youth and beauty shine,
Belie a godhead's form divine,
Scatter thy gifts, and fly to those   220
Where thine own humor may dispose;
But when to good men thou art sent
By Jove's direct commandement,
Thou then art agèd, lame and blind,
And canst nor path nor persons find.   225
Go, honest spirit, chase him hence
T' his caves, and there let him dispense,
For murders, treasons, rapes, his bribes
Unto the discontented tribes,
Where let his heaps grow daily less,   230
And he and they still want success.
The majesty that here doth move
Shall triumph, more secured by love
Than all his earth, and never crave
His aids, but force him as a slave.   235
To those bright beams I owe my life,
And I will pay it in the strife

223 COMMANDEMENT *four syllables.*
231 WANT *lack.*

Of duty back. See, here are ten,
The spirits of court and flower of men,
240 Led on by me, with flamed intents,
To figure the ten ornaments
That do each courtly presence grace.
Nor will they rudely strive for place,
One to precede the other, but
245 As music them in form shall put,
So will they keep their measures true,
And make still their proportions new,
Till all become one harmony
Of honor and of courtesy,
250 True valor and urbanity,
Of confidence, alacrity,
Of promptness and of industry,
Hability, reality.
Nor shall those graces ever quit your court,
255 Or I be wanting to supply their sport.

Dances.

SONG

This motion was of love begot,
It was so airy, light and good,
260 His wings into their feet he shot,
Or else himself into their blood.
But ask not how. The end will prove
That love's in them, or they're in love.

240 FLAMED *ardent.*
241 FIGURE *represent.*
246 MEASURES *(1) formations. (2) dances. The word also implies decorum and temperance.*
247 PROPORTIONS *in the dance figure, relationships to each other.*
250 URBANITY *refinement.*
253 HABILITY *ability.* REALITY *loyalty.*

SONG

Have men beheld the Graces dance,   265
  Or seen the upper orbs to move?
So did these turn, return, advance,
  Drawn back by doubt, put on by love.
And now, like earth, themselves they fix,
Till greater powers vouchsafe to mix   270
  Their motions with them. Do not fear,
  You brighter planets of this sphere:
    Not one male heart you see
      But rather to his female eyes
      Would die a destined sacrifice   275
    Than live at home and free.

SONG

Give end unto thy pastimes, Love,
  Before they labors prove;
A little rest between   280
Will make thy next shows better seen.
  Now let them close their eyes and see
  If they can dream of thee,
Since morning hastes to come in view,
And all the morning dreams are true.   285

270, 272 GREATER POWERS, BRIGHTER PLANETS *the ladies in the audience.*
270–71 MIX . . . THEM *dance with them in the revels.*
285 MORNING . . . TRUE *a belief persisting since classical times.*

Mercury Vindicated
from the Alchemists at Court

By Gentlemen, the King's Servants.

After the loud music, the scene discovered, being a laboratory, or alchemist's
workhouse; Vulcan looking to the registers, while a Cyclope, tending the
fire, to the cornets began to sing.

Cyclope.　Soft, subtile fire, thou soul of art,
　　　　　　Now do thy part　　　　　　　　　　　　　　5
　　　　On weaker Nature, that through age is lamed.
　　　　　Take but thy time, now she is old,
　　　　　And the sun her friend grown cold,
　　　　She will no more in strife with thee be named.
　　　　Look but how few confess her now　　　　　　10
　　　　　In cheek or brow!
　　　　From every head, almost, how she is frighted!
　　　　　The very age abhors her so
　　　　　That it learns to speak and go
　　　　As if by art alone it could be righted.　　　　15

Title BY . . . SERVANTS *performed by the theatrical company The King's Men.*
2 REGISTERS *sliding doors on a furnace to regulate the draft.*
6 WEAKER NATURE N.

The song ended, Mercury appeared, thrusting out his head and afterward his body at the tunnel of the middle furnace, which, Vulcan espying, cried out to the Cyclope.

Vulcan. Stay, see! our Mercury is coming forth; art and all the
20   elements assist. Call forth our philosophers. He will be gone,
he will evaporate. Dear Mercury! Help! He flies. He is 'scaped.
Precious golden Mercury, be fixed; be not so volatile. Will
none of the sons of art appear?

In which time Mercury, having run once or twice about the room, takes
25   *breath and speaks.*

Mercury. Now the place and goodness of it protect me. One tender-
hearted creature or other save Mercury and free him. Ne'er an
old gentlewoman i' the house that has a wrinkle about her to
hide me in? I could run into a serving-woman's pocket now,
30   her glove, any little hole. Some merciful farthingale among so
many be bounteous and undertake me: I will stand close up
anywhere to escape this polt-footed philosopher, old Smug
here of Lemnos, and his smoky family. Has he given me time
to breathe? O the variety of torment that I have endured in the
35   reign of the Cyclops, beyond the most exquisite wit of tyrans.
The whole household of 'em are become alchemists (since their
trade of armor-making failed them) only to keep themselves in
fire for this winter; for the mischief of a secret that they know,

16 MERCURY *or Hermes, patron of alchemy.*
20 PHILOSOPHERS *i.e. experts in "hermetic" knowledge.*
28 WRINKLE *in her face: mercury was used in cosmetics.*
30 FARTHINGALE *hoopskirt.*
32 POLT-FOOTED *club-footed.* SMUG *blacksmith.*
33 LEMNOS *Vulcan, the smith of the gods, was flung from heaven by Jove, and landed on the isle of Lemnos, laming himself in his fall.*
35 TYRANS *tyrants.*
37 ARMOR-MAKING ... THEM *because King James was a pacifist.*
38 MISCHIEF ... KNOW *i.e. they know no secrets.*

above the consuming of coals and drawing of usquebagh. Howsoever they may pretend under the specious names of Geber, Arnold, Lully, Bombast of Hohenheim to commit miracles in art and treason again' nature. And as if the title of philosopher, that creature of glory, were to be fetched out of a furnace, abuse the curious and credulous nation of metal-men through the world, and make Mercury their instrument. I am their crude and their sublimate, their precipitate and their unctuous, their male and their female, sometimes their hermaphrodite; what they list to style me. It is I that am corroded and exalted and sublimed and reduced and fetched over and filtered and washed and wiped; what between their salts and their sulfurs, their oils and their tartars, their brines and their vinegars, you might take me out now a soused Mercury, now a salted Mercury, now a smoked and dried Mercury, now a powdered and pickled Mercury: never herring, oyster, or cucumber passed so many vexations; my whole life with 'em hath been an exercise of torture; one, two, three, four and five times an hour ha' they made me dance the philosophical circle, like an ape through a hoop, or a dog in a wheel. I am their turn-spit indeed: they eat or smell no roast meat but in my

40

45

50

55

---

39 USQUEBAGH *whiskey.*

40 SPECIOUS NAMES *of famous alchemists: Geber, or Jaber, Arabian, eighth century; Arnold (Arnoldus de Villa Nova), French, thirteenth century; Lully (Raymond Lull), Majorcan, thirteenth century; Bombast of Hohenheim, or Paracelsus (1493–1541), the great Swiss physician and chemist.*

46 CRUDE . . . SUBLIMATE *mercury before and after being refined by the alchemists.*

46–7 PRECIPITATE . . . UNCTUOUS *mercury in solid and gaseous states.*

47 MALE . . . FEMALE *mercury and sulfur, the two basic substances in the alchemical process, were said to have male and female properties respectively; mercury was even thought to have both.*

49 EXALTED *intensified.* SUBLIMED *perfected.*

58–9 DOG . . . TURN-SPIT *a common kitchen engine. The dog ran inside the wheel and provided power to turn the spit.*

60   name. I am their bill of credit still, that passes for their victuals
and house-room. It is through me they ha' got this corner o'
the court to cozen in, where they shark for a hungry diet below
stairs, and cheat upon your under-officers, promising moun-
tains for their meat, and all upon Mercury's security. A poor
65   page o' the larder they have made obstinately believe he shall
be physician for the household next summer; they will give
him a quantity of the quintessence, shall serve him to cure
kibes, or the mormal o' the shin, take away the pustules i' the
nose, and Mercury is engaged for it. A child o' the scullery
70   steals all their coals for 'em too, and he is bid sleep secure, he
shall find a corner o' the philosophers' stone for't under his
bolster one day, and have the proverb inverted. Against which,
one day I am to deliver the buttery in, so many firkins of *aurum
potabile* as it delivers out bombards of budge to them between
75   this and that. For the pantry, they are at a certainty with me,
and keep a tally: an ingot, a loaf, or a wedge of some five
pound weight, which is a thing of nothing, a trifle. And so the

---

67 QUINTESSENCE *the purest essence of matter, the substance of which the heavenly
bodies were composed; but also used in the period to mean simply an alcoholic
tincture.*

68 KIBES *chapped or ulcerated chilblains.* MORMAL *an inflamed sore.*

71 PHILOSOPHERS' STONE *which would turn base metals into gold.*

72 PROVERB *The proverb is* "carbonem pro thesauro invenire," *to find coal instead
of a treasure, to have one's hopes disappointed.* AGAINST WHICH *in anticipation of the discovery of the philosophers' stone.*

73 FIRKINS *small casks.*

73–4 AURUM POTABILE *literally drinkable gold, a medicinal cordial made from gold.*
BOMBARDS OF BUDGE *leather bags of provisions (budge = bouge).*

75 THIS *this day.* FOR . . . ME *as for the menials in the pantry, they have made sure of
me.*

76 TALLY *account (of how much they have supplied the alchemists with).* INGOT,
LOAF, ETC. *of the philosophers' stone: this is what they expect in
exchange.*

blackguard are pleased with a toy, a lease of life (for some 999), especially those o' the boiling house: they are to have Medea's kettle hung up, that they may souse into it when they will and come out renewed like so many stripped snakes at their pleasure. But these are petty engagements, and (as I said) below the stairs; marry, above here, perpetuity of beauty (do you hear, ladies?), health, riches, honors, a matter of immortality is nothing. They will calcine you a grave matron (as it might be a mother o' the maids) and spring up a young virgin out of her ashes, as fresh as a phoenix; lay you an old courtier o' the coals like a sausage or a bloat-herring, and after they ha' broiled him enough, blow a soul into him with a pair of bellows till he start up into his galliard that was made when Monsieur was here. They profess familiarly to melt down all the old sinners o' the suburbs once in half a year into fresh gamesters again. Get all the cracked maidenheads and cast 'em into new ingots; half the wenches o' the town are alchemy. See, they begin to muster again and draw their forces out against me! The genius of the place defend me! You that are both the Sol and Jupiter of this sphere, Mercury invokes your majesty against the sooty tribe here; for in your favor only I grow recovered and warm.

80

85

90

95

78 BLACK GUARD *the menials of the court.* 999 *the number of years of the lease (vs. "perpetuity of beauty," line 83).*

79–80 MEDEA'S KETTLE *in which she restored the youth of her father-in-law, Aeson.*

81 STRIPPED SNAKES *snakes that have shed their skins.*

85 CALCINE *reduce to a powder by means of intense heat.*

86 MOTHER . . . MAIDS *chief of the queen's maids of honor.*

87 PHOENIX *a fabulous Arabian bird that consumed itself in fire at the moment of death and was reborn from the ashes.*

88 BLOAT-HERRING *bloater, smoked herring.*

90 GALLIARD *a lively dance.* MONSIEUR *the Duc d'Alençon, who came as a suitor for the hand of Queen Elizabeth in 1579.*

95 GENIUS *tutelary spirit.*

96 SOL AND JUPITER *sun and ruler, i.e. King James.*

At which time Vulcan entering with a troupe of threadbare alchemists
100   *prepares them to the first antimasque.*

Vulcan. Begin your charm, sound music, circle him in and take him:
if he will not obey, bind him.

They all danced about Mercury with variety of changes, whilst he defends
himself with his caduceus, and after the dance spake.

105 *Mercury.* It is in vain, Vulcan, to pitch your net in the sight of the
fowl thus: I am no sleepy Mars to be catched i' your subtile
toils. I know what your aims are, sir, to tear the wings from
my head and heels, and lute me up in a glass with my own
seals, while you might wrest the caduceus out of my hand to
110 the adultery and spoil of Nature, and make your accesses by it
to her dishonor more easy. Sir, would you believe it should be
come to that height of impudence in mankind that such a nest
of fire-worms as these are (because their patron Mulciber heretofore has made stools stir and statues dance, a dog of brass to
115 bark, and—which some will say was his worst act—a woman
to speak) should therefore with their heats called *balnei cineris,*
or horse dung, profess to outwork the sun in virtue and contend to the great act of generation, nay, almost creation? It is

104 CADUCEUS *Mercury's wand.*
106–07 SLEEPY . . . TOILS *Vulcan devised a net in which he trapped his adulterous*
    wife Venus in bed with Mars.
108 LUTE *close with an airtight seal.*
108–09 WITH . . . SEALS *with the seals of Hermes, i.e. hermetically.*
113 MULCIBER *Vulcan.*
114 MADE . . . DANCE *Both feats are described by Homer in* Iliad *XVIII.373ff.*
    DOG OF BRASS *guarding the palace of Alcinoüs, in* Odyssey *VII.91ff. (But*
    Jonson is in error: there are two dogs, of silver and gold.)
115 WOMAN *Pandora, created by Vulcan out of clay.*
116 BALNEI CINERIS *"baths of ash," in which vessels containing substances to be*
    heated were immersed to slow the heating process.
117 HORSE DUNG *used to generate low heat.* VIRTUE *power.*
117–18 CONTEND *strive.*

so, though. For in yonder vessels which you see in their laboratory they have enclosed materials to produce men, beyond the   120
deeds of Deucalion or Prometheus (of which one, they say, had
the philosophers' stone and threw it over his shoulder, the other
the fire, and lost it). And what men are they, they are so busy
about, think you? Not common or ordinary creatures, but of
rarity and excellence, such as the times wanted and the age had   125
a special deal of need of: such as there was a necessity they
should be artificial, for nature could never have thought or
dreamt o' their composition. I can remember some o' their
titles to you, and the ingredients: do not look for Paracelsus'
man among 'em, that he promised you out of white bread and   130
deal-wine, for he never came to light. But of these, let me see;
the first that occurs, a master of the duel, a carrier of the differencies. To him went spirit of ale, a good quantity, with the
amalgama of sugar and nutmegs, oil of oaths, sulfur of quarrel,
strong waters, valor precipitate, vapored o'er the helm with   135
tobacco, and the rosin of Mars with a dram o' the business, for
that's the word of tincture, the business. Let me alone with the

---

121 DEUCALION *a Greek Noah, who survived the universal flood and, on advice
from the oracle, repeopled the earth by throwing behind him stones that
miraculously became men and women.* PROMETHEUS *stole fire from Jupiter
and taught men to use it.*

128 REMEMBER *mention.*

129–30 PARACELSUS' MAN *Paracelsus gives a formula for the creation of a man in
the laboratory through chemical means.* N.

131 DEAL-WINE *a kind of Rhenish wine.*

132–33 DIFFERENCIES *disputes.*

134 AMALGAMA *mixture.*

135 VAPORED . . . HELM *The helm was the top of the retort used for distilling; vapor
was carried through a pipe "o'er the helm" into the vessel in which condensa-
tion took place.*

136 BUSINESS *great affair, a pretentious way of referring to any small quarrel.*

137 TINCTURE *essence.*

business, I will carry the business. I do understand the business. I do find an affront i' the business. Then another is a fencer i' the mathematics, or the town's cunning man, a creature of art too; a supposed secretary to the stars, but indeed, a kind of lying intelligencer from those parts. His materials, if I be not deceived, were juice of almanacs, extraction of *ephemerides*, scales of the globe, filings of figures, dust o' the twelve houses, conserve of questions, salt of confederacy, a pound of adventure, a grain of skill, and a drop of truth. I saw vegetals too, as well as minerals, put into one glass there, as adder's tongue, title-bane, niter of clients, tartar of false conveyance, *aurum palpabile*, with a huge deal of talk, to which they added tincture of conscience with the feces of honesty; but for what this was I could not learn, only I have overheard one o' the artists say, out o' the corruption of a lawyer was the best generation of a broker in suits: whether this were he or no, I know not.

Vulcan. Thou art a scorner, Mercury, and out of the pride of thy protection here mak'st it thy study to revile art, but it will turn to thine own contumely soon. Call forth the creatures of the first class and let them move to the harmony of our heat, till the slanderer have sealed up his own lips to his own torment.

150 feces] faces Ff.

139–40 FENCER . . . MATHEMATICS *one who plans his strategies according to geometric projections.*

141 SECRETARY . . . STARS *astrologer.*

143 EPHEMERIDES *astrological almanacs.*

144 FIGURES *diagrams of the position of the planets, used for casting horoscopes.* TWELVE HOUSES *signs of the zodiac.*

146 VEGETALS *plants.*

148 TITLE-BANE *lawyer's poison (cf. ratsbane).* FALSE CONVEYANCE *illegal transfer of property.*

148–49 AURUM PALPABILE *"touchable gold," i.e. money; a pun on* aurum potabile, *lines 73–4.*

Mercury. Let 'em come, let 'em come, I would not wish a greater
    punishment to thy impudence.   160

There enters the second antimasque of imperfect creatures, with helms of
    limbecks on their heads, whose dance ended, Mercury proceeded.

[*Mercury.*] Art thou not ashamed, Vulcan, to offer in defense of thy
    fire and art, against the excellence of the sun and Nature, crea-
    tures more imperfect than the very flies and insects that are her 165
    trespasses and scapes? Vanish with thy insolence, thou and thy
    impostors, and all mention of you melt before the majesty of
    this light, whose Mercury henceforth I profess to be, and never
    again the philosophers'. Vanish, I say, that all who have but
    their senses may see and judge the difference between thy 170
    ridiculous monsters and his absolute features.

At which the whole scene changed to a glorious bower wherein Nature was
placed with Prometheus at her feet, and the twelve masquers standing about
them. After they had been a while viewed, Prometheus descended, and
    Nature after him, singing.   175

Nature.   How young and fresh am I tonight,
          To see't kept day by so much light,
        And twelve my sons stand in their maker's sight!
         Help, wise Prometheus, something must be done
         To show they are the creatures of the sun, 180
             That each to other
             Is a brother,
         And Nature here no stepdame, but a mother.
Chorus.   Come forth, come forth, prove all the numbers then
         That make perfection up, and may absolve you men. 185

161–62 HELMS OF LIMBECKS *See line 135.*
166 SCAPES *transgressions.*
171 FEATURES *creations.*
184 PROVE *try.* NUMBERS *rhythmical units—here, the dances.*
185 ABSOLVE YOU *make you absolute or perfect.*

[*Nature.*]   But show thy winding ways and arts,
Thy risings and thy timely starts
Of stealing fire from ladies' eyes and hearts.
Those softer circles are the young man's heaven,

190   And there more orbs and planets are than seven,
To know whose motion
Were a notion
As worthy of youth's study as devotion.

Chorus.   Come forth, come forth, prove all the time will gain,

195   For Nature bids the best, and never bade in vain.

The first dance, after which this song.

Prometheus. How many 'mongst these ladies here
Wish now they such a mother were!

Nature.   Not one, I fear,

200   And read it in their laughters.
There's more, I guess, would wish to be my daughters.

Prometheus. You think they would not be so old
For so much glory.

Nature.   I think that thought so told

205   Is no false piece of story.
'Tis yet with them but beauty's noon,
They would not grandams be too soon.

Prometheus.   Is that your sex's humor?
'Tis then since Niobe was changed that they have left
that tumor.

188 STEALING FIRE *as Prometheus did from the gods.*

190 ORBS . . . SEVEN *In Ptolemaic astronomy, the orbs were seven transparent spheres that rotated about earth, each containing one of the heavenly bodies that were seen to move: the five planets, the sun and moon.*

194 PROVE *experience.* GAIN *allow.*

209 NIOBE *mother of six sons and six daughters, who boasted herself happier than Leto, mother of Apollo and Artemis. As punishment for this hubris, Apollo killed the sons, and Artemis all but one of the daughters. Niobe weeping became a rock with a fountain running from it.* TUMOR *passion.*

Chorus. Move, move again in forms as heretofore.   210
Nature.   'Tis form allures.
          Then move; the ladies here are store.
Prometheus. Nature is motion's mother, as she is yours;
Chorus. The spring whence order flows, that all directs,
          And knits the causes with th'effects.   215

The main dance. Then dancing with the ladies; then their last dance. After
which, Prometheus calls to them in song.

Prometheus.   What, ha' you done
               So soon?
          And can you from such beauty part?   220
               You'll do a wonder more than I.
               I woman with her ills did fly,
               But you their good and them deny.
Chorus.   Sure, each hath left his heart
          In pawn to come again, or else he durst not start.   225
Nature.   They are loath to go,
               I know,
               Or sure they are no sons of mine.
               There is no banquet, boys, like this,
               If you hope better, you will miss;   230
               Stay here, and take each one a kiss.
Chorus.   Which if you can refine
          The taste knows no such cates, nor yet the palate wine.
               No cause of tarrying shun:
          They are not worth his light, go backward from the sun.   235

212 STORE *both many, and treasure.*
222 WOMAN *To revenge himself on Prometheus for the loss of the gods' fire, Zeus*
     commanded Hephaestos, or Vulcan, to create Pandora, the first woman, and
     offered her to Prometheus as a gift. But Prometheus wisely refused, and
     Pandora was accepted instead by his brother Epimetheus.
233 CATES *delicacies.*
235 GO *who go.*

The Golden Age Restored

In a Masque at Court, 1615, by the Lords, and Gentlemen, the
King's Servants.

> *Loud music. Pallas in her chariot descending.*
>
> *To a softer music.*

[*Pallas.*] Look, look! rejoice and wonder!
       That you offending mortals are,
       For all your crimes, so much the care
Of him that bears the thunder!

Jove can endure no longer
       Your great ones should your less invade,
       Or that your weak, though bad, be made
A prey unto the stronger;

And therefore means to settle
       Astraea in her seat again,
       And let down in his golden chain
The age of better metal.

5

10

14 metal] mettle Ff.

Title GENTLEMEN . . . SERVANTS *the theatrical company The King's Men.*
1 PALLAS *Athena.*
12 ASTRAEA *goddess of justice.*
14 METAL *or mettle, the same word in Jonson's time.*

Which deed he doth the rather   15
    That even Envy may behold
    Time not enjoyed his head of gold
Alone beneath his father;

But that his care conserveth,
    As Time, so all Time's honors too,   20
    Regarding still what heav'n should do,
And not what earth deserveth.

    A tumult and clashing of arms heard within.

But hark, what tumult from yond' cave is heard!
    What noise, what strife, what earthquake and alarms!   25
As troubled Nature for her maker feared,
    And all the Iron Age were up in arms!
Hide me, soft cloud, from their profaner eyes,
    Till insolent rebellion take the field,
And as their spirits with their counsels rise,   30
    I frustrate all with showing but my shield.

    Iron Age presents itself, calling forth the evils.

[*Iron Age.*] Come forth, come forth, do we not hear
    What purpose, and how worth our fear,
      The king of gods hath on us?   35
    He is not of the iron breed
    That would, though Fate did help the deed,
      Let shame in so upon us.
    Rise, rise then up, thou grandame vice
    Of all my issue, Avarice,   40

17–18 TIME . . . FATHER *i.e. Jove's age is golden too. Jove's father was Saturn, or Kronos, whose reign was the Golden Age.*
20 TIME *Jonson, following both late classical and Renaissance etymologists, identified Kronos with Time (Chronos).*
21 STILL *always.*
26 AS *as if.*

Bring with thee Fraud and Slander,
Corruption with the golden hands,
Or any subtler ill that stands
    To be a more commander.
Thy boys, Ambition, Pride and Scorn,
Force, Rapine, and thy babe last born,
    Smooth Treachery, call hither,
Arm Folly forth, and Ignorance,
And teach them all our pyrrhic dance,
    We may triumph together
Upon this enemy so great,
Whom if our forces can defeat,
    And but this once bring under,
We are the masters of the skies,
Where all the wealth, height, power lies,
    The scepter and the thunder.
Which of you would not in a war
Attempt the price of any scar
    To keep your own states even?
But here, which of you is that he,
Would not himself the weapon be
    To ruin Jove and heaven?
About it then, and let him feel
The Iron Age is turned to steel,
    Since he begins to threat her;
And though the bodies here are less
Than were the giants, he'll confess
    Our malice is far greater.

The antimasque and their dance, two drums, trumpets, and a confusion of
martial music; at the end of which, Pallas, showing her shield.

49 PYRRHIC DANCE *war dance.*
67 GIANTS *titans, overthrown by Jove.*

142

[*Pallas.*] So change and perish, scarcely knowing how,
   That 'gainst the gods do take so vain a vow,
   And think to equal with your mortal dates
   Their lives that are obnoxious to no fates.
   'Twas time t'appear, and let their follies see   75
   'Gainst whom they fought, and with what destiny.
   Die all that can remain of you but stone,
   And that be seen awhile, and then be none.

They metamorphosed and the scene changed, she calls Astraea and the
          Golden Age.   80

   Now, now, descend, you both beloved of Jove,
   And of the good on earth no less the love,
   Descend, you long long wished and wanted pair,
   And as your softer times divide the air,
   So shake all clouds off with your golden hair,   85
   For spite is spent: the Iron Age is fled,
   And, with her power on earth, her name is dead.

   Astraea [and the Golden] Age descending.

Astraea,   ⎫ And are we then
Golden Age⎭   To live again   90
       With men?
Astraea. Will Jove such pledges to the earth restore
   As justice?
Golden Age.   Or the purer ore?
Pallas.   Once more.   95
Golden Age. But do they know
   How much they owe
    Below?
Astraea. And will of grace receive it, not as due?
Pallas. If not, they harm themselves, not you.   100

74 OBNOXIOUS *subject.*

Astraea.   True.

Golden Age.   True.

Choir. Let narrow natures, how they will, mistake;
       The great should still be good for their own sake.

They are descended.

105   *Pallas.* Welcome to earth and reign.

    Astraea,   ⎫   But how without a train
    Golden Age. ⎭   Shall we our state sustain?

    Pallas. Leave that to Jove; therein you are
           No little part of his Minerva's care.

110   Expect awhile.

She calls the poets.

       You far-famed spirits of this happy isle,
       That for your sacred songs have gained the style
       Of Phoebus' sons, whose notes the air aspire
115   Of th'old Egyptian, or the Thracian lyre,
       That Chaucer, Gower, Lydgate, Spenser hight,
       Put on your better flames and larger light
       To wait upon the age that shall your names new nourish,
       Since virtue pressed shall grow, and buried arts shall flourish.

120   *Poets descend.*

    Two Poets.   We come.

    Two Poets.   We come.

    All Four.   Our best of fire
           Is that which Pallas doth inspire.

---

109 MINERVA *Roman name of Pallas Athena.*

114 PHOEBUS *Apollo, god of poetry.* ASPIRE *breathe.*

115 EGYPTIAN *hermetic.* THRACIAN *Thrace was Orpheus' home.*

116 HIGHT *are named.*

119 PRESSED *oppressed.*

144

Pallas. Then see you yonder souls, set far within the shade,
    And in Elysian bowers the blessèd seats do keep,   125
    That for their living good now semigods are made,
        And went away from earth, as if but tamed with sleep:
    These must we join to wake, for these are of the strain
    That justice dare defend, and will the age sustain.
Choir. Awake, awake, for whom these times were kept,   130
    O wake, wake, wake, as you had never slept;
    Make haste and put on air to be their guard,
    Whom once but to defend is still reward.
Pallas. Thus Pallas throws a lightning from her shield.
Choir. To which let all that doubtful darkness yield.   135

                    The scene of light discovered.

Astraea. Now peace,
Golden Age.   And love,
Astraea.   Faith,
Golden Age.   Joys,
Both.   All, all increase;
Two Poets. And strife,
Two Poets.   And hate,
Two Poets.   And fear,
Two Poets.   And pain
All Four.   All cease:

                            A pause.

Pallas. No tumor of an iron vein.   140
        The causes shall not come again.
Choir.   But, as of old, all now be gold.
        Move, move then to these sounds.

131 AS *as if.*
132 PUT . . . BE *act as.*
140 TUMOR *passion.*

                            145

And do not only walk your solemn rounds,
145   But give those light and airy bounds
That fit the *genii* of these gladder grounds.

The first dance; after which Pallas.

[*Pallas.*] Already? Do not all things smile?
Astraea. But when they have enjoyed awhile
150   The age's quickening power—
Golden Age. That every thought a seed doth bring,
And every look a plant doth spring,
And every breath a flower—
Pallas. Then earth unplowed shall yield her crop,
155   Pure honey from the oak shall drop,
The fountain shall run milk;
The thistle shall the lily bear,
And every bramble roses wear,
And every worm make silk.
160 *Choir.* The very shrub shall balsam sweat,
And nectar melt the rock with heat,
Till earth have drunk her fill,
That she no harmful weed may know,
Nor barren fern, nor mandrake low,
165   Nor mineral to kill.

The main dance, after which,

Pallas. But here's not all; you must do more,
Or else you do but half restore
The age's liberty.
170 *Poets.* The male and female used to join,
And into all delight did coin
That pure simplicity.

146 GENII *guardian spirits.*

Then feature did to form advance,
And youth called beauty forth to dance,
 And every grace was by.   175
It was a time of no distrust,
So much of love had nought of lust,
 None feared a jealous eye.
The language melted in the ear,
Yet all without a blush might hear;   180
 They lived with open vow.
Choir. Each touch and kiss was so well placed,
 They were as sweet as they were chaste,
  And such must yours be now.

     Dance with ladies.   185

   Pallas ascending calls them.

[*Pallas.*] 'Tis now enough. Behold you here
 What Jove hath built to be your sphere;
  You hither must retire.
And as his bounty gives you cause,   190
Be ready still without your pause
  To show the world your fire.

Like lights about Astraea's throne
You here must shine, and all be one
  In fervor and in flame;   195
That by your union she may grow,
And, you sustaining her, may know
  The age still by her name;

186–206 *so revised* F[1] *and* F[2]; *originally followed line 224 in* F[1]. *N.*

---

173 FEATURE . . . ADVANCE *Platonic terminology: individual shapes were perfected to
  ideal ones.*
186–206 N.

Who vows, against all heat or cold,
200 To spin you garments of her gold,
That want may touch you never;
And making garlands every hour,
To write your names in some new flower,
That you may live forever.

205 *Choir.* To Jove, to Jove be all the honor given
That thankful hearts can raise from earth to heaven.

Astraea. What change is here! I had not more
Desire to leave the earth before
Than I have now to stay;
210 My silver feet, like roots, are wreathed
Into the ground, my wings are sheathed,
And I cannot away.

Of all there seems a second birth;
It is become a heav'n on earth,
215 And Jove is present here:
I feel the godhead! nor will doubt
But he can fill the place throughout,
Whose power is everywhere.

This, this, and only such as this,
220 The bright Astraea's region is,
Where she would pray to live;
And in the midst of so much gold,
Unbought with grace or fear unsold,
The law to mortals give.

225 *Galliards and corantos.*

The End.

---

208 LEAVE . . . BEFORE *Justice fled from earth when Saturn's reign was overthrown.*
223 FEAR *with fear.*
225 GALLIARDS *quick dances.* CORANTOS *dances with running or gliding steps.*

The Vision of Delight

Presented at court in Christmas, 1617.

The scene: a street in perspective of fair building discovered. Delight is seen to come as afar off, accompanied with Grace, Love, Harmony, Revel, Sport, Laughter; Wonder following.

Delight. (Spake in song, stilo recitativo.)

Let us play and dance and sing,   5
   Let us now turn every sort
O' the pleasures of the spring
   To the graces of a court.
From air, from cloud, from dreams, from toys,
   To sounds, to sense, to love, to joys;   10
Let your shows be new, as strange,
   Let them oft and sweetly vary;
Let them haste so to their change
   As the seers may not tarry;
Too long t'expect the pleasing'st sight   15
   Doth take away from the delight.

Here the first antimasque entered, a she-monster delivered of six burratines that dance with six pantaloons; which done, Delight spoke again.

4 STILO RECITATIVO *The music was by Nicholas Lanier.*
17, 18 BURRATINES, PANTALOONS *grotesque figures from the Italian comedy. The burratines are young men, the pantaloons old.*

Yet hear what your Delight doth pray:
20   All sour and sullen looks away
That are the servants of the day;
Our sports are of the humorous night,
Who feeds the stars that give her light,
And useth than her wont more bright
25   To help the vision of Delight.

Here the Night rises, and took her chariot bespangled with stars.
Delight proceeds.

See, see, her scepter and her crown
Are all of flame, and from her gown
30   A train of light comes waving down.
This night in dew she will not steep
The brain nor lock the sense in sleep,
But all awake with phantoms keep,
And those to make delight more deep.

35 *By this time the Night and Moon being both risen, Night, hovering over*
the place, sung.

[*Night.*] Break, Fant'sy, from thy cave of cloud
And spread thy purple wings;
Now all thy figures are allowed,
40   And various shapes of things;
Create of airy forms a stream;
It must have blood and nought of phlegm,
And though it be a waking dream,

22 HUMOROUS *fantastic.*
42 BLOOD . . . PHLEGM *Blood and phlegm are two of the four bodily humors, producing*
temperaments that are respectively hot and lively (sanguine), and moist and
dull (phlegmatic).

The Choir.	Yet let it like an odor rise
	To all the senses here,	45
	And fall like sleep upon their eyes,
	Or music in their ear.

The scene here changed to cloud, and Fant'sy breaking forth spake.

[*Fant'sy.*] Bright Night, I obey thee, and am come at thy call,
But it is no one dream that can please these all;   50
Wherefore I would know what dreams would delight 'em,
For never was Fant'sy more loath to affright 'em.
And Fant'sy, I tell you, has dreams that have wings,
And dreams that have honey, and dreams that have stings;
Dreams of the maker and dreams of the teller,   55
Dreams of the kitchen and dreams of the cellar;
Some that are tall, and some that are dwarfs,
Some that are haltered, and some that wear scarfs;
Some that are proper and signify o' thing,
And some another, and some that are nothing.   60
For say the French farthingale and the French hood
Were here to dispute; must it be understood
A feather, for a wisp, were a fit moderator?

58 are haltered] *so* MS; were haltered F.

49–106 N.

55 MAKER *poet.* TELLER *clerk.*

58 SOME . . . HALTERED *prisoners.* SOME . . . SCARFS *soldiers or courtiers.*

59 PROPER *both elegant and literal, not metaphorical.* O' *one.*

61 FARTHINGALE . . . HOOD *new and old styles in women's dress. The farthingale, or hoopskirt, had recently become popular, and spectators at masques were forbidden to wear it because of its bulkiness. But also, the dispute is between the body below the waist and the head, just as the speech as a whole concerns the rival claims of lechery and gluttony to be the prime source of delight.*

61–6 N.

63 FEATHER *The ostrich feather was the courtier's plume.* WISP *a straw man for a scold to rail at; "for a wisp" means "serving as a wisp."*

Your ostrich, believe it, 's no faithful translator
Of perfect Utopian; and then it were an odd piece
To see the conclusion peep forth at a codpiece.
   The politic pudding hath still his two ends,
Though the bellows and bagpipe were nev'r so good friends;
And who can report what offence it would be
For the squirrel to see a dog climb a tree?
If a dream should come in now to make you afeard,
With a windmill on his head and bells at his beard,
Would you straight wear your spectacles here at your toes,
And your boots o' your brows, and your spurs o' your nose?
Your whale he will swallow a hogshead for a pill;
But the maker o' the mousetrap is he that hath skill.

64 OSTRICH *emblematic of both gluttony (because it digests iron) and garrulousness; but also of justice, hence its appearance as "moderator" of the dispute.* N.

65 UTOPIAN *literally, "of nowhere," the language of the dream world.*

66 CONCLUSION . . . CODPIECE *i.e. for a man to settle women's disputes, with a pun on "concluding a peace," and obvious obscene overtones.*

67 POLITIC *expedient, pragmatic.* PUDDING *sausage, but here, phallus, continuing the image of the stuffed codpiece.* STILL *always.* ENDS *with an equivocation on "purposes."*

67–70 N.

68 BELLOWS . . . BAGPIPE *Bellows are the lungs; but the bagpipe is a traditional symbol of lechery, and often directly represents the male genitals. The bellows, then, is "that which blows up or fans the fire of passion" (OED). Cf.* Antony and Cleopatra *I.i.9–10.*

70 SQUIRREL . . . TREE *i.e. for the natural situation to be reversed.*

71–8 N.

72 WINDMILL . . . BEARD *The windmill-head is an emblem of gluttony: the head becomes merely a device for grinding up food.* N. *The bells imply frivolity.*

73–4 WOULD . . . NOSE *Cf. line 70. The image of the normal world inverted is now applied to human behavior.*

75 WHALE *a traditional symbol of gluttony.* HOGSHEAD *huge cask.*

76 MAKER . . . MOUSETRAP *slang for lecher, the man who can catch "mice," or women.*

And the nature of the onion is to draw tears,
As well as the mustard—peace, pitchers have ears,
And shuttlecocks wings; these things, do not mind 'em.
If the bell have any sides, the clapper will find 'em.   80
There's twice so much music in beating the tabor
As i' the stockfish, and somewhat less labor.
Yet all this while no proportion is boasted
'Twixt an egg and an ox, though both have been roasted;
For grant the most barbers can play o' the cittern,   85
Is it requisite a lawyer should plead to a gittern?
   You will say now the morris-bells were but bribes
To make the heel forget that ev'r it had kibes;
I say let the wine make nev'r so good jelly,
The conscience o' the bottle is much i' the belly: 90
For why? do but take common counsel i' your way,
And tell me who'll then set a bottle of hay

77–8 ONION . . . MUSTARD *i.e. things, too, act according to their natures.*
78 PITCHERS . . . EARS *proverbial: "we are being overheard."*
79 SHUTTLECOCKS WINGS *i.e. light banter is flying around. But pitchers and shuttlecocks also carry overtones of gluttony and lechery.*
80 IF . . . 'EM *If there is any point to this, it will become apparent.*
81–2 BEATING . . . STOCKFISH *The tabor is a drum used to accompany a dance; the stockfish is a dried fish that must be beaten before cooking. The point is that it is better to enjoy oneself than work.*
83–4 NO . . . OX *i.e. I am not claiming that small things are equal to great.*
85–6 BARBERS . . . GITTERN *Both cittern and gittern are old forms of guitar. Barbers kept citterns in their shops for customers to amuse themselves with while waiting. The point of the line is that not all occasions are suitable for music.*
86 TO *to the accompaniment of.*
87 MORRIS–BELLS *bells worn by morris dancers.*
87–95 N.
88 KIBES *chilblains.*
89 JELLY *also means semen (and is.thus appropriate to both glutton and lecher).*
92 BOTTLE *bundle.*

Before the old usurer, and to his horse
A slice of salt butter, perverting the course
95   Of civil society? Open that gap,
And out skip your fleas, four and twenty at a clap,
With a chain and a trundle bed following at th' heels,
And will they not cry then, the world runs a-wheels?
As for example, a belly and no face
100   With the bill of a shoveler may here come in place,
The haunches of a drum with the feet of a pot
And the tail of a Kentishman to it—why not?
Yet would I take the stars to be cruel
If the crab and the ropemaker ever fight duel
105   On any dependence, be it right, be it wrong—
But mum; a thread may be drawn out too long.

Here the second antimasque of phantasms came forth, which danced.

Fant'sy proceeded.

Why, this you will say was fantastical now,
110   As the cock and the bull, the whale and the cow;
But vanish away; I have change to present you,
And such as I hope will more truly content you.
Behold the gold-haired Hour descending here,

94 SALT BUTTER *a luxury.*

95–8 OPEN . . . WHEELS *The perversion of "civil society" produces an image of the world first as a flea circus, and then as controlled by its vermin.*

98 WORLD . . . WHEELS *proverbial (and ironic): "everything is running smoothly," i.e. toward perdition.* N.

99–102 BELLY . . . KENTISHMAN *an emblematic figure representing gluttony.*

100 SHOVELER *spoonbill.*

102 TAIL . . . KENTISHMAN N.

104 CRAB *capstan or winch, and thus relevant to the* ROPEMAKER. *But also, the two are emblematic of gluttony and sloth respectively.* N.

105 DEPENDENCE *the grounds of a quarrel.*

113 GOLD-HAIRED HOUR *Peace, one of the three Horae, daughters of Zeus and Themis, who control the seasons and give laws, justice, and peace to men.*

That keeps the gate of heaven and turns the year,
    Already with her sight how she doth cheer,   115
And makes another face of things appear.

Here one of the Hours descending, the whole scene changed to the bower of
        Zephyrus, whilst Peace sung as followeth.

[*Peace.*]   Why look you so, and all turn dumb,
        To see the opener of the new year come?   120
    My presence rather should invite,
        And aid, and urge, and call to your delight.
    The many pleasures that I bring
        Are all of youth, of heat, of life and spring,
    And were prepared to warm your blood,   125
        Not fix it thus as if you statues stood.

The Choir. We see, we hear, we feel, we taste,
    We smell the change in every flower;
    We only wish that all could last
    And be as new still as the hour.   130

        The song ended, Wonder spake.

Wonder must speak or break: what is this? Grows
The wealth of nature here, or art? It shows
As if Favonius, father of the spring,
Who in the verdant meads doth reign sole king,   135
Had roused him here and shook his feathers, wet
With purple-swelling nectar, and had let
The sweet and fruitful dew fall on the ground
To force out all the flowers that might be found;
    Or a Minerva with her needle had   140
    Th'enamored earth with all her riches clad,

126 you statues] your statutes F.

---

118 ZEPHYRUS *the west wind.*
134 FAVONIUS *Latin name for Zephyrus.*
140 MINERVA *goddess of the arts.*

And made the downy Zephyr as he flew
Still to be followed with the spring's best hue.
    The gaudy peacock boasts not in his train
So many lights and shadows, nor the rain-
Resolving Iris when the Sun doth court her,
Nor purple pheasant while his aunt doth sport her
To hear him crow, and with a perchèd pride
Wave his discolored neck and purple side.
    I have not seen the place could more surprise;
It looks, methinks, like one of Nature's eyes,
Or her whole body set in art. Behold!
How the blue bindweed doth itself enfold
With honeysuckle, and both these entwine
Themselves with bryony and jessamine,
To cast a kind and odoriferous shade!

Fant'sy. How better than they are are all things made
By Wonder! But awhile refresh thine eye;
I'll put thee to thy oftener what and why.

160 *Here, to a loud music, the bower opens, and the masquers discovered as the*
glories of the spring.

Wonder again spake.

Thou wilt indeed. What better change appears?
Whence is it that the air so sudden clears,
And all things in a moment turn so mild?
Whose breath or beams have got proud Earth with child
Of all the treasure that great Nature's worth,

145

150

155

165

146 IRIS *the rainbow.*
147 AUNT *mistress.*
148 PERCHÈD *exalted.*
149 DISCOLORED *highly colored.*
153 BLUE BINDWEED *bittersweet or woody nighshade.*
159 I'LL . . . WHY *i.e. I'll make you ask more questions.*

And makes her every minute to bring forth?
How comes it winter is so quite forced hence,
And locked up under ground? that every sense   170
Hath several objects? trees have got their heads,
The fields their coats? that now the shining meads
Do boast the paunce, the lily and the rose;
And every flower doth laugh as Zephyr blows?
That seas are now more even than the land?   175
The rivers run as smoothèd by his hand;
Only their heads are crispèd by his stroke:
How plays the yearling with his brow scarce broke
Now in the open grass? and frisking lambs
Make wanton salts about their dry-sucked dams,   180
Who to repair their bags do rob the fields?
   How is't each bough a several music yields?
The lusty throstle, early nightingale
Accord in tune, though vary in their tale?
The chirping swallow called forth by the sun,   185
And crested lark doth his division run?
The yellow bees the air with murmur fill?
The finches carol, and the turtles bill?
Whose power is this? what god?

Fant'sy.   Behold a king
Whose presence maketh this perpetual spring,   190
The glories of which spring grow in that bower,
And are the marks and beauties of his power.

171 HEADS *leaves.*
173 PAUNCE *pansy.*
178 WITH . . . BROKE *whose horns have barely begun to sprout.*
180 SALTS *jumps.*
181 REPAIR . . . BAGS *replenish their udders.*
183 THROSTLE *thrush.*
186 DIVISION *a quick variation on a ground, or given melody.*
188 TURTLES *doves.*

To which the choir answered.

'Tis he, 'tis he, and no power else,
That makes all this what Fant'sy tells;
   The founts, the flowers, the birds, the bees,
The herds, the flocks, the grass, the trees
Do all confess him; but most these
Who call him lord of the four seas,
King of the less and greater isles,
And all those happy when he smiles.
   Advance, his favor calls you to advance,
And do your this night's homage in a dance.

Here they danced their entry, after which they sung again.

Again, again; you cannot be
Of such a true delight too free,
   Which who once saw would ever see;
And if they could the object prize,
Would, while it lasts, not think to rise,
   But wish their bodies all were eyes.

They danced their main dance, after which they sung.

In curious knots and mazes so
The spring at first was taught to go,
And Zephyr when he came to woo
His Flora had their motions too,
   And thence did Venus learn to lead
   Th' Idalian brawls, and so to tread

195

200

205

210

215

217 to] *not in* F.

---

212 CURIOUS *complex.*
215 FLORA *goddess of flowers.*
217 IDALIAN *from Idalium in Cyprus, a place sacred to Venus.* BRAWLS *group dances.*

> As if the wind, not she, did walk;
> Nor pressed a flower, nor bowed a stalk.

They danced with ladies, and the whole revels followed; after which Aurora 220
appeared, the Night and Moon descended, and this epilogue followed.

[*Aurora.*] I was not wearier where I lay
    By frozen Tithon's side tonight,
    Than I am willing now to stay
    And be a part of your delight.   225
      But I am urgèd by the day,
    Against my will, to bid you come away.
The Choir. They yield to time, and so must all.
    As night to sport, day doth to action call,
      Which they the rather do obey   230
    Because the morn with roses strews the way.

Here they danced their going off, and ended.

220 AURORA *dawn.*
223 TITHON *Tithonus, husband of Aurora, who was granted immortality but not
eternal youth.*

Pleasure Reconciled to Virtue

A Masque. As it was presented at court before King James. 1618.

The scene was the mountain Atlas, who had his top ending in the figure of an old man, his head and beard all hoary and frost as if his shoulders were covered with snow; the rest wood and rock. A grove of ivy at his feet, out of which, to a wild music of cymbals, flutes and tabers, is brought forth Comus, the god of cheer, or the belly, riding in triumph, his head crowned with roses and other flowers, his hair curled; they that wait upon him crowned with ivy, their javelins done about with it; one of them going with Hercules his bowl bare before him, while the rest presented him with this 5

HYMN

Room, room, make room for the bouncing belly, 10
First father of sauce, and deviser of jelly,
Prime master of arts, and the giver of wit,
That found out the excellent engine, the spit,
The plow, and the flail, the mill, and the hopper,
The hutch, and the bolter, the furnace, and copper, 15

9 hymn] song MS.

---

10 ROOM, ROOM *the usual opening of mummers' plays.*
14 FLAIL *thresher.* HOPPER *in a grain mill, the funnel into which the grain is poured.*
15 HUTCH *bin.* BOLTER *grain sifter.* COPPER *pot.*

The oven, the bavin, the mawkin, the peel,
The hearth, and the range, the dog and the wheel.
He, he first invented the hogshead and tun,
The gimlet and vice too, and taught 'em to run.
20 And since, with the funnel, an Hippocras bag
He's made of himself, that now he cries swag.
Which shows, though the pleasure be but of four inches,
Yet he is a weasel, the gullet that pinches,
Of any delight, and not spares from this back
25 Whatever to make of the belly a sack.
Hail, hail, plump paunch, O the founder of taste
For fresh meats, or powdered, or pickle, or paste;
Devourer of broiled, baked, roasted or sod,
And emptier of cups, be they even or odd;
30 All which have now made thee so wide i' the waist
As scarce with no pudding thou art to be laced;

18 the] both MS.

---

16 BAVIN *bundle of wood used in bakers' ovens.* MAWKIN *malkin, baker's mop.*
   PEEL *baker's shovel.*
17 DOG . . . WHEEL *an ingenious kitchen engine: the dog supplied the power and the*
   wheel turned the spit. Cf. Mercury Vindicated, *lines 58–9.*
18 HOGSHEAD, TUN *both large casks for liquor.*
19 GIMLET . . . VICE *comprise the tap of a cask.*
20 HIPPOCRAS BAG *a cone of cloth used to filter wine.*
21 CRIES SWAG *reveals his swag-belly, or drooping paunch.*
22–5 THOUGH . . . SACK *Though the pleasure result only in an increase in girth,*
   yet the gullet will not forgo any delight or make it in any way easier for the
   back to support the great belly.
28 SOD *boiled.*
29 EVEN . . . ODD *in whatever quantity; alluding to a classical superstition that to*
   consume an even number of drinks was unlucky.
31 SCARCE . . . LACED *A pudding is a thick rope tied about the mast of a ship as a*
   support; lace with (as in "lace with brandy") means add. The line means
   both "your girdle can scarcely be laced up with a sailor's rope," and "you
   can scarcely have any more pudding added to you."

But eating and drinking until thou dost nod,
Thou break'st all thy girdles, and break'st forth a god.

To this, the Bowl-bearer.

Do you hear, my friends? to whom did you sing all this now?　35
Pardon me only that I ask you, for I do not look for an answer;
I'll answer myself. I know it is now such a time as the saturnals
for all the world, that every man stands under the eaves of his
own hat and sings what please him; that's the right and the
liberty of it. Now you sing of god Comus here, the Belly-god.　40
I say it is well, and I say it is not well. It is well as it is a ballad,
and the belly worthy of it, I must needs say, an 'twere forty
yards of ballad more—as much ballad as tripe. But when the
belly is not edified by it, it is not well; for where did you ever
read or hear that the belly had any ears? Come, never pump　45
for an answer, for you are defeated. Our fellow Hunger there,
that was as ancient a retainer to the belly as any of us, was
turned away for being unseasonable—not unreasonable, but
unseasonable—and now is he (poor thin-gut) fain to get his
living with teaching of starlings, magpies, parrots and jack-　50
daws, those things he would have taught the belly. Beware of
dealing with the belly; the belly will not be talked to, especially when he is full. Then there is no venturing upon Venter;
he will blow you all up; he will thunder indeed, la: some in
derision call him the father of farts. But I say he was the first　55
inventor of great ordnance, and taught us to discharge them
on festival days. Would we had a fit feast for him, i'faith, to
show his activity: I would have something now fetched in to
please his five senses, the throat, or the two senses, the eyes.

37　SATURNALS *The Roman saturnalia was a time of complete festive license, and
Twelfth-night, culmination of the season of masques and revels, took on its
character.*

53　VENTER *paunch (Latin).*

56　GREAT ORDNANCE *large artillery.*

60   Pardon me for my two senses; for I that carry Hercules' bowl
        i' the service may see double by my place, for I have drunk like
        a frog today. I would have a tun now brought in to dance, and
        so many bottles about him. Ha! You look as if you would
        make a problem of this. Do you see? Do you see? a problem:
65   why bottles? and why a tun? and why a tun? and why bottles
        to dance? I say that men that drink hard and serve the belly in
        any place of quality (as The Jovial Tinkers, or The Lusty
        Kindred) are living measures of drink, and can transform
        themselves, and do every day, to bottles or tuns when they
70   please; and when they ha' done all they can, they are, as I say
        again (for I think I said somewhat like it afore) but moving
        measures of drink; and there is a piece i' the cellar can hold
        more than all they. This will I make good if it please our new
        god but to give a nod; for the belly does all by signs, and I
75   am all for the belly, the truest clock i' the world to go by.

*Here the first antimasque [danced by men dressed as bottles and a cask],
after which,*

Hercules. What rites are these? Breeds earth more monsters yet?
        Antaeus scarce is cold: what can beget
80   This store?—and stay! such contraries upon her?
        Is earth so fruitful of her own dishonor?
        Or 'cause his vice was inhumanity,

64 Do you see? Do you see?] Do you see? MS.
67 The Lusty] a lusty MS.

67–8 JOVIAL TINKERS, LUSTY KINDRED N.

79 ANTAEUS *a giant, son of the earth goddess, who gained his strength from contact with
        the earth. Hercules defeated him by lifting him off the ground and crushing
        him.*

80 STORE *plenty.* AND STAY *an expression of surprise.* SUCH . . . HER *such monsters
        upon earth.*

82 HIS *Antaeus's.*

Hopes she by vicious hospitality
To work an expiation first? and then
(Help, Virtue!) these are sponges, and not men.   85
Bottles? mere vessels? half a tun of paunch?
How? and the other half thrust forth in haunch?
Whose feast? the belly's? Comus'? and my cup
Brought in to fill the drunken orgies up?
And here abused? that was the crowned reward   90
Of thirsty heroës after labor hard?
Burdens and shames of nature, perish, die;
For yet you never lived, but in the sty
Of vice have wallowed, and in that swine's strife
Been buried under the offense of life.   95
Go, reel and fall under the load you make,
Till your swoll'n bowels burst with what you take.
Can this be pleasure, to extinguish man?
Or so quite change him in his figure? Can
The belly love his pain, and be content   100
With no delight but what's a punishment?
These monsters plague themselves, and fitly, too,
For they do suffer what and all they do.
But here must be no shelter, nor no shroud
For such: sink grove, or vanish into cloud!   105

At this the whole grove vanished, and the whole music was discovered,
sitting at the foot of the mountain, with Pleasure and Virtue seated above
them. The choir invited Hercules to rest with this

SONG

Great friend and servant of the good,   110
Let cool awhile thy heated blood,

91 heroës] *so* MS; heroes F.

___

83 VICIOUS HOSPITALITY *hospitality to vice.*

And from thy mighty labor cease.
Lie down, lie down,
And give thy troubled spirits peace,
115   Whilst Virtue, for whose sake
Thou dost this godlike travail take,
May of the choicest herbage make,
Here on this mountain bred,
A crown, a crown
120   For thy immortal head.

Here Hercules being laid down at their feet, the second antimasque, which was of pigmies, appeared.

1st Pigmy. Antaeus dead! and Hercules yet live!
Where is this Hercules? What would I give
125   To meet him now? Meet him? nay three such other,
If they had hand in murder of our brother?
With three? with four? with ten? nay, with as many
As the name yields? Pray anger there be any
Whereon to feed my just revenge, and soon:
130   How shall I kill him? Hurl him 'gainst the moon,
And break him in small portions? Give to Greece
His brain, and every tract of earth a piece?
2nd Pigmy. He is yonder.
1st Pigmy.   Where?
3rd Pigmy.   At the hill foot, asleep.
1st Pigmy. Let one go steal his club.
2nd Pigmy.   My charge, I'll creep.
4th Pigmy. He's ours.
1st Pigmy.   Yes, peace.
135 *3rd Pigmy.*   Triumph, we have him, boy.

126 BROTHER *Like Antaeus, the pigmies are "contraries" begotten on the earth goddess.*
127–28 MANY . . . YIELDS *Numerous ancient heroes were named Hercules, and though separate figures, were considered part of a single cult.*

4th Pigmy. Sure, sure, he is sure.
1st Pigmy.   Come, let us dance for joy.

At the end of their dance they thought to surprise him, when suddenly, being awaked by the music, he roused himself, they all run into holes.

SONG

[*Choir.*] Wake, Hercules, awake: but heave up thy black eye,   140
        'Tis only asked from thee to look and these will die,
                        Or fly.
                    Already they are fled,
                    Whom scorn had else left dead.

At which Mercury descended from the hill with a garland of poplar to 145
        crown him.

Mercury. Rest still, thou active friend of Virtue: these
        Should not disturb the peace of Hercules.
        Earth's worms and honor's dwarfs, at too great odds,
        Prove, or provoke the issue of the gods.   150
        See, here a crown the agèd hill hath sent thee,
        My grandsire Atlas, he that did present thee
        With the best sheep that in his fold were found,
        Or golden fruit in the Hesperian ground,
        For rescuing his fair daughters, then the prey   155
        Of a rude pirate, as thou cam'st this way;
        And taught thee all the learning of the sphere,
        And how, like him, thou might'st the heavens up-bear,
        As that thy labor's virtuous recompense.

153–54 SHEEP . . . FRUIT N.
157 LEARNING . . . SPHERE *astronomy, which Atlas knew because he bore the heavens on his shoulders.*
158 LIKE HIM *Hercules briefly relieved Atlas of his burden.*
159 THAT *The demonstrative is used as an intensive, and is syntactically unnecessary; a Latinism.*

160 He, though a mountain now, hath yet the sense
Of thanking thee for more, thou being still
Constant to goodness, guardian of the hill;
Antaeus, by thee suffocated here,
And the voluptuous Comus, god of cheer,
165 Beat from his grove, and that defaced. But now
The time's arrived that Atlas told thee of: how
By unaltered law, and working of the stars,
There should be a cessation of all jars
'Twixt Virtue and her noted opposite
170 Pleasure; that both should meet here in the sight
Of Hesperus, the glory of the west,
The brightest star, that from his burning crest
Lights all on this side the Atlantic seas
As far as to thy pillars, Hercules.
175 See where he shines: Justice and Wisdom placed
About his throne, and those with Honor graced,
Beauty and Love. It is not with his brother
Bearing the world, but ruling such another
Is his renown. Pleasure, for his delight
180 Is reconciled to Virtue, and this night
Virtue brings forth twelve princes have been bred
In this rough mountain and near Atlas' head,
The hill of knowledge; one and chief of whom
Of the bright race of Hesperus is come,

171 HESPERUS *Atlas' brother, the evening star; here representing King James.*
174 PILLARS *The pillars of Hercules were the straits of Gibraltar, the entrance to the Mediterranean.*
178 SUCH ANOTHER *alluding to the tradition that Britain was a separate, specially favored world.*
181 HAVE *who have.*
183 ONE . . . CHIEF *This was Prince Charles's first masque, and he was the chief masquer.*

Who shall in time the same that he is be,   185
And now is only a less light than he.
These now she trusts with Pleasure, and to these
She gives an entrance to the Hesperides,
Fair Beauty's garden: neither can she fear
They should grow soft or wax effeminate here,   190
Since in her sight and by her charge all's done,
Pleasure the servant, Virtue looking on.

Here the whole choir of music called the twelve masquers forth from the lap
of the mountain, which then opened with this

SONG   195

Ope agèd Atlas, open then thy lap,
And from thy beamy bosom strike a light,
That men may read in thy mysterious map
        All lines
        And signs   200
Of royal education and the right.
        See how they come and show,
        That are but born to know.
            Descend,
            Descend,   205
        Though pleasure lead,
            Fear not to follow:
They who are bred
        Within the hill
        Of skill   210
    May safely tread
        What path they will,
No ground of good is hollow.

188 HESPERIDES *nymphs who guarded the golden apples of immortality; obtaining*
the apples was one of the labors of Hercules.

In their descent from the hill Daedalus came down before them, of whom
215   *Hercules questioned Mercury.*

Hercules.   But Hermes, stay a little, let me pause.
                  Who's this that leads?
Mercury.   A guide that gives them laws
             To all their motions: Daedalus the wise.
Hercules.   And doth in sacred harmony comprise
             His precepts?
Mercury.   Yes.
220 *Hercules.*   They may securely prove
             Then any labyrinth, though it be of love.

Here, while they put themselves in form, Daedalus had his first

SONG

      Come on, come on; and where you go,
225   So interweave the curious knot,
      As ev'n th' observer scarce may know
         Which lines are Pleasure's and which not.
      First, figure out the doubtful way
         At which awhile all youth should stay,
230   Where she and Virtue did contend
         Which should have Hercules to friend.
      Then, as all actions of mankind
         Are but a labyrinth or maze,
      So let your dances be entwined,

216 stay . . . pause] *so* MS; stay, a little let me pause F.

---

214 DAEDALUS *the archetype artisan, builder of the labyrinth of Minos in Crete.*
216 HERMES *Greek name for Mercury.*
220 PROVE *attempt.*
225 CURIOUS *complex.*
230–31 WHERE . . . FRIEND N.

Yet not perplex men unto gaze; 235
But measured, and so numerous too,
  As men may read each act you do,
And when they see the graces meet,
  Admire the wisdom of your feet.
For dancing is an exercise 240
  Not only shows the mover's wit,
But maketh the beholder wise,
  As he hath power to rise to it.

The first dance.

After which Daedalus again. 245

SONG 2

O more, and more; this was so well
  As praise wants half his voice to tell;
    Again yourselves compose;
And now put all the aptness on 250
  Of figure, that proportion
    Or color can disclose.
That if those silent arts were lost,
  Design and picture, they might boast
    From you a newer ground, 255
Instructed to the height'ning sense
  Of dignity and reverence

237 you] thcy F.
256 to] by F.

---

235 PERPLEX . . . GAZE *cause confusion.*
236 NUMEROUS *composed of numbers, or rhythmical units.*
251 PROPORTION *architecture.*
252 COLOR *painting.*
255 GROUND *(1) architectural foundation. (2) underpainting or background color. (3) musical ground-bass.*

In your true motions found:
Begin, begin; for look, the fair

260

Do longing listen to what air
You form your second touch,
That they may vent their murmuring hymns
Just to the tune you move your limbs,
And wish their own were such.

265

Make haste, make haste, for this
The labyrinth of beauty is.

The second dance.

That ended, Daedalus.

SONG 3

270

It follows now you are to prove
The subtlest maze of all, that's love,
And if you stay too long,
The fair will think you do 'em wrong.
Go choose among—but with a mind

275

As gentle as the stroking wind
Runs o'er the gentler flowers.
And so let all your actions smile
As if they meant not to beguile
The ladies, but the hours.

280

Grace, laughter and discourse may meet,
And yet the beauty not go less:
For what is noble should be sweet,
But not dissolved in wantonness.

258 your] their F.

---

261 TOUCH *attempt.*
270 PROVE *try.*
276 RUNS *that runs.*
281 GO *be worth.*

Will you that I give the law
    To all your sport, and sum it?   285
It should be such should envy draw,
    But ever overcome it.

Here they danced with the ladies, and the whole revels followed; which
ended, Mercury called to him in this following speech, which was after
repeated in song by two trebles, two tenors, a bass and the whole chorus.   290

SONG 4

An eye of looking back were well,
    Or any murmur that would tell
        Your thoughts, how you were sent
            And went,   295
To walk with Pleasure, not to dwell.
These, these are hours by Virtue spared
Herself, she being her own reward,
        But she will have you know
            That though   300
Her sports be soft, her life is hard.
    You must return unto the hill,
            And there advance
    With labor, and inhabit still
            That height and crown   305
From whence you ever may look down
            Upon triumphèd Chance.
She, she it is, in darkness shines.
    'Tis she that still herself refines,
            By her own light, to every eye   310
More seen, more known when Vice stands by.
    And though a stranger here on earth,
        In heaven she hath her right of birth.

289 HIM *presumably Daedalus, but perhaps we should read " them."*

> There, there is Virtue's seat,
315 > Strive to keep her your own;
> 'Tis only she can make you great,
> Though place here make you known.

After which, they danced their last dance, and returned into the scene, which closed and was a mountain again as before.

320 > *The End.*

This pleased the king so well, as he would see it again, when it was presented with these additions.

321–22 THIS . . . ADDITIONS *The additions were* For the Honor of Wales. N.

Chloridia: Sir Jeffrey Hudson as the Dwarf Postilion.

Dutch Post

News from the New World Discovered in the Moon

A masque, as it was presented at court before King James, 1620.

Nascitur e tenebris, et se sibi vindicat orbis.

Enter first herald, second herald, printer, chronicler, factor.

1st Herald. News, news, news!

2nd Herald. Bold and brave news!

1st Herald. New as the night they are born in—

5   *2nd Herald.* Or the fant'sy that begot 'em.

1st Herald. Excellent news!

2nd Herald. Will you hear any news?

Printer. Yes, and thank you too, sir. What's the price of 'em?

1st Herald. Price, cockscomb! What price but the price o' your ears?

10   As if any man used to pay for anything here!

2nd Herald. Come forward. You should be some dull tradesman by
      your pigheaded sconce now, that think there's nothing good
      anywhere but what's to be sold.

Title DISCOVERED N.

Epigraph NASCITUR . . . ORBIS *A world is born out of darkness and sets itself free.*
    (*Untraced.*)

1 FACTOR *literally, agent; here, newspaper columnist. See lines 30ff.*

12 SCONCE *head.*

Printer. Indeed I am all for sale, gentlemen, you say true. I am a printer, and a printer of news, and I do hearken after 'em 15 wherever they be, at any rates; I'll give anything for a good copy now, be't true or false, so't be news.

1st Herald. A fine youth!

Chronicler. And I am for matter of state, gentlemen, by consequence, story, to fill up my great book, my chronicle, which must be 20 three ream of paper at least: I have agreed with my stationer aforehand to make it so big, and I want for ten quire yet. I ha' been here ever since seven o'clock i' the morning to get matter for one page, and I think I have it complete; for I have both noted the number and the capacity of the degrees here, and 25 told twice over how many candles there are i' th' room lighted, which I will set you down to a snuff precisely, because I love to give light to posterity in the truth of things.

1st Herald. This is a finer youth!

Factor. Gentlemen, I am neither printer nor chronologer, but one 30 that otherwise take pleasure i' my pen: a factor of news for all the shires of England. I do write my thousand letters a week ordinary, sometime twelve hundred, and maintain the business at some charge, both to hold up my reputation with mine own ministers in town and my friends of correspondence in the 35 country. I have friends of all ranks and of all religions, for which I keep an answering catalogue of dispatch wherein I have my Puritan news, my Protestant news and my Pontifical news.

2nd Herald. A superlative, this! 40

20 to . . . chronicle] *H. A. Evans*; my chronicle, to fill up my great book F.

20 CHRONICLE N.
25 DEGREES *tiers (of seats).*
29 FINER *i.e. than the "fine youth" of line 18.*
33 ORDINARY *ordinarily.*

Factor. And I have hope to erect a staple for news ere long, whither all shall be brought and thence again vented under the name of staple-news, and not trusted to your printed conundrums of the serpent in Sussex, or the witches bidding the devil to
45 dinner at Derby—news that, when a man sends them down to the shires where they are said to be done, were never there to be found.

Printer. Sir, that's all one, they were made for the common people, and why should not they ha' their pleasure in believing of lies
50 are made for them, as you have in Paul's that make 'em for yourselves?

1st Herald. There he speaks reason to you, sir.

Factor. I confess it, but it is the printing I am offended at. I would have no news printed; for when they are printed they leave to
55 be news. While they are written, though they be false, they remain news still.

Printer. See men's divers opinions! It is the printing of 'em makes 'em news to a great many, who will indeed believe nothing but what's in print. For those I do keep my presses and so many
60 pens going to bring forth wholesome relations, which once in half a score years (as the age grows forgetful) I print over again with a new date, and they are of excellent use.

Chronicler. Excellent abuse, rather.

Printer. Master Chronicler, do not you talk; I shall—
65 *1st Herald.* Nay, gentlemen, be at peace one with another. We have enough for you all three, if you dare take upon trust.

Printer. I dare, I assure you.

41 STAPLE *central office.*
42 VENTED *published.*
43 CONUNDRUMS *absurdities.*
44 SERPENT IN SUSSEX N.
50 PAUL'S *St. Paul's churchyard, the popular haunt of gossip mongers.*
60 RELATIONS *stories.*

Factor. And I, as much as comes.

Chronicler. I dare too, but nothing so much as I ha' done. I have been
so cheated with false relations i' my time as I ha' found it a far   70
harder thing to correct my book than collect it.

Factor. Like enough. But to your news, gentlemen; whence come
they?

1st Herald. From the moon ours, sir.

Factor. From the moon! Which way? By sea? or by land?   75

1st Herald. By moonshine, a nearer way, I take it.

Printer. Oh, by a trunk! I know it, a thing no bigger than a flute case.
A neighbor of mine, a spectacle maker, has drawn the moon
through it at the bore of a whistle and made it as great as a
drumhead twenty times and brought it within the length of   80
this room to me I know not how often.

Chronicler. Tut, that's no news; your perplexive glasses are common. No, it will fall out to be Pythagoras' way, I warrant
you, by writing and reading i' th' moon.

Printer. Right, and as well read of you, i' faith; for Cornelius Agrippa   85
has it, *in disco lunae*, there 'tis found.

1st Herald. Sir, you are lost, I assure you; for ours came to you
neither by the way of Cornelius Agrippa nor Cornelius
Dribble.

2nd Herald. Nor any glass of—   90

1st Herald. No philosopher's fantasy—

2nd Herald. Mathematician's perspicil—

---

77 TRUNK *tube, i.e. telescope.*

82 PERPLEXIVE *confusing; the chronicler's mistake for "perspective."*

83-4 PYTHAGORAS ... MOON *Pythagoras was said to have been able to reflect
messages onto the moon by writing in blood on a mirror.*

85 CORNELIUS AGRIPPA ... LUNAE N.

86 IN ... LUNAE *on the moon's disk.*

88-9 CORNELIUS DRIBBLE N.

92 PERSPICIL *lens.*

179

1st Herald. Or brother of the Rosy Cross's intelligence; no forced
way, but by the neat and clean power of poetry—

95 *2nd Herald.* The mistress of all discovery—

1st Herald. Who after a world of these curious uncertainties hath
employed thither a servant of hers in search of truth, who has
been there—

2nd Herald. In the moon—

100 *1st Herald.* In person—

2nd Herald. And is this night returned.

Factor. Where? Which is he? I must see his dog at his girdle and the
bush of thorns at his back ere I believe it.

1st Herald. Do not trouble your faith then; for if that bush of thorns

105 should prove a goodly grove of oaks, in what case were you
and your expectation?

2nd Herald. Those are stale ensigns o' the stage's man i' th' moon,
delivered down to you by musty antiquity, and are of as
doubtful credit as the makers.

110 *Chronicler.* Sir, nothing again antiquity, I pray you; I must not hear
ill of antiquity.

1st Herald. Oh! you have an old wife belike, or your venerable
jerkin there, make much of 'em. Our relation, I tell you still,
is news.

115 *2nd Herald.* Certain and sure news—

1st Herald. Of a new world—

2nd Herald. And new creatures in that world—

1st Herald. In the orb of the moon—

2nd Herald. Which is now found to be an earth inhabited!

120 *1st Herald.* With navigable seas and rivers!

2nd Herald. Variety of nations, polities, laws!

---

93 BROTHER . . . CROSS *Rosicrucian (see lines 189–91).*

102–03 DOG . . . THORNS *properties of the man in the moon.*

104–06 IF . . . EXPECTATION *i.e. mere symbols do not prove anything.*

110 AGAIN *against.*

1st Herald. With havens in't, castles and port towns!

2nd Herald. Inland cities, boroughs, hamlets, fairs and markets!

1st Herald. Hundreds, and wapentakes! Forests, parks, cony-ground, meadow-pasture, what not?　　　　　　　　　　　　　　　125

2nd Herald. But differing from ours.

Factor. And has your poet brought all this?

Chronicler. Troth, here was enough; 'tis a pretty piece of poetry as 'tis.

1st Herald. Would you could hear on, though.　　　　　　　　130

2nd Herald. Gi' your minds to't a little.

Factor. What inns or alehouses are there there? Does he tell you?

1st Herald. Truly, I have not asked him that.

2nd Herald. Nor were you best, I believe.

Factor. Why, in travel a man knows these things without offense. 135
I am sure if he be a good poet he has discovered a good tavern in his time.

1st Herald. That he has; I should think the worse of his verse else.

Printer. And his prose too, i' faith.

Chronicler. Is he a man's poet or a woman's poet, I pray you?　140

2nd Herald. Is there any such difference?

Factor. Many, as betwixt your man's tailor and your woman's tailor.

1st Herald. How, may we beseech you?

Factor. I'll show you. Your man's poet may break out strong and deep i' th' mouth, as he said of Pindar, *Monte decurrens velut* 145
amnis. But your woman's poet must flow and stroke the ear, and (as one of them said of himself sweetly)

　　Must write a verse as smooth and calm as cream,
　　In which there is no torrent, nor scarce stream.

---

124 HUNDREDS, WAPENTAKES *subdivisions of English counties.* CONY-GROUND *rabbit warrens.*

145–46 MONTE . . . AMNIS *like a torrent rushing down from the mountain.* (Horace, Odes *IV.ii.*5)

148–49 MUST . . . STREAM N.

150 *2nd Herald.* Ha' you any more on't?

Factor. No, I could never arrive but to this remnant.

1st Herald. Pity! Would you had had the whole piece for a pattern to all poetry.

Printer. How might we do to see your poet? Did he undertake this
155   journey, I pray you, to the moon o' foot?

1st Herald. Why do you ask?

Printer. Because one of our greatest poets (I know not how good a one) went to Edinburgh o' foot, and came back. Marry, he has been restive, they say, ever since, for we have had nothing from
160   him; he has set out nothing, I am sure.

1st Herald. Like enough; perhaps he has not all in. When he has all in, he will set out (I warrant you) at least those from whom he had it; it is the very same party that has been i' th' moon now.

Printer. Indeed! has he been there since? Belike he rid thither then.

165 *Factor.* Yes, post, upon the poet's horse for a wager.

1st Herald. No, I assure you, he rather flew upon the wings of his muse. There are in all but three ways of going thither: one is Endymion's way, by rapture in sleep or a dream. The other Menippus his way, by wing, which the poet took. Then the
170   third, old Empedocles' way, who when he leaped into Aetna, having a dry, sere body and light, the smoke took him and whift him up into the moon, where he lives yet, waving up and down like a feather, all soot and embers coming out of that coal pit. Our poet met him and talked with him.

157–58 ONE . . . BACK *Jonson himself, in 1618. "Greatest" plays on Jonson's fatness.*

159 RESTIVE *inactive.*

160 SET OUT *sent out (for publication).*

161 ALL *i.e. all his information.*

162 SET OUT *(1) publish. (2) disclose the names of (his informants). (3) translate (his sources).*

168 ENDYMION *shepherd loved by Diana, the moon.*

168, 169 MENIPPUS, EMPEDOCLES N.

Chronicler. In what language, good sir? 175

2nd Herald. Only by signs and gestures; for they have no articulate voices there, but certain motions to music. All the discourse there is harmony.

Factor. A fine lunatic language, i' faith. How do their lawyers then?

2nd Herald. They are Pythagoreans, all dumb as fishes; for they 180 have no controversies to exercise themselves in.

Factor. How do they live then?

1st Herald. O' th' dew o' th' moon, like grasshoppers, and confer with the Doppers.

Factor. Ha' you Doppers? 185

2nd Herald. A world of Doppers! But they are there as lunatic persons, walkers only, that have leave only to hum and ha, not daring to prophesy or start up upon stools to raise doctrine.

1st Herald. The brethren of the Rosy Cross have their college within a mile o' the moon, a castle i' th' air that runs upon wheels 190 with a winged lanthorn—

Printer. I ha' seen 't in print.

2nd Herald. All the fantastical creatures you can think of are there.

Factor. 'Tis to be hoped there are women there then?

1st Herald. And zealous women, that will out-groan the groaning 195 wives of Edinburgh.

Factor. And lovers as fantastic as ours?

2nd Herald. But none that will hang themselves for love, or eat candles' ends, or drink to their mistress' eyes till their own bid 'em goodnight, as the sublunary lovers do. 200

Factor. No, sir?

---

180 PYTHAGOREANS *As novices, these ruputedly had to remain silent for five years.*
184 DOPPERS *literally* "*dippers*"; *Anabaptists.*
189 BRETHREN . . . CROSS *Rosicrucians.*
190–92 CASTLE . . . PRINT *See* The Fortunate Isles, *lines 57–60 and note.*
200 SUBLUNARY "*beneath the moon,*" *earthly.*

2nd Herald. No, some few you shall have that sigh or whistle themselves away, and those are presently hung up by the heels like
meteors, with squibs i' their tails, to give the wiser sort
205   warning.

Printer. Excellent!

Factor. Are there no self-lovers there?

2nd Herald. There were, but they are all dead of late for want of
tailors.

210 *Factor.* 'Slight, what luck is that? We could have spared them a
colony from hence.

2nd Herald. I think some two or three of them live yet, but they are
turned moon-calves by this.

Printer. O, aye, moon-calves! What monster is that, I pray you?

215 *2nd Herald.* Monster? None at all; a very familiar thing, like our
fool here on earth.

1st Herald. The ladies there play with them instead of little dogs.

Factor. Then there are ladies?

2nd Herald. And knights, and squires.

220 *Factor.* And servants, and coaches?

1st Herald. Yes, but the coaches are much o' the nature of the ladies,
for they go only with wind.

Chronicler. Pretty, like China wagons.

Factor. Ha' they any places of meeting with their coaches, and taking
225   the fresh open air, and then covert when they please, as in our
Hyde Park, or so?

2nd Herald. Above all the Hyde Parks in Christendom, far more
hiding and private; they do all in clouds there. They walk i'
the clouds, they sit i' the clouds, they lie i' the clouds, they ride
230   and tumble i' the clouds, their very coaches are clouds.

204 SQUIBS *firecrackers.*
213 MOON-CALVES *congenital idiots.* BY THIS *by this time.*
223 CHINA WAGONS *which had sails.*

Printer. But ha' they no carmen to meet and break their coaches?

2nd Herald. Alas, carmen! They will over a carman there, as he will
do a child here. You shall have a coachman with cheeks like a
trumpeter and a wind in his mouth blow him afore him as far
as he can see him, or skirr over him with his bat's wings a mile   235
and a half ere he can steer his wry neck to look where he is.

Factor. And they ha' their new Wells too, and physical waters, I
hope, to visit all time of year?

1st Herald. Your Tunbridge, or the Spa itself, are mere puddle to 'em.
When the pleasant months o' the year come, they all flock to   240
certain broken islands which are called there the Isles of
Delight.

Factor. By clouds still?

1st Herald. What else? Their boats are clouds too.

2nd Herald. Or in a mist; the mists are ordinary i' the moon; a man   245
that owes money there needs no other protection; only buy a
mist and walk in't, he's never discerned—a matter of a baubee
does it.

1st Herald. Only one island they have is called the Isle of the Epicoenes, because there under one article both kinds are signified;   250
for they are fashioned alike, male and female the same, not-
heads and broad hats, short doublets and long points; neither

231 CARMEN *porters.* BREAK *either bring to a halt (cf. brake), or unload.*
232 OVER *run over.*
235 SKIRR *skim.*
237 NEW WELLS *Epsom, where the mineral waters were discovered in 1618.*
239 SPA *Liège, Belgium.*
241 BROKEN *scattered.*
247 BAUBEE *small Scottish coin.*
249–50 EPICOENES *here, people having the characteristics of both sexes.*
250 KINDS *genders.*
251–52 NOT-HEADS *short haircuts.*
252 POINTS *laces.*

do they ever untruss for distinction, but laugh and lie down in
moonshine, and stab with their poniards; you do not know the
255   delight of the Epicoenes in moonshine.

2nd Herald. And when they ha' tasted the springs of pleasure enough,
and billed and kissed, and are ready to come away, the shes
only lay certain eggs (for they are never with child there) and
of those eggs are disclosed a race of creatures like men, but are
260   indeed a sort of fowl, in part covered with feathers (they call
'em Volatees), that hop from island to island. You shall see a
covey of 'em if you please presently.

1st Herald. Yes, faith, 'tis time to exercise their eyes; for their ears
begin to be weary.

265 *2nd Herald.* Then know we do not move these wings so soon,
On which our poet mounted to the moon
Menippus-like, but all 'twixt it and us
Thus clears and helps to the presentment, thus.

The antimasque of Volatees.

270 *2nd Herald.* We have all this while, though the muses' heralds,
adventured to tell your majesty no news; for hitherto we have
moved rather to your delight than your belief. But now be
pleased to expect a more noble discovery worthy of your ear,
as the object will be your eye: a race of your own, formed,
275   animated, lightened and heightened by you, who, rapt above
the moon far in speculation of your virtues, have remained
there entranced certain hours with wonder of the piety, wisdom, majesty reflected by you on them from the divine light,
to which only you are less. These, by how much higher they

---

253 FOR DISTINCTION *to determine sex.* LAUGH . . . DOWN *an off-color pun on
the card game "Laugh and Lay Down."*

254, 255 MOONSHINE "*an appearance without substance; something unsubstantial
or unreal*" (OED).

have been carried from earth to contemplate your greatness, 280
have now conceived the more haste and hope in this their
return home to approach your goodness; and led by that
excellent likeness of yourself, the Truth, imitating Procritus'
endeavor, that all their motions be formed to the music of
your peace and have their ends in your favor, which alone is 285
able to resolve and thaw the cold they have presently contracted in coming through the colder region.

They descend and shake off their icicles.

SONG 1

Howe'er the brightness may amaze,   290
Move you, and stand not still at gaze,
   As dazzled with the light;
But with your motions fill the place,
And let their fullness win your grace
   Till you collect your sight.   295
So while the warmth you do confess,
And temper of these rays, no less
   To quicken than refine,
You may by knowledge grow more bold,
And so more able to behold   300
   The body whence they shine.

The first dance follows.

SONG 2

Now look and see in yonder throne
How all those beams are cast from one.   305

283 TRUTH *danced by Prince Charles.* PROCRITUS *not a proper name, but the Greek
form of the Latin title* Princeps Iuventutis (*leader of the youth*), *bestowed in
imperial Rome on the son of the emperor when he adopted the toga of man-
hood and entered fully into the ranks of the Roman nobility.* N.

This is that orb so bright
Has kept your wonder so awake,
Whence you as from a mirror take
The sun's reflected light.
310 Read him as you would do the book
Of all perfection, and but look
What his proportions be;
No measure that is thence contrived,
Or any motion thence derived,
315 But is pure harmony.

Main dance and revels.

SONG 3

Not that we think you weary be,
For he
320 That did this motion give,
And made it so long live,
Could likewise give it perpetuity.
Nor that we doubt you have not more,
And store
325 Of changes to delight;
For they are infinite,
As is the power that brought forth those before.
But since the earth is of his name
And fame
330 So full you cannot add,
Be both the first and glad
To speak him to the region whence you came.

313 MEASURE (1) *standard* (2) *slow dance.*
319–22 FOR . . . PERPETUITY *See note to lines 88–9.*
324 STORE *plenty.*
332 SPEAK *describe.*

The last dance.

SONG 4

Look, look already where I am,   335
        Bright Fame,
    Got up unto the sky
        Thus high
   Upon my better wing
        To sing   340
    The knowing king,
And make the music here
    With yours on earth the same.
Chorus. Join then to tell his name,
      And say but James is he;   345
   All ears will take the voice,
   And in the tune rejoice,
   Or Truth hath left to breathe, and Fame hath left to be.
1st Herald. See, what is that this music brings,
   And is so carried in the air about?   350
2nd Herald. Fame, that doth nourish the renown of kings,
   And keeps that fair which envy would blot out.

The End.

Pan's Anniversary,
or the Shepherds' Holiday
The Scene: Arcadia

As it was presented at court before King James. 1620.
The Inventors
Inigo Jones   Ben Jonson

The first presentation is of three nymphs strewing several sorts of flowers,
followed by an old shepherd with a censer and perfumes.

1st Nymph. Thus, thus begin the yearly rites
       Are due to Pan on these bright nights;
5   His morn now riseth and invites
       To sports, to dances and delights:
          All envious and profane, away;
          This is the shepherds' holiday.
2nd Nymph. Strew, strew the glad and smiling ground
10   With every flower, yet not confound
       The primrose drop, the spring's own spouse;

Bright day's-eyes and the lips of cows;
  The garden star, the queen of May,
  The rose to crown the holiday.
3rd Nymph. Drop, drop, you violets, change your hues,   15
  Now red, now pale, as lovers use,
  And in your death go out as well
  As when you lived, unto the smell,
   That from your odor all may say
   This is the shepherds' holiday.   20
Shepherd. Well done, my pretty ones; rain roses still,
  Until the last be dropped. Then hence, and fill
  Your fragrant prickles for a second shower;
  Bring corn-flag, tulips and Adonis' flower,
  Fair ox-eye, goldilocks and columbine,   25
  Pinks, goulands, king-cups and sweet sops-in-wine,
  Blue harebells, paigles, pansies, calaminth,
  Flower-gentle, and the fair-haired hyacinth;
  Bring rich carnations, flower-de-luces, lilies,
  The checked and purple-ringèd daffodillies,   30
  Bright crown-imperial, king's spear, hollyhocks,
  Sweet Venus' navel, and soft lady's-smocks;
  Bring too some branches forth of Daphne's hair,
  And gladdest myrtle for these posts to wear

12 DAY'S-EYES *daisies.* LIPS OF COWS *cowslips; Jonson's etymology is fanciful.*
23 PRICKLES *wicker flower baskets.*
24 CORN-FLAG *gladiolus.* ADONIS' FLOWER *variously, the anemone and the rose.*
26 GOULANDS, KING-CUPS *types of buttercups.* SOPS-IN-WINE *gillyflowers.*
27 BLUE HAREBELLS *bluebells.* PAIGLES *cowslips.*
28 FLOWER-GENTLE *amaranth.*
29 FLOWER-DE-LUCES *white iris.*
30–1 CHECKED . . . DAFFODILLIES, CROWN-IMPERIAL *types of fritillaries.*
31 KING'S SPEAR *yellow asphodel.*
32 VENUS' NAVEL *wall pennywort.* LADY'S-SMOCKS *cuckooflower.*
33 DAPHNE'S HAIR *laurel.*

35 With spikenard weaved, and marjoram between,
And starred with yellow-golds and meadow's queen,
That when the altar, as it ought, is dressed,
More odor come not from the Phoenix' nest;
The breath thereof Panchaia may envy,
40 The colors China, and the light the sky.

Loud music.

The scene opens, and in it are the masquers discovered sitting about the fountain of light. The musicians attired like the priests of Pan standing in the work beneath them, when entereth to the old shepherd a fencer
45 *flourishing.*

[*Fencer.*] Room for an old trophy of time, a son of the sword, a
servant of Mars, the minion of the muses and a master of
fence! One that hath shown his quarters and played his prizes
at all the games of Greece in his time, as fencing, wrestling,
50 leaping, dancing, what not; and hath now ushered hither by
the light of my long sword certain bold boys of Boeotia, who
are come to challenge the Arcadians at their own sports, call
them forth on their own holiday and dance them down on
their own greensward.
55 *Shepherd.* 'Tis boldly attempted, and must be a Boeotian enterprise
by the face of it, from all the parts of Greece else, especially at
this time when the best and bravest spirits of Arcadia, called
together by the excellent Arcas, are yonder sitting about the
fountain of light in consultation of what honors they may do

36 YELLOW-GOLDS *marigolds.* MEADOW'S QUEEN *meadowsweet.*
38 PHOENIX' NEST *which gave off an exquisite perfume as the bird was consumed and reborn.*
39 PANCHAIA *a mythical island off the Arabian coast famous for spices and scents.*
40 CHINA *colored china was first being imported at this period.*
48 QUARTERS *body.*

the great Pan by increase of anniversary rites fitted to the   60
music of his peace.

Fencer. Peace to thy Pan, and mum to thy music, swain. There is a
tinker of Thebes a-coming, called Epam, with his kettle will
make all Arcadia ring of him. What are your sports for the
purpose, say? If singing, you shall be sung down, if dancing,   65
danced down. There is no more to be done with you but
know what, which it is; and you are in smoke, gone, vapored,
vanished, blown, and, as a man would say in a word of two
syllables, nothing.

Shepherd. This is short, though not so sweet. Surely the better part of   70
the solemnity here will be dancing.

Fencer. Enough: they shall be met with instantly in their own sphere,
the sphere of their own activity, a dance. But by whom, expect: no Cynaetheian, nor satyrs, but, as I said, boys of Boeotia,
things of Thebes (the town is ours, shepherd) mad merry   75
Greeks, lads of life that have no gall in us, but all air and sweetness. A tooth-drawer is our foreman, that if there be but a
bitter tooth in the company it may be called out at a twitch;
he doth command any man's teeth out of his head upon the
point of his poniard, or tickles them forth with his riding rod;   80
he draws teeth a-horseback in full speed, yet he will dance
afoot, he hath given his word: he is yeoman of the mouth to
the whole brotherhood, and is charged to see their gums be
clean and their breath sweet at a minute's warning. Then
comes my learned Theban, the tinker I told you of, with his   85
kettle drum before and after, a master of music and a man of

60–1 PAN ... PEACE N.
63 EPAM *see line 88*.
73–4 EXPECT *wait*.
74 CYNAETHEIAN *from Cynaetha, a town in Arcadia*.
80 PONIARD *dagger*.
82 YEOMAN ... MOUTH *a real court title belonging to officers of the royal pantry*.

mettle; he beats the march to the tune of "Ticklefoot, pam, pam, pam, brave Epam with a nondas." That's the strain.

Shepherd. A high one.

90 *Fencer.* Which is followed by the trace and tract of an excellent juggler, that can juggle with every joint about him from head to heel. He can do tricks with his toes, wind silk and thread pearl with them, as nimble a fine fellow of his feet as his hands; for there is a noble corn-cutter, his companion, hath so pared 95 and finified them—. Indeed, he hath taken it into his care to reform the feet of all and fit their footing to a form: only one splay-foot in the company, and he is a bellows-mender, allowed, who hath the looking to of all their lungs by patent, and by his place is to set that leg afore still, and with his puffs 100 keeps them in breath during pleasure; a tinder box man to strike new fire into them at every turn, and where he spies any brave spark that is in danger to go out, ply him with a match presently.

Shepherd. A most politic provision!

105 *Fencer.* Nay, we have made our provisions beyond example, I hope. For to these there is annexed a clock-keeper, a grave person as Time himself, who is to see that they all keep time to a nick and move every elbow in order, every knee in compass. He is to wind them up and draw them down as he sees cause. Then is 110 there a subtle shrewd-bearded sir, that hath been a politician

---

87 mettle] metal F.

---

87 METTLE *with a pun on* "*metal,*" *the same word in Jonson's time.*

88 EPAM . . . NONDAS *playing on the name of Epaminondas, Theban hero (4th century* B.C.*), who introduced Spartan gymnastic exercises into the training of the youth, and led Thebes to victory against Sparta.*

90 TRACE . . . TRACT *steps.*

95 FINIFIED *spruced up*

98 ALLOWED *officially licensed.*

103 PRESENTLY *at once.*

but is now a maker of mousetraps, a great inginer yet, and he is
to catch the ladies' favors in the dance with certain cringes he
is to make, and to bait their benevolence. Nor can we doubt of
the success, for we have a prophet amongst us of that peremp-
tory pate, a tailor or master fashioner, that hath found it out in   115
a painted cloth, or some old hanging (for those are his library),
that we must conquer in such a time and such a half time;
therefore bids us go on cross-legged, or however thread the
needles of our own happiness, go through-stitch with all,
unwind the clew of our cares; he hath taken measure of our   120
minds and will fit our fortune to our footing. And to better
assure us, at his own charge brings his philosopher with him, a
great clerk who (they say) can write, and it is shrewdly suspected but he can read too; and he is to take the whole dances
from the foot by brachygraphy, and so make a memorial, if   125
not a map of the business. Come forth, lads, and do your own
turns.

The antimasque is danced, after which,

Fencer. How like you this, shepherd? Was not this gear gotten on a
holiday?   130
Shepherd. Faith, your folly may well deserve pardon because it hath
delighted; but beware of presuming, or how you offer comparison with persons so near deities. Behold where they are
that have now forgiven you, whom should you provoke again
with the like, they will justly punish that with anger which   135
they now dismiss with contempt. Away!

---

111 MAKER OF MOUSETRAPS *slang for lecher.* INGINER *engineer.*
119 GO . . . ALL *go through with everything.*
120 CLEW *ball of yarn.*
125 BRACHYGRAPHY *shorthand, but Jonson uses it here to mean dance notation.*
132–33 COMPARISON . . . DEITIES N.

And come you prime Arcadians forth, that taught
By Pan the rites of true society,
From his loud music all your manners wrought,
140   And made your commonwealth a harmony,
Commending so to all posterity
Your innocence from that fair fount of light,
As still you sit without the injury
Of any rudeness folly can, or spite;
145   Dance from the top of the Lycaean mountain
Down to this valley, and with nearer eye
Enjoy what long in that illumined fountain
You did far off, but yet with wonder, spy.

HYMN I

150   *1st Arcadian.* Of Pan we sing, the best of singers, Pan,
That taught us swains how first to tune our lays,
And on the pipe more airs than Phoebus can.
Chorus.   Hear, O you groves, and hills resound his praise.
2nd Arcadian. Of Pan we sing, the best of leaders, Pan,
155   That leads the Naiads and the Dryads forth,
And to their dances more than Hermes can.
Chorus.   Hear, O you groves, and hills resound his worth.
3rd Arcadian. Of Pan we sing, the best of hunters, Pan,
That drives the hart to seek unusèd ways,
160   And in the chase more than Sylvanus can.
Chorus.   Hear, O you groves, and hills resound his praise.
4th Arcadian. Of Pan we sing, the best of shepherds, Pan,
That keeps our flocks and us, and both leads forth
To better pastures than great Pales can.

145 LYCAEAN MOUNTAIN *Lycaeus, Pan's native mountain in Arcadia.*
152 PHOEBUS *Apollo, god of music.*
160 SYLVANUS *god of the forest.*
164 PALES *goddess of the country.*

Chorus. Hear, O you groves, and hills resound his worth. 165
        And while his powers and praises thus we sing,
        The valleys let rebound, and all the rivers ring.

The masquers descend and dance their entry.

HYMN 2

Pan is our all, by him we breathe, we live, 170
We move, we are; 'tis he our lambs doth rear,
Our flocks doth bless, and from the store doth give
The warm and finer fleeces that we wear.
   He keeps away all heats and colds,
   Drives all diseases from our folds, 175
   Makes everywhere the spring to dwell,
   The ewes to feed, their udders swell;
   But if he frown, the sheep (alas),
   The shepherds wither, and the grass.
Strive, strive to please him then by still increasing thus 180
The rites are due to him, who doth all right for us.

The main dance.

HYMN 3

   If yet, if yet
   Pan's orgies you will further fit, 185
See where the silver-footed fays do sit,
    The nymphs of wood and water,
    Each tree's and fountain's daughter.
   Go take them forth, it will be good
   To see some wave it like a wood, 190
   And others wind it like a flood,
      In springs
      And rings,
    Till the applause it brings

197

195   Wakes Echo from her seat,
                    The closes to repeat.

(*Echo.*   The closes to repeat.)

         Echo, the truest oracle on ground,
               Though nothing but a sound,

200 (*Echo.*   Though nothing but a sound,)

          Beloved of Pan, the valley's queen,

(*Echo.*   The valley's queen,)

          And often heard, though never seen.

(*Echo.*   Though never seen.)

205   *Revels.*

Fencer. Room, room there; where are you, shepherd? I am come again with my second part of my bold bloods, the brave gamesters, who assure you by me that they perceive no such wonder in all is done here but that they dare adventure another

210 trial. They look for some sheepish devices here in Arcadia, not these, and therefore a hall, a hall they demand.

Shepherd. Nay, then they are past pity; let them come, and not expect the anger of a deity to pursue them, but meet them. They have their punishment with their fact. They shall be sheep.

215 *Fencer.* O spare me by the law of nations; I am but their ambassador.

Shepherd. You speak in time, sir.

                Second antimasque.

Shepherd. Now let them return with their solid heads, and carry their stupidity into Boeotia, whence they brought it, with an

220 emblem of themselves and their country. This is too pure an air for so gross brains.

        End you the rites, and so be eased
        Of these, and then great Pan is pleased.

196 CLOSES *cadences.*
211 A HALL *i.e. space to perform in.*
214 FACT *crime.*

HYMN 4

Great Pan, the father of our peace and pleasure,   225
   Who giv'st us all this leisure,
Hear what thy hallowed troop of herdsmen pray
  For this their holiday,
And how their vows to thee they in Lycaeum pay.

So may our ewes receive the mounting rams,   230
And we bring thee the earliest of our lambs;
So may the first of all our fells be thine,
And both the beestning of our goats and kine:
  As thou our folds dost still secure,
  And keep'st our fountains sweet and pure,   235
  Driv'st hence the wolf, the tod, the brock,
  Or other vermin from the flock;
That we preserved by thee, and thou observed by us,
May both live safe in shade of thy loved Maenalus.

Shepherd. Now each return unto his charge,   240
  And though today you have lived at large,
  And well your flocks have fed their fill,
  Yet do not trust your hirelings still.
  See, yond' they go, and timely do
  The office you have put them to,   245
  But if you often give this leave,
  Your sheep and you they will deceive.

The End.

229 LYCAEUM *Lycaeus, Pan's native mountain.*
232 FELLS *fleeces.*
233 BEESTNING *first milk.*
236 TOD *fox.* BROCK *badger.*
239 MAENALUS *an Arcadian mountain.*
243 STILL *always.*

A Masque of the Metamorphosed Gypsies

As it was thrice presented to King James; first at Burley-on-the-Hill,
next at Belvoir, and lastly at Windsor. August, 1621.

The speech at the king's entrance at Burley.

[*Porter.*] If for our thoughts there could but speech be found,
    And all that speech be uttered in one sound,
    So that some power above us would afford
5   The means to make a language of a word,
    It should be, Welcome! In that only voice
    We would receive, retain, enjoy, rejoice,
    And all affects of love and life dispense,
    Till it were called a copious eloquence;
10   For should we vent our spirits, now you are come,
    In other syllables, were as to be dumb.
    Welcome, O welcome, then, and enter here,
    The house your bounty'ath built, and still doth rear

8 affects] effects H, F.
13 bounty'ath] bounty'hath Ne; bounty D; bounty hath H, F.

Title THRICE N. BURLEY-ON-THE-HILL *estate of the Marquis (later Duke) of
    Buckingham.* BELVOIR *estate of the Earl of Rutland.*
6 ONLY VOICE *single word.*
8 AFFECTS *feelings.*
13 YOUR BOUNTY *Buckingham was James's favorite.*

With those high favors, and those heaped increases,
Which shows a hand not grieved but when it ceases.   15
The master is your creature, as the place,
And every good about him is your grace,
Whom, though he stand by silent, think not rude,
But as a man turned all to gratitude
For what he nev'r can hope how to restore,   20
Since while he meditates one, you heap on more.
Vouchsafe to think he only is oppressed
With their abundance, not that in his breast
His pow'rs are stupid grown; for please you enter
Him, and his house, and search them to the center;   25
You'll find within no thanks or vows there shorter,
For having trusted thus much to his porter.

The Prologue at Windsor.

As many blessings as there be bones
In Ptolemy's fingers, and all at once   30
Held up in an Andrew's cross for the nonce,
    Light on you, good master!
    I dare be no waster
    Of time or of speech
      Where you are in place;   35
    I only beseech
      You take in good grace
    Our following the court,
    Since 'tis for your sport,

21 heap] pour D, H.
25 them] him D, H.

---

20 RESTORE *repay.*
24 STUPID *inoperative.*
30 PTOLEMY'S *Gypsies were thought to have come from Egypt; the name is a corruption of "Egyptians."*
31 ANDREW'S CROSS *shaped like an X.*

40   To have you still merry,
            And not make you weary.
            We may strive to please,
        So long, some will say, till we grow a disease.
            But you, sir, that twice
45   Have graced us already, encourage to thrice;
          Wherein if our boldness your patience invade,
          Forgive us the fault that your favor hath made.

THE GYPSIES METAMORPHOSED

Enter a gypsy leading a horse laden with five little children bound in a trace
50 *of scarfs upon him; a second leading another horse laden with stolen*
    poultry, etc. The first leading gypsy speaks, being the

Jackman. Room for the five princes of Egypt, mounted all upon one
horse, like the four sons of Aymon, to make the miracle the
more by a head, if it may be. Gaze upon them, as on the off-
55 spring of Ptolemy, begotten upon several Cleopatras in their
several counties; especially on this brave spark struck out of
Flintshire upon Justice Jug's daughter, then sheriff of the
county, who running away with a kinsman of our captain's,
and her father pursuing her to the marches, he great with
60 justice, she great with juggling, they were both for the time
turned stone upon the sight of each other in Chester, till at last
(see the wonder!) a jug of the town ale reconciling them, the
memorial of both their gravities, his in beard and hers in belly,
hath remained ever since preserved in picture upon the most
65 stone jugs of the kingdom. The famous imp yet grew a

43 grow] prove Ne.

---

43 GROW *grow to be.*
49 TRACE *halter.*
52 JACKMAN *educated beggar.* N.
53 FOUR . . . AYMON *a medieval romance about four brothers, knights, who rode
one magic horse.*

wretchock, and though for seven years together he were very
carefully carried at his mother's back, rocked in a cradle of
Welsh cheese, like a maggot, and there fed with broken beer
and blown wine o' the best daily, yet looks he as if he never
saw his *quinquennium*. 'Tis true he can thread needles o' horse- 70
back, or draw a yard of inkle through his nose; but what's that
to a grown gypsy, one o' the blood, and of his time, if he had
thrived! Therefore, till with his painful progenitors he be able
to beat it on the hard hoof to the bene bowse or the stalling ken,
to nip a jan and cly the jark, 'tis thought fit he march in the 75
infants' equipage,

> With the convoy, cheats and peckage,
> Out of clutch of harman-beckage,
> To their libkens at the crackman's,
> Or some skipper of the blackman's. 80

2nd Gypsy. Where the cacklers, but no grunters,
> Shall uncased be for the hunters;
> Those we still must keep alive,

---

66 very] *not in* D, H.

66 WRETCHOCK *the smallest or weakest of the brood.*

68 BROKEN *leftover.*

69 BLOWN *stale.*

69–70 NEVER . . . QUINQUENNIUM *i.e. though he is seven years old, he looks not yet five.*

71 INKLE *linen tape.*

72 TO *compared with.*

73 PAINFUL *diligent.*

74 BENE BOWSE *good drink; here, tavern.* N. STALLING KEN *receiver of stolen goods, "fence."*

75 NIP A JAN *cut a purse.* CLY THE JARK *get a fake license.·*

77 CHEATS *stolen goods.* PECKAGE *food.*

78 HARMAN-BECKAGE *from* harman beck, *a constable.*

79 LIBKENS *sleeping place.* CRACKMAN's *hedge.*

80 SKIPPER *barn.* BLACKMAN's *night's.*

81 CACKLERS *fowl.* GRUNTERS *pigs. (King James's dislike of pork was well known.)*

Aye, and put them out to thrive
85 In the parks and in the chases,
And the finer wallèd places,
As Saint James's, Greenwich, Tibbal's,
Where the acorns, plump as chibols,
Soon shall change both kind and name,
90 And proclaim 'em the king's game;
So the act no harm may be
Unto their keeper Barnaby:
It will prove as good a service
As did ever gypsy Gervase,
95 Or our captain, Charles the tall man,
And a part too of our salmon.

Jackman. If we be a little obscure, it is our pleasure; for rather than
we will offer to be our own interpreters, we are resolved not
to be understood: yet if any man doubt of the significancy of
100 the language, we refer him to the third volume of reports set
forth by the learned in the laws of canting, and published in the
gypsies' tongue. Give me my guitarra, and room for our chief!

DANCE
which is the entrance of the Captain with six more attendant. After which,
105 *the Jackman sings.*

---

84 out] forth D, H.
104 which is] being D, H. attendant] to a stand D, H.

---

87 SAINT JAMES'S, GREENWICH, TIBBAL'S *all royal parks stocked with game.
"Tibbal's" represents Jonson's pronunciation of Theobald's.*
88 CHIBOLS *a kind of onion.*
92 BARNABY *presumably the king's gamekeeper.*
94 GERVASE *presumably the gentleman who played the 5th gypsy.* N.
95 CHARLES N.
96 SALMON *sacrament.*
100–01 THIRD . . . CANTING *a parody of legal titles.*

SONG

[*Jackman.*]   From the famous Peak of Derby
   And the Devil's Arse there hard by,
   Where we yearly keep our musters,
   Thus th'Egyptians throng in clusters.   110

   Be not frighted with our fashion,
   Though we seem a tattered nation;
   We account our rags our riches,
   So our tricks exceed our stitches.

   Give us bacon, rinds of walnuts,   115
   Shells of cockles and of small nuts,
   Ribbons, bells and saffroned linen;
   All the world is ours to win in.

   Knacks we have that will delight you,
   Slights of hand that will invite you   120
   To endure our tawny faces,
   And not cause you cut your laces. *Windsor:* [And not cause you] quit your places.

   All your fortunes we can tell ye,
   Be they for the back or belly,
   In the moods too, and the tenses   125
   That may fit your fine five senses.

[*Burley/Belvoir*]   Draw but then your gloves, we pray you,
   And sit still, we will not fray you;
[*Burley*]   For though we be here at Burley,
   We'd be loath to make a hurly.   130

---

107 PEAK OF DERBY *a hilly district in the north of Derbyshire.*
108 DEVIL'S ARSE *a famous cave in Castleton, Derbyshire, now more politely called Peak Cavern.*
122 CUT . . . LACES *i.e. faint (the laces are on the ladies' bodices).* QUIT . . . PLACES *get up and leave.* N.
127–30 DRAW . . . HURLY N.

Patrico.   Stay, my sweet singer,
          The touch of thy finger
          A little, and linger
          For me, that am bringer
135   Of bound to the border,
          The rule and recorder,
          And mouth of the order,
          As priest of the game,
          And prelate of the same.

140   *[Burley]*   *[Belvoir/Windsor]*
There's a gentry-cove here   [There be gentry-coves here
Is the top of the shire   Are the chief of the shire;]
Of the Bever-ken,
A man among men;
145   You need not to fear,
          I have an eye and an ear
          That turns here and there
          To look to our gear.
[Burley]   Some say that there be
150   One or two, if not three,
          That are greater than he.

137 the] your D, H.
140b–42b H *only, headed* At Beaver.

---

131 PATRICO *nedge-priest* N.

135 BOUND *order.*

141a GENTRY-COVE *nobleman, the Earl of Rutland, Buckingham's father-in-law, and owner of Belvoir.*

141a–44a THERE'S . . . MEN N.

142 SHIRE *Leicestershire, where Belvoir was, and of which Rutland was Lord Lieutenant.*

143 BEVER-KEN *Belvoir house.*

149–51 SOME . . . HE N.

150 ONE . . . THREE *the king, Prince Charles, and Buckingham.*

And for the room-morts,
I know by their ports
And their jolly resorts,
They are of the sorts   155
That love the true sports
Of King Ptolemaeus,
Our great coryphaeus,
And Queen Cleopatra,
The gypsies' grand matra.   160
Then if we shall shark it,
Here fair is, and market.

Leave pig by, and goose,
And play fast and loose,
A short cut, and long,   165
[With (ever and among)]
Some inch of a song,
Pythagoras' lot
Drawn out of a pot,
With what says Alchindus,   170
And Pharaotes Indus,

166 Ne, F, *om.*

152 ROOM-MORTS *rum (fine) ladies.*
154 RESORTS *gatherings.*
158 CORYPHAEUS *leader of the chorus.*
161 SHARK IT *seize our opportunity.*
163 LEAVE . . . BY *i.e. stop stealing.*
164 FAST AND LOOSE *a trick roughly analogous to the shell game, with which gypsies cheated yokels.*
165 SHORT . . . LONG *the game of drawing straws.*
168 PYTHAGORAS' LOT *a method of divination.*
170, 172 ALCHINDUS, JOHN DE INDAGINE *authorities on palmistry: Alchindus (Abu Yusuf al Kindi), tenth-century Arabian philosopher; John de Indagine (Johannes ab Indagine, or Johann van Hagen), early sixteenth-century writer on chiromancy, astrology, and natural magic.*
171 PHARAOTES INDUS *properly Phraotes, Indian king from whom Apollonius of Tyana learned the uses of physiognomy in judging character.* N.

John de Indagine,
With all their *paginae*
Of faces and palmistry,
And this is all myst'ry.

Lay by your wimbles,
Your boring for thimbles,
Or using your nimbles
In diving the pockets
And sounding the sockets
Of simper-the-cockets,
Or angling the purses
Of such as will curse us.
But in the strict duel,
Be merry and cruel,
Strike fair at some jewel,
That mint may accrue well,
For that is the fuel
To make the tun brew well,
And the pot ring well,
And the brain sing well,
Which we may bring well
About by a string well,
And do the thing well.
It is but a strain

174 Of . . . and] faces and D; treating of H.

---

173 PAGINAE *pages.*
176 WIMBLES *gimlets.*
177 BORING *through a purse, to steal thimbles.*
178 NIMBLES *fingers.*
180 SOUNDING . . . SOCKETS *obscene.*
181 SIMPER-THE-COCKETS *coquettes.*
187 MINT *money.*
193 BY A STRING *i.e. easily.*

Of true legerdemain,
Once, twice and again.

[*Burley/Belvoir*]	[*Windsor*]	
Or what will you say now	Or what will you say now	
If with our fine play now,	If with our fine play now,	200
Our knacks and our dances,	Our feats and our fingering,	
We work on the fancies	Here without lingering,	
Of some of these nancies,	Cosening the sights	
These trickets and tripsies,	Of the lords and the knights,	
And make 'em turn gypsies?	Some one of their Georges	205
	Come off to save charges?	

Here's no Justice Lippus
Will seek for to nip us
In cramp-ring or cippus,
And then for to strip us, 210
And after to whip us,
His justice to vary,
While here we do tarry.

[*Burley/Belvoir*]	[*Windsor*]	
But be wise and wary,	But be wise and wary,	215
And we may both carry	And we may both carry	
The Kate and the Mary,	The George and the Garter	

201a knacks . . . our] knackets and D; knacks and H.

203a NANCIES *girls.*

204a TRICKETS *"trickers."* TRIPSIES *dancers.*

205b GEORGES *half-crowns (which bore the image of Saint George), with a quibble on Buckingham's name. (Cf. line 217b.)*

207 LIPPUS *literally, blear-eyed (Latin).*

209 CRAMP-RING *fetters.* CIPPUS *the stocks.*

217a KATE, MARY *names of Buckingham's wife and mother, the Marchioness and Countess of Buckingham.*

217b GEORGE . . . GARTER *the order of the garter, with its George, or jewel, depicting Saint George on horseback fighting the dragon.*

And all the bright aerie
Away to the quarry,
220
                  Into our own quarter;
                  Or durst I go farther
                  In method and order,
                  There's a purse and a seal
                  I've a great mind to steal,
                  That when our tricks are done
                  We might seal our own pardon.
225
                  All this we may do,
                  And a great deal more too,
        If our brave Ptolemy
        Will but say, follow me.
3rd Gypsy. Captain, if ever at the bowsing ken
230
        You have in draughts of Darby drilled your men,
        And we have served there armèd all in ale,
        With the brown bowl, and charged in bragget stale;
        If mustered thus and disciplined in drink,
        In our long watches we did never shrink,
235
        But so, commanded by you, kept our station,
        As we preserved ourselves a royal nation,
        And never yet did branch of statute break
        Made in your famous palace of the Peak;
        If we have deemed that mutton, lamb or veal,
240
        Chick, capon, turkey, sweetest we did steal,

234 shrink] wink D, H.
236 royal] loyal D, H.

218a AERIE *here used figuratively for the other ladies.*
221 PURSE . . . SEAL *the lord keeper's purse and the Great Seal.*
229 CAPTAIN *addressed to Buckingham.* BOWSING KEN *alehouse.*
230 DARBY *Derby ale.*
232 CHARGED *loaded, with a military pun.* BRAGGET *drink made of ale fermented with honey.* STALE *strong.*
238 PALACE . . . PEAK *Buckingham's home, Burley-on-the-Hill.*

As being by our Magna Carta taught
To judge no viands wholesome that are bought;
If for our linen we still used the lift,
And with the hedge, our *Trade's Increase*, made shift,
And ever at your solemn feasts and calls   245
We have been ready with th' Egyptian brawls,
To set Kit Callet forth in prose or rhyme,
Or who was Cleopatra for the time:
   If we have done this, that, more, such or so,
   Now lend your ear but to the Patrico.   250
Captain. Well, dance another strain, and we'll think how.
[*4th Gypsy.* Meantime in song do you conceive some vow.]

Dance 2. Strain 1.

SONG 2

[*Patrico.*]   The fairy beam upon you,   255
             The stars to glister on you,
               A moon of light
               In the noon of night,
             Till the firedrake hath o'er-gone you.

             The wheel of fortune guide you,   260
             The boy with the bow beside you

252 4th . . . vow] *Greg*; 1st . . . vow D; H, Ne, F *om.*

---

243 USED . . . LIFT *i.e. stole it.*
244 WITH . . . SHIFT *i.e. the linen they stole had been left to dry and bleach on the*
     hedges. TRADE'S INCREASE *the largest ship of its time (1100 tons), owned*
     by the East India Company, and christened by King James and Prince
     Henry in 1609.
246 BRAWLS *dances.*
247 KIT CALLET *a gypsy version of Maid Marian, and cant for a whore.*
248 CLEOPATRA *i.e. the gypsy queen.*
259 FIREDRAKE *either meteor or will-o'-the-wisp.*
261 BOY . . . BOW *Cupid.*

211

Run aye in the way
Till the bird of day
And the luckier lot betide you.

265 *Captain.* Bless my sweet masters, the old and the young,
From the gall of the heart and the stroke of the tongue.
With you, lucky bird, I begin: let me see;
I aim at the best, and I trow you are he.
Here's some luck already; if I understand
270 The grounds of mine art, here's a gentleman's hand.
I'll kiss it for luck's sake; you should by this line
Love a horse and a hound, but no part of a swine;
To hunt the brave stag not so much for the food
As the weal of your body and the health o' your blood.
275 You're a man of good means and have territories store
Both by sea and by land, and were born, sir, to more,
Which you, like a lord, and the prince of your peace,
Content with your havings, despise to increase.
You are no great wencher, I see by your table,
280 Although your *mons Veneris* says you are able;
You live chaste and single, and have buried your wife,
And mean not to marry, by the line of your life.
Whence he that conjectures your quality learns
You're an honest good man and have care of your bairns.

271 should] shall Ne, F.
273 the food] your food H, Ne.
277 the prince] a prince H.

---

262 AYE *always.*
267 YOU *King James.*
275 STORE *many.*
276 BORN . . . MORE *the English crown still claimed France.*
279 TABLE *a technical term from palmistry denoting a particular area of the hand.*
280 MONS VENERIS *on the palm just below the thumb.*
281 BURIED . . . WIFE *Queen Anne died in 1619.*
284 BAIRNS *children.*

Your Mercury's hill too a wit doth betoken,   285
Some book-craft you have, and are pretty well spoken.
But stay! in your Jupiter's mount what's here?
A king? A monarch? What wonders appear!
High, bountiful, just, a Jove for your parts,
A master of men, and that reign in their hearts.   290
      I'll tell it my train
      And come to you again.

SONG 3

   To the old, long life and treasure,
   To the young, all health and pleasure,   295
      To the fair, their face
      With eternal grace,
   And the foul to be loved at leisure.

   To the witty, all clear mirrors,
   To the foolish, their dark errors,   300
      To the loving sprite,
      A secure delight,
   To the jealous, his own false terrors.

After which the king's fortune is pursued by the
Captain. Could any doubt that saw this hand   305
   Or who you are, or what command
     You have upon the fate of things,
   Or would not say you were let down
   From heaven on earth to be the crown
     And top of all your neighbor kings?   310

   To see the ways of truth you take
   To balance business, and to make
     All Christian differences cease,

285 MERCURY'S HILL *below the little finger.*
287 JUPITER'S MOUNT *below the forefinger.*
291 TRAIN *followers.*

Or till the quarrel and the cause
315 You can compose, to give them laws,
As arbiter of war and peace.

For this, of all the world you shall
Be stylèd James the Just, and all
Their states dispose, their sons and daughters;
320 And for your fortune, you alone
Among them all shall work your own
By peace, and not by human slaughters.

[Windsor] But why do I presume, though true,
To tell a fortune, sir, to you,
325 Who are the maker here of all;
Where none do stand or sit in view,
But owe their fortune unto you,
At least what they good fortune call?

Myself a gypsy here do shine,
330 Yet are you maker, sir, of mine.
O, that confession could content
So high a bounty, that doth know
No part of motion but to flow,
And giving, never to repent!

335 May still the matter wait your hand,
That it not feel or stay or stand,
But all desert still overcharge;
And may your goodness ever find
In me, whom you have made, a mind
340 As thankful as your own is large.

327 fortune] fortunes H.
331 could] would H.

323–40 N.
330 MINE *i.e. my fortune.*
337 OVERCHARGE *fill to excess.*

Dance 2. Strain 2.

After which the prince's fortune is offered at by the

2nd Gypsy. As my captain hath begun
                With the sire, I take the son:
                    Your hand, sir!   345
                Of your fortune be secure,
                Love and she are both at your
                    Command, sir.

                See what states are here at strife
                Who shall tender you a wife,   350
                    A brave one;
                And a fitter for a man
                Than is offered here you can—
                    Not have one.

                She is sister of a star,   355
                One the noblest now that are,
                    Bright Hesper,
                Whom the Indians in the east
                Phosphor call, and in the west
                    Hight Vesper.   360

                Courses even with the sun
                Doth her mighty brother run
                    For splendor;
                What can to the marriage night

---

343 2ND GYPSY *played by William, Lord Feilding (later Earl of Denbigh), Bucking-*
        ham's brother-in-law.
355 SHE *the Infanta Maria, sister of Philip IV of Spain. See* Neptune's Triumph,
        note to lines 90–7.
357 HESPER *Venus as the evening star.*
359 PHOSPHOR *Venus as the morning star.*
360 VESPER *Latin form of the Greek Hesper.*

365 More than morn and evening light
    Attend her,

[*Windsor*] Save the promise before day
    Of a little James to play
        Hereafter
370 Twixt his grandsire's knees, and move
    All the pretty ways of love
        And laughter?

    Whilst with care you strive to please
    In your giving his cares ease,
375   And labors,
    And by being long the aid
    Of the empire, make afraid
        Ill neighbors;

    Till yourself shall come to see
380 What we wish yet far to be
        Attending,
    For it skills not when or where
    That begins, which cannot fear
        An ending;

385 Since your name in peace or wars
    Nought shall bound until the stars
        Up take you,
    [And to all succeeding view,
    Heaven a constellation new
390   Shall make you.]

388–90 D, Ne, F *om.*

---

366 N.
382 SKILLS *matters.*
389 CONSTELLATION NEW N.

Dance 2. Strain 3.

After which the Lady Marquess Buckingham's by the

3rd Gypsy.   Hurl after an old shoe,
   I'll be merry whate'er I do;   395
    Though I keep no time,
    My words shall chime,
   I'll overtake the sense with a rhyme.
     Face of a rose,
     I pray thee depose   400
 Some small piece of silver; it shall be no loss,
 But only to make the sign of the cross:
  If your hand you hallow,
  Good fortune will follow;
   I swear by these ten   405
   You shall have it again,
   I do not say when.
  But lady, either I am tipsy,
  Or you are to fall in love with a gypsy;
   Blush not, dame Kate,   410
   For early or late
  I do assure you it will be your fate.

  Nor need you be once ashamed of it, madam,
  He's as handsome a man as ever was Adam;
   A man out of wax   415

400 depose] *so* D, F; dispose H; despose Ne.

---

391 BURLEY/BELVOIR N.
394 3RD GYPSY *played by the poet Endymion Porter, a member of Buckingham's household.* HURL . . . SHOE *for good luck.*
400 DEPOSE *put down.*
405 THESE TEN *fingers.*
415 MAN . . . WAX *"a term of emphatic commendation"* (OED).

As a lady would ax;
Yet he's not to wed ye,
He's enjoyed you already,
And I hope he has sped ye:
420   A dainty young fellow,
And though he look yellow,
He never will be jealous,
But love you most zealous,
There's never a line in your hand but doth tell us.

425   And you are a soul so white and so chaste,
A table so smooth and so newly 'rased,
 As nothing called foul
  Dare approach with a blot,
  Or any least spot,
430   But still you control,
  Or make your own lot,
Preserving love pure, as it first was begot.

 But, dame, I must tell ye,
 The fruit of your belly
435   Is that you must tender,
  And care so to render,
  That as yourself came
  In blood and in name
  From one house of fame,
440   So that may remain
   The glory of twain.

416 AX *ask.*
419 SPED YE *caused you to thrive.*
421 LOOK YELLOW *because of his gypsy makeup.*
426 NEWLY 'RASED *free from markings, as if new.*
439 HOUSE OF FAME *She was the daughter of the Earl of Rutland.*

Dance 2. Strain 4.

After which the Countess of Rutland's by the

3rd Gypsy. You, sweet lady, have a hand too,
And a fortune you may stand to,   445
[*Belvoir*] Both your bravery and your bounty
Style you mistress of the county.
You will find it from this night
Fortune shall forget her spite,
And heap all the blessings on you   450
That she can pour out upon you.
To be loved where most you love
Is the worst that you shall prove,
And by him to be embraced,
Who so long hath known you chaste,   455
Wise and fair, whilst you renew
Joys to him, and he to you:
And when both your years are told,
Neither think the other old.

[*Belvoir*]   *And the Countess of Exeter's by the*   460

Patrico. Madam, we knew of your coming so late,
We could not well fit you a nobler fate
Than what you have ready made;
An old man's wife
Is the light of his life,   465
A young one's is but his shade.

446–47 BOTH . . . COUNTY N.
449 FORTUNE . . . SPITE *Her two sons had died in infancy.*
453 PROVE *experience.*
460 COUNTESS OF EXETER *wife of the Earl, the grandfather of Buckingham's sister-in-law Lady Purbeck (see lines 497ff).*
461 COMING SO LATE N.
464 OLD . . . WIFE *She was thirty-eight years younger than the earl.*

> You will not importune
> The change of your fortune;
> For if you dare trust to my forecasting,
470 'Tis presently good, and will be lasting.

Dance 2. Strain 5.

After which the Countess of Buckingham's by the

4th Gypsy. Your pardon, lady, here you stand,
If some should judge you by your hand,
475 The greatest felon in the land
Detected.
I cannot tell you by what arts,
But you have stol'n so many hearts,
As they would make you at all parts
480 Suspected.

Your very face, first; such a one
As being viewed, it was alone
Too slippery to be looked upon,
And threw men;
485 But then your graces they were such
As none could e'er behold too much,
Both every taste and every touch
So drew men.

Still blessed in all you think or do,
490 Two of your sons are gypsies too;
You shall our queen be, and see who
Importunes

470 will] it will H.

___

472 COUNTESS OF BUCKINGHAM *Buckingham's mother. If Viscount Purbeck is the
4th Gypsy, her fortune is being told by her eldest son.*
483 SLIPPERY *dangerous (alluding to Horace, Odes I.xix.8).*
492 IMPORTUNES *intends.*

The hurt of either yours or you,
And doth not wish both George and Sue,
And every bairn besides, all new   495
 Good fortunes.

   The Lady Purbeck's by the

2nd Gypsy. Help me, wonder! here's a book
Where I would forever look;
Never yet did gypsy trace   500
Smoother lines in hand or face.
Venus here doth Saturn move
That you should be queen of love,
And the other stars consent;
Only Cupid's not content;   505
For though you the theft disguise,
You have robbed him of his eyes;
And to show his envy further,
Here he chargeth you with murder,
Says, although that at your sight   510
He must all his torches light,
Though your either cheek discloses
Mingled baths of milk and roses,
Though your lips be banks of blisses,
Where he plants and gathers kisses,   515
And yourself the reason why
Wisest men for love may die,
 You will turn all hearts to tinder,
 And shall make the world one cinder.

493 hurt] heart D, Ne, F.

---

494 GEORGE, SUE *Buckingham (George Villiers) and his sister Susanna, wife of the 2nd Gypsy, Baron Feilding.*
497 LADY PURBECK *wife of Buckingham's elder brother John, perhaps the 4th Gypsy.*
502 SATURN *the coldest planet, and therefore hardest to win over.*

520   *And the Lady Elizabeth Hatton's by the*

5th Gypsy. Mistress of a fairer table
     Hath no history nor fable;
     Others' fortunes may be shown,
     You are builder of your own;
525   And whatever heav'n hath giv'n you,
     You preserve the state still in you;
     That which time would have depart,
     Youth, without the help of art
     You do keep still, and the glory
530   Of your sex is but your story.

[*Windsor*]

[*Dance 2. Strain 3.*]

The Lord Chamberlain's by the

Jackman. Though you, sir, be Chamberlain, I have a key
535   To open your fortune a little by the way:
         You are a good man,
         Deny it that can,
         And faithful you are,
         Deny it that dare;
540   You know how to use your sword and your pen,
     And you love not alone the arts, but the men;
     The graces and muses everywhere follow
     You, as you were their second Apollo;

532 Dance . . . 3] *Greg; after line 550 in all texts.*
534–50 *after line 639 in* H.

---

520 LADY . . . HATTON *mother of Lady Purbeck, and daughter of the Earl of Exeter* (*see line 464*).
531 WINDSOR N.
533 LORD CHAMBERLAIN *Jonson's patron, the Earl of Pembroke.*
543 AS *as if.*

Only your hand here tells you to your face
    You have wanted one grace   545
To perform what has been a right of your place;
For by this line, which is Mars his trench,
You never yet helped your master to a wench:
    'Tis well for your honor he's pious and chaste,
    Or you had most certainly been displaced.   550

     The Lord Keeper's fortune by the

Patrico. As happy a palm, sir, as most i' the land;
    It should be a pure and an innocent hand,
               And worthy the trust,
               For it says you'll be just,   555
               And carry that purse
               Without any curse
               Of the public weal
               When you take out the seal;
               You do not appear   560
               A judge of a year.
               I'll venture my life
               You never had wife,
               But I'll venture my skill
               You may when you will.   565
You have the king's conscience too in your breast,
         And that's a good guest,
      Which you'll have true touch of,
      And yet not make much of,
More than by truth yourself forth to bring   570
The man that you are, for God and the king.

562–65 I'll . . . will] H *om.*

---

551 LORD KEEPER *of the Great Seal, John Williams, Bishop of Lincoln. It was*
    rumored that he was to marry Buckingham's mother (hence line 565).
556 PURSE *in which the Great Seal is carried.*

The Lord Treasurer's fortune by the

3rd Gypsy. I come to borrow, and you'll grant my demand, sir,
　　　　　Since 'tis for no money; pray lend me your hand, sir:
575　　　And yet this good hand, if you please to stretch it,
　　　　　Had the errand been money, could easily fetch it.
　　　　　You command the king's treasure, and yet, o' my soul,
　　　　　You handle not much, for your palm is not foul;
　　　　　Your fortune is good, and will be to set
580　　　The office upright and the king out of debt,
　　　　　To put all that have pensions soon out of their pain
　　　　　By bringing th'exchequer in credit again.

[Dance 2. Strain 4.]

The Lord Privy Seal's [by the]

585　*2nd Gypsy.*　　　　Honest and old:
　　　　　In those the good part of a fortune is told.
　　　　　　God send you your health!
　　　　　The rest is provided, honor and wealth,
　　　　　　All which you possess
590　　　Without the making of any man less;
　　　　　Nor need you my warrant, enjoy it you shall,
　　　　　For you have a good privy seal for it all.

The Earl Marshal's [by the]

3rd Gypsy. Next the great master who is the donor,
595　　　I read you here the preserver of honor,

573 come] come, sir H.
574 for no] not for H.
583 Dance . . . 4] *Greg; all texts om.*

572 LORD TREASURER *Henry, Baron Montagu and Viscount Mandeville, later the Earl of Manchester.*
581 PENSIONS *All pensions, including Jonson's, had been suspended for over a year.* N.
584 LORD PRIVY SEAL *Edward Somerset, Earl of Worcester.*
593 EARL MARSHAL *Thomas Howard, Earl of Arundel and Earl of Surrey.*

And spy it in all your singular parts
What a father you are, and a nurse of the arts;
By cherishing which, a way you have found
How they, free to all, to one may be bound,
And they again love their bonds; for to be   600
Obligèd to you is the way to be free.
But this is their fortune; hark to your own:
Yours shall be to make true gentry known
From the fictitious; not to prize blood
So much by the greatness as by the good;   605
To show and to open clear virtue the way
Both whither she should and how far she may;
And whilst you do judge twixt valor and noise,
T'extinguish the race of the roaring boys.

The Lord Steward's by the   610

4th Gypsy.   I find by this hand
                    You have the command
Of the very best man's house i' the land.
                    Our captain and we
                    Ere long will see   615
                    If you keep a good table;
                    Your master's able,
And here be bountiful lines that say
You'll keep no part of his bounty away.
                    There's written frank   620
                    On your Venus' bank,

597 NURSE . . . ARTS *Arundel was a great collector and patron.*
609 ROARING BOYS *riotous fellows.*
610 LORD STEWARD *Lodovick Stuart, Duke of Lennox.*
620 FRANK *clearly.*
621 VENUS' BANK *mons Veneris (see line 280).*

225

To prove a false steward you'll find much ado,
Being a true one by blood and by office too.

[*Dance 2. Strain 5.*]

625   *The Lord Marquis Hamilton's by the*

3rd Gypsy. Only your hand, sir, and welcome to court!
Here is a man both for earnest and sport.
You were lately employed,
And your master is joyed
630   To have such in his train
So well can sustain
His person abroad
And not shrink for the load.
But had you been here,
635   You should have been a gypsy, I swear;
Our captain had summoned you by a doxy
To whom you would not have answered by proxy,
One, had she come in the way of your sceptre,
'Tis odds you had laid it by to have leapt her.

640   *The Earl of Buccleuch's by the*

Patrico. A hunter you have been heretofore,
And had game good store;
But ever you went
Upon a new scent,

624 Dance . . . 5] *Greg;* Dance 2. 4 Strain H; D, Ne, F *om.*
626 sir] *so* H; D, Ne, F *om.* and] and you're H.
640–54 H *om.*

623 BLOOD . . . OFFICE *playing on his surname.*
625 LORD . . . HAMILTON *James, second Marquis, a privy councillor.*
628 LATELY EMPLOYED *as Lord High Commissioner to the Scottish parliament in July 1621.*
640 EARL OF BUCCLEUCH *Walter, Lord Scott of Buccleuch.*
642 GOOD STORE *very much.*

And shifted your loves   645
As often as they did their smocks or their gloves.
But since that your brave intendments are
    Now bent for the war,
    The world shall see
    You can constant be   650
    One mistress to prove,
    And court her for your love:
Pallas shall be both your sword and your gage,
Truth bear your shield, and fortune your page.

Dance 2. Strain 6,   655

which leads into Dance 3.

Dance 3.

During which enter the clowns,

Cockerel, Clod, Townshead, Puppy,

[whilst the Patrico and Jackman   660

sing this song.]

SONG

Patrico.   Why, this is a sport,
                    See it north, see it south,
                    For the taste of the court,   665

655–59 Dance . . . Puppy] *so* H; *after line 688 in* D, Ne, F.
660–61 whilst . . . song] D, Ne, F *om.*

---

647 INTENDMENTS *purposes.*
648 BENT . . . WAR *He commanded a Dutch regiment.*
653 PALLAS *representing wisdom.* GAGE *glove (thrown down as a challenge in battle).*
654 TRUTH . . . PAGE N.
659 COCKEREL . . . PUPPY *townspeople. (At Burley and Belvoir their entrance and the preceding dance came before line 689).*

227

Jackman.		For the court's own mouth.
		Come Windsor, the town,
		With the mayor, and oppose;
		We'll put 'em all down,
670	*Patrico.*	Do-do-down like my hose.

Jackman.   For the court's own mouth.
                           Come Windsor, the town,
                           With the mayor, and oppose;
                           We'll put 'em all down,
670 *Patrico.*   Do-do-down like my hose.
                           A gypsy in his shape
                           More calls the beholder
                           Than the fellow with the ape,
Jackman.   Or the ape on his shoulder.
675   He's a sight that will take
                           An old judge from his wench,
                           Aye, and keep him awake,
Patrico.   Yes, awake o' the bench;
                           And has so much worth,
680   Though he sit i' the stocks,
                           He will draw the girls forth,
Jackman.   Aye, forth i' their smocks.
                           Tut, a man's a man;
                           Let the clowns with their sluts
685   Come mend us if they can,
Patrico.   If they can for their guts.
           Come mend us, come lend us their shouts and their noise,
Both.   Like thunder, and wonder at Ptolemy's boys.

Cockerel. Oh the lord! what be these? Tom, dost thou know? Come
690   hither, come hither, Dick, didst thou ever see such? the finest
       olive-colored spirits; they have so danced and jingled here as if
       they had been a set of overgrown fairies.

689 (*All three versions now continue.*)

228

Clod. They should be morris-dancers by their jingle, but they have
no napkins.

Cockerel. No, nor a hobbyhorse.   695

Clod. Oh, he's often forgotten, that's no rule; but there is no Maid
Marian nor friar amongst them, which is the surer mark.

Cockerel. Nor a fool, that I see.

Clod. Unless they be all fools.

Townshead. Well said, Tom Fool! why, thou simple parish ass thou,   700
didst thou never see any gypsies? These are a covey of gypsies,
and the bravest new covey that ever constable flew at; goodly
game, gypsies! they are gypsies o' this year, o' this moon, in
my conscience.

Clod. Oh, they are called the moon men, I remember now.   705

Cockerel. One shall hardly see such gentlemanlike gypsies though,
under a hedge, in a whole summer's day, if they be gypsies.

Townshead. Male gypsies all, not a mort among them.

Puppy. Where, where? I could never endure the sight of one of these
rogue gypsies; which be they? I would fain see 'em.   710

Clod. Yonder they are.

Puppy. Can they cant or mill? are they masters of their arts?

Townshead. No, bachelors these; they cannot have proceeded so far;
they have scarce had their time to be lousy yet.

712 of] in D, H.

693–94 THEY ... NAPKINS *Morris-dancers wore bells and carried kerchiefs in their*
hands or tied them on their shoulders.

695–96 HOBBYHORSE ... FORGOTTEN *refrain of a popular ballad, often quoted (e.g.*
in Hamlet, *III.ii.130).*

696–97 MAID ... FRIAR *The characters in the morris-dance were from the Robin*
Hood story.

703 MOON *month.*

705 MOON MEN *madmen, a common term for gypsies.* N.

708 MORT *woman.*

712 CANT *beg.* MILL *steal.*

715 *Puppy.* All the better; I would be acquainted with them while they
    are in clean life, they'll do their tricks the cleanlier.

    Cockerel. We must have some music then, and take out the wenches.

    Puppy. Music! we'll have a whole poverty of pipers. Call Cheeks
    upon the bagpipe and Tom Ticklefoot with his tabor; see
720   where he comes!

    Cockerel. Aye, and all the good wenches of Windsor after him.
    Yonder's Prue o' the Park.

    Townshead. And Frances o' the Castle.

    Puppy. And Long Meg of Eton.

725 *Clod.* And Christian o' Dorney.

    Townshead. See the miracle of a minstrel!

    Cockerel. He's able to muster up the smocks o' the two shires.

    Puppy. And set the codpieces and they by th'ears at pleasure.

    Townshead. I cannot hold now; there's my groat. Let's have a fit for
730   mirth's sake.

    Cockerel. Yes, and they'll come about us for luck's sake.

    Puppy. But look to our pockets and purses for our own sake.

    Clod. Aye, I have the greatest charge; gather the money.

    Cockerel. Come, girls, here be gypsies come to town; let's dance
735   'em down!

719–20 *N.*
733 gather] if I gather H.
734 let's] if we can, let's H.

---

717 TAKE OUT *to dance.*

718 POVERTY *"An alleged name for a company of pipers."* OED, *s.v.* 7. N.

719–20 SEE . . . COMES N.

721–35 N.

724, 725 ETON, DORNEY *across the river from Windsor.*

727 TWO SHIRES *Windsor is in Berkshire, and Eton and Dorney are in Buckingham-*
    shire. But the allusion is obviously left over from the versions for Burley
    (Rutland) and Belvoir (Leicestershire), where it had more point.

729 HOLD *hold back.* GROAT *a coin worth fourpence.* FIT *bit of music.*

Pipers.

The clowns take out their wenches, Prudence, Frances, Meg, Christian.

COUNTRY DANCE

During which the gypsies come about them prying, and after, the

Patrico.

Sweet doxies and dells,	740
My Roses and Nells,	
Scarce out of the shells,	
Your hands, nothing else.	
We ring you no knells	
With our Ptolemy's bells,	745
Though we come from the fells,	
But bring you good spells,	
And tell you some chances	
In midst of your dances	
That fortune advances	750
To Prudence or Frances,	
To Cicely or Harry,	
To Roger or Mary,	
Or Peg of the dairy,	
To Maudlin or Thomas;	755
Then do not run from us;	
Although we look tawny,	
We're healthy and brawny;	
Whate'er your demand is,	
We'll give you no jaundice.	760

Puppy. Say you so, old gypsy? 'Slid, these go to't in rhymes; this is
better than canting by t'one half.

---

736 Pipers] *so* D, Ne; minstrel H; F *om.*
761 rhymes] rhyme D, H. this] that H.

---

740 DELLS *virgins (as opposed to doxies).*
746 FELLS *fens.*
762 CANTING *begging.*

Townshead. Nay, you shall hear 'em; peace, they begin with
    Prudence, mark that.

765 *Puppy.* The wiser gypsies they, marry.

Townshead. Are you advised?

Puppy. Yes, and I'll stand to't that a wise gypsy (take him at time o'
    year) is as politic a piece of flesh as most justices in the county
    where he stalks.

770 *3rd Gypsy.* To love a keeper your fortune will be,
        But the doucets better than him or his fee.

Townshead. Ha, Prue, has he hit you i' the teeth with a sweet bit?

Puppy. Let her alone; she'll swallow't well enough! A learned gypsy.

Townshead. You'll hear more hereafter.

775 *Puppy.* Marry, and I'll listen. Who stands next? Jack Cock'rel?

[*2nd Gypsy.*] You'll ha' good luck to horse flesh, o' my life,
        You plowed so late with the vicar's wife!

Puppy. A prophet, a prophet! no gypsy, or if he be a gypsy, a divine
    gypsy.

780 *Townshead.* Mark Frances, now she's going to't, the virginity o' the
    parish!

Patrico.   Fear not, in hell you'll never lead apes,
        A mortified maiden of five scapes.

Puppy. By'r lady, he touched the virgin string there a little too hard.

---

772 a] the D, H.
773 her] it D, H.
776 2nd Gypsy] Ne, F *om.*
776–77 *N.*

767–68 TAKE . . . YEAR *i.e. catch him at the right time.*

771 DOUCETS *sweets.*

776–77 YOU'LL . . . WIFE N.

778 DIVINE *divining, prophetic.*

780 VIRGINITY *arch-virgin.*

782 IN . . . APES "To lead apes in hell: *the fancied consequence of dying an old
    maid.*" (OED)

They are arrant learned men all, I see. What say they upon 785
Tom Clod? list!

4th Gypsy. Clod's feet will in Christmas go near to be bare,
        When he has lost all his hobnails at post and pair.

Puppy. He's hit the right nail o' the head, his own game.

Townshead. And the very metal he deals in at play, if you mark it. 790

Puppy. Peace, who's this? Long Meg?

Townshead. Long and foul Meg, if she be a Meg, as ever I saw of her
    inches! Pray God they fit her with a fair fortune.

Puppy. They slip her, and treat upon Ticklefoot.

4th Gypsy. On Sundays you rob the poor's box with your tabor; 795
        The collectors would do it, you save 'em a labor.

Puppy. Faith, but little, they do it *non upstante.*

Townshead. Here's my little Christian forgot! Ha' you any fortune
    left for her, a strait-laced Christian of sixteen?

Patrico.   Christian shall get her a loose-bodied gown 800
        In trying how a gentleman differs from a clown.

Puppy. Is that a fortune for a Christian? A Turk gypsy could not
    have told her a worse.

Townshead. Come, I'll stand myself, and once venture the poor head
    o' the town. Do your worst; my name's Townshead, and here's 805
    my hand I'll not be angry.

3rd Gypsy. A cuckold you must be, and that for three lives,
        Your own, the parson's, and your wife's.

---

794 *N.*
797 little, they] a little, they'll Ne, F.
802 Turk] *so* D; Turk with a H; Turk or a Ne, F.

---

788 POST . . . PAIR *a card game.*
791 LONG MEG "*a virago whose exploits were famous in the 16th c.*" (OED)
    Cf. The Fortunate Isles, *line 260.*
794 THEY . . . TICKLEFOOT N. SLIP *pass by.*
797 NON UPSTANTE *anyway.*
802 TURK *i.e. un-Christian.*

Townshead. I swear I'll never marry for that, an't be but to give
810   fortune my foe the lie. Come, Paul Puppy, you must in too.

Puppy. No, I'm well enough; I would ha' no good fortune an I
      might.

[*4th Gypsy.*] Yet look to yourself, you'll ha' some ill luck—
      And shortly, for I have his purse at a pluck!

815 *Patrico.*   Away, birds, mum!
                    I hear by the hum
                    If beck-harman come
                    He'll strike us all dumb
                    With a noise like a drum.
820   Let's give him our room
                    Here, this way some,
                    And that way others;
                    We are not all brothers:
                    Leave me to the cheats,
825   I'll show 'em some feats.

Puppy. What? are they gone? flown all of a sudden? This is fine, i'
      faith. A covey call ye 'em? they are a covey soon scattered,
      methinks; who sprung 'em I marle?

Townshead. Marry, yourself, Puppy, for aught I know; you quested
830   last.

Clod. Would he had quested first and sprung 'em an hour ago for
      me.

813 4th Gypsy] *so* D; Patrico H, Ne, F.
831 first] first, for me, H.
831–32 for me] H *om.*

---

810 FORTUNE . . . FOE *an Elizabethan popular song, preserved in a setting by
      William Byrd in the* Fitzwilliam Virginal Book.
817 BECK-HARMAN *harman beck, the constable.*
824 TO THE CHEATS *i.e. to do the tricks.*
828 MARLE *wonder.*
831–32 FOR ME *for all I care.*

Townshead. Why, what's the matter, man?

Clod. 'Slid, they ha' sprung my purse and all I had about me.

Townshead. They ha' not, ha' they?   835

Clod. As I am true Tom Clod, ha' they, and ransacled me of every
    penny; outcept I were with child of an owl (as they say), I
    never saw such luck! It's enough to make a man a whore.

Puppy. Hold thy peace; thou talk'st as if thou hadst a license to lose
    thy purse alone in this company. 'Slid, here be those can lose a   840
    purse in honor of the gypsies as well as thou, for thy heart, and
    never make word of it: I ha' lost my purse too.

Cockerel. What was there i' thy purse thou keep'st such a whining?
    Was the lease of thy house in it?

Puppy. Or thy grannam's silver ring?   845

Clod. No, but a mill sixpence [of my mother's] I loved as dearly, and
    two pence I had to spend over and above, besides the harper
    that was gathered amongst us to pay the piper.

Townshead. Our whole stock, is that gone? How will Tom Tickle-
    foot do to wet his whistle then?   850

Puppy. Marry, a new collection, there's no music else, masters; he
    can ill pipe that wants his upper lip: money.

Prudence. They have robbed me too of a dainty race of ginger and a
    jet ring I had to draw Jack Straw hither a holidays.

Townshead. Is't possible? fine fingered gypsies, i' faith!   855

---

843 whining] whimpering H.
846 of . . . mother's] H, Ne, F *om.*
852 money] D, H *om.*
853 dainty] D, H *om.*

---

837 OUTCEPT *except.* WITH . . . OWL *i.e. bewitched.*
846 MILL SIXPENCE *Milling produced a finer coin than the old method of hammering.
    The technique was introduced into England in 1561.*
847 HARPER *an Irish coin worth ninepence.*
853 RACE *root.*

Meg. And I have lost an enchanted nutmeg all gilded over, was enchanted at Oxford for me, to put i' my sweetheart's ale a-mornings, with a row of white pins that prick me to the very heart, the loss of 'em.

860 *Clod.* And I have lost, besides my purse, my best bride-lace I had at Joan Turnip's wedding, and a halp'orth of hobnails. Frances Addlebreech has lost somewhat too, besides her maidenhead.

Frances. I have lost my thimble and a skein of Coventry blue I had to work Gregory Litchfield a handkerchief.

865 *Christian.* And I, unhappy Christian as I am, have lost my *Practice of Piety*, with a bowed groat and the ballad of *Whoop Barnaby*, which grieves me ten times worse.

Clod. And Ticklefoot has lost his clout, he says, with a threepence and four tokens in't, besides his taboring stick even now.

870 *Cockerel.* And I my knife and sheath and my fine dog's-leather gloves.

Townshead. Ha' we lost never a dog amongst us: where's Puppy?

Puppy. Here, goodman Townshead; you have nothing to lose, it seems, but the town-brains you are trusted with.

875 [*Patrico.*]   O, my dear marrows,
                          No shooting of arrows

856–57 was . . . me] *so* Ne, F; enchanted at Oxford, I had H.
861 Turnip's] *so* H; Turner's Ne, F.
875 Patrico] Ne, F *om.*

---

856 GILDED *glazed with egg yolk. The nutmeg was used to spice ale.*

858 WHITE *silver.*

861 HALP'ORTH *half-pennyworth.*

863 COVENTRY BLUE *blue embroidery thread.*

865–66 PRACTICE OF PIETY *a popular devotional work by King James's chaplain Lewes Bayly, first published in 1612.* BOWED *bent (as a love token).*

868 CLOUT *rag.*

869 TABORING STICK *drumstick.*

875 MARROWS *companions.*

Or shafts of your wit,
Each other to hit
In your skirmishing fit.
Your store is but small,   880
Then venture not all;
Remember each mock
Doth spend o' the stock.
And what was here done,
Being under the moon   885
And at afternoon,
Will prove right soon
Deceptio visus
Done *gratia risus*.
There's no such thing   890
As the loss of a ring,
Or what you count worse,
The miss of a purse,
But hey for the main,
And pass o' the strain,   895
Here's both come again.
And there's an old twinger
Can show ye the ginger;
The pins and the nutmeg
Are safe here with slut Meg;   900
Then strike up your tabor,

885–86 UNDER . . . AFTERNOON *i.e. the performance is at night, but the fictive time is during the day. But also, "under the moon" = subject to mutability and deception.*

888 DECEPTIO VISUS *deception of the sight.*

889 GRATIA RISUS *for a laugh.*

894–95 HEY . . . STRAIN *The Patrico makes a conjurer's gesture while repeating the conjurer's formula, "hey, pass."*

897 TWINGER *nuisance (literally, one who makes you twinge, or smart).*

And there's for your labor;
The sheath and the knife,
I'll venture my life,
905 Shall breed you no strife,
But like man and wife,
Or sister and brother,
Keep one with another,
And light as a feather,
910 Make haste to come hither.
The Coventry blue
Hangs there upon Prue;
And here's one opens
The clout and the tokens;
915 Deny the bowed groat
And you lie i' your throat;
Or the taborer's ninepence,
Or the six fine pence.
As for the ballad,
920 Or book what-you-call-it,
Alas, our society
Mells not with piety;
Himself hath forsook it
That first undertook it;
925 For thimble or bride-lace,
Search yonder side lass.
All's to be found
If you look yourselves round;
We scorn to take from ye,
930 We had rather spend on ye;
If any man wrong ye,
The thief's among ye.

922 MELLS *meddles.*

Townshead. Excellent, i' faith, a most restorative gypsy. All's here
    again; and yet by his learning of legerdemain he would make
    us believe we had robbed ourselves.   935

Cockerel. A gypsy of quality, believe it, and one of the king's
    gypsies this, a drinkalian or a drink-braggetan; ask him. The
    king has his noise of gypsies as well as of bear wards and other
    minstrels.

Puppy. What sort or order of gypsies, I pray sir?   940

[*Patrico.*]   A flagonfekian,
               A Devil's-Arse-a-Peakian,
               Born first at Nigglington,
               Bred up at Filchington,
               Boarded at Tappington,   945
               Bedded at Wappington.

Townshead. 'Fore me, a dainty derived gypsy!

Puppy. But I pray, sir, if a man might ask on you, how came your
    captain's place first to be called the Devil's Arse?

Patrico.   For that take my word,   950
               We have a record
               That doth it afford,
               And says our first lord,

---

935 *N.*
938 has his] hath a D; has a H.
938–39 of bear . . . minstrels] of bear wards D; bear wards H.
941 Patrico] Ne, F *om.*

---

935 OURSELVES *N.*
937 DRINKALIAN *great drinker.* DRINK-BRAGGETAN *drinker of bragget (ale fermented
    with honey).*
941 FLAGONFEKIAN *flagon-beater* (*?*)
942 DEVIL'S . . . PEAKIAN *See lines 107–08.*
943 NIGGLINGTON *from* niggle, "*to have to do with a woman carnally.*" (OED)
945 TAPPINGTON *suggesting the taps of liquor casks, hence taverns.*
946 WAPPINGTON *wapping= niggling.*

Cock Lorel he hight,
On a time did invite
The devil to a feast;
The tail of the jest
(Though since it be long)
Lives yet in a song,
Which if you would hear,
Shall plainly appear
[Like a chime in your ear:]
I'll call in my clerk,
Shall sing like a lark.

955

960

965 [*Cockerel.* Oh, aye, the song, the song in any case; if you want
music, we'll lend him our minstrel.]

Patrico.

Come in, my long shark,
With thy face brown and dark,
With thy tricks and thy toys,
Make a merry, merry noise
To these mad country boys,
And chant out the farce
Of the grand Devil's Arse.

970

SONG

975 [*Jackman.*] Cock Lorel would needs have the devil his guest,
And bade him once into the Peak to dinner,

962 D, Ne, F *om.*
965–66 D, Ne, F *om.*

---

954 COCK LOREL *literally, arch-rogue; the name of a legendary knave and thief.*
HIGHT *was called.*
958 SINCE *i.e. since that time.*
963 CLERK *presumably the literate gypsy, the Jackman.*

Where never the fiend had such a feast
    Provided him yet at the charge of a sinner.

His stomach was queasy for coming there coached;
    The jogging had caused some crudities rise;   980
To help it he called for a Puritan poached,
    That used to turn up the eggs of his eyes.

And so, recovered unto his wish,
    He sat him down, and he fell to eat;
Promoter in plum broth was the first dish;   985
    His own privy kitchen had no such meat.

Yet though with this he much were taken,
    Upon a sudden he shifted his trencher
As soon as he spied the bawd and bacon,
    By which you may note the devil's a wencher.   990

Six pickled tailors sliced and cut,
    Sempsters, tirewomen, fit for his palate,
With feathermen and perfumers put
    Some twelve in a charger to make a grand salad.

A rich fat usurer stewed in his marrow,   995
    And by him a lawyer's head and green sauce,
Both which his belly took in like a barrow,
    As if till then he never had seen sauce.

979 for . . . coached] (he came thither coached) H.
980 caused] made H.
985 the] his H.
998 never had] had never D, F.

---

985 PROMOTER *informer.*
989 BAWD *also means hare.* BACON *cant for both body, or flesh, and prize.*
992 SEMPSTERS *seamstresses.* TIREWOMEN *dressmakers.*
993 FEATHERMEN *dealers in feathers.*
996 GREEN SAUCE *" Sauce for mutton, veal and kid is green sauce, made in summer
    with vinegar . . . , with a few spices, and without garlic." (OED, citing Sir
    John Harington, 1612)*

Then carbonadoed and cooked with pains,
1000   Was brought up a cloven sergeant's face;
The sauce was made of his yeoman's brains
    That had been beaten out with his own mace.

Two roasted sheriffs came whole to the board
    (The feast had nothing been without 'em);
1005 Both living and dead they were foxed and furred,
    Their chains like sausages hung about 'em.

The very next dish was the mayor of a town,
    With a pudding of maintenance thrust in his belly,
Like a goose in the feathers dressed in his gown,
1010   And his couple of hinch-boys boiled to a jelly.

A London cuckold, hot from the spit,
    And when the carver up had broke him,
The devil chopped up his head at a bit,
    But the horns were very near like to have choked him.

1015 The chine of a lecher too there was roasted,
    With a plump harlot's haunch and garlic,
A pander's pettitoes, that had boasted
    Himself for a captain, yet never was warlike.

A large fat pasty of midwife hot;
1020   And for a cold baked meat into the story,

---

999 CARBONADOED *scored or slashed.* PAINS *The word also means side dishes made with bread.*

1005 FOXED AND FURRED *i.e. their clothes were trimmed with fox fur. But* foxed *also means drunk.*

1008 PUDDING OF MAINTENANCE *alluding to the cap of maintenance, carried before the Lord Mayor in official processions.*

1010 HINCH-BOYS *hench-boys, pages.*

1015 CHINE *back.*

1017 PETTITOES *pig's trotters.*

A reverend painted lady was brought,
　　Was coffined in crust till now she was hoary.

To these, an overgrown justice of peace,
　　With a clerk like a gizzard trussed under each arm,
And warrants for sippets laid in his own grease,　　　　1025
　　Set over a chafing dish to be kept warm.

The jowl of a jailor, served for fish,
　　A constable soused with vinegar by,
Two alderman lobsters asleep in a dish,
　　A deputy tart, a churchwarden pie.　　　　1030

All which devoured, he then for a close
　　Did for a full draught of Darby call;
He heaved the huge vessel up to his nose,
　　And left not till he had drunk up all.

Then from the table he gave a start,　　　　1035
　　Where banquet and wine were nothing scarce,
All which he flirted away with a fart,
　　From whence it was called the Devil's Arse.

[Windsor.] And there he made such a breech with the wind,
　　The hole too standing open the while,　　　　1040
That the scent of the vapor before and behind
　　Hath foully perfumed most part of the isle.

1022 was coffined] and coffined D, Ne, F.
1024 trussed] thrust D, Ne, F.
1037 flirted] blew H.
1039–50 H *om.*
1041 before . . . behind] he left behind Ne.

1025 SIPPETS *croutons.*
1030 CHURCHWARDEN PIE *with a pun on warden, a kind of pear.*
1032 DARBY *Derby ale.*
1037 FLIRTED *flicked.*
1039–50 AND . . . END N.

And this was tobacco, the learnèd suppose,
　　Which since in country, court and town,
1045　In the devil's glister-pipe smokes at the nose
　　Of polecat and madam, of gallant and clown.

From which wicked weed, with swine's flesh and ling,
　　Or anything else that's feast for the fiend,
Our captain and we cry God save the king,
1050　And send him good meat, and mirth without end.

Puppy. An excellent song and a sweet songster, and would ha' done
　rarely in a cage with a dish of water and hemp seed; a fine
　breast of his own! Sir, you are a prelate of the order, I under-
　stand, and I have a terrible grudging now upon me to be one
1055　of your company: will your captain take a prentice, sir? I
　would bind myself to him, body and soul, either for one and
　twenty years, or as many lives as he would.

Clod. Aye, and put in my life for one, for I am come about too. I am
　sorry I had no more money i' my purse when you came first
1060　upon us, sir; if I had known you would have picked my pocket
　so like a gentleman, I would have been better provided. I shall
　be glad to venture a purse with your worship at any time you'll
　appoint, so you would prefer me to your captain. I'll put in
　security for my truth and serve out my time, though I die
1065　tomorrow.

1060 us] me H.

1043 TOBACCO *King James was a strong opponent of smoking.*
1045 GLISTER-PIPE *clyster.*
1046 POLECAT *whore.*
1047 LING *a fish especially disliked by the king.*
1052 N.
1053 BREAST *voice.*
1054 GRUDGING *longing.*
1063 PREFER *recommend.*

Cockerel. Aye, upon those terms, sir, and in hope your captain keeps
better cheer than he made the devil (for my stomach will never
agree with that diet) we'll be all his followers. I'll go home and
fetch a little money, sir, all I have, and you shall pick my
pocket to my face, and I'll avouch it, a man would not desire 1070
to have his pocket picked in better company.

Puppy. Tut, they have other manner of gifts than picking of pockets
or telling fortunes, if they would but please to show 'em, or
thought us poor country mortals worthy of them. What
might a man do to be a gentleman of your company, sir? 1075

[*Cockerel.*] Aye, a gypsy in ordinary, or nothing.

Patrico. Friends, not to refel ye
Or any way quell ye,
To buy or to sell ye,
I only must tell ye 1080
Ye aim at a mystery
Worthy a history.
There's much to be done
Ere you can be a son
Or brother o' the moon; 1085
'Tis not so soon
Acquired as desired.
You must be bene-bowsy,
And sleepy and drowsy,
And lazy and lousy 1090
Before ye can rouse ye

1071 POCKET] purse H.
1072–74 N.
1076 Cockerel] Ne, F *om.*

1066–67 KEEPS . . . CHEER *eats better.*
1072–74 TUT . . . THEM N.
1076 IN ORDINARY *regular.*
1077 REFEL *reject.*
1088 BENE-BOWSY *from* bene bowse, *good drink.*

In shape that avows ye.
And then ye may stalk
The gypsies' walk
1095   To the coops and the pens,
And bring in the hens;
Though the cock be sullen
For loss o' the pullen,
Take turkey and capon
1100   And gammons of bacon,
Let nought be forsaken.
We'll let you go loose
Like a fox to a goose,
And show you the sty
1105   Where the little pigs lie,
Whence if you can take
One or two, and not wake
The sow in her dreams,
But by the moonbeams
1110   So warily hie
As neither do cry,
You shall the next day
Have license to play
At the hedge a flirt
1115   For a sheet or a shirt.
If your hand be light,
I'll show ye the slight
Of our Ptolemy's knot;
It is, and 'tis not;
1120   To change your complexion

1092 AVOWS YE *you approve.*
1098 PULLEN *chickens.*
1113–15 PLAY . . . SHIRT *i.e. flick the linen from the hedge.*
1118 PTOLEMY'S KNOT *gypsy trick.*

With the noble confection
Of walnuts and hog's grease,
Better than dog's grease;
And to milk the kine
Ere the milkmaid fine   1125
Have opened her eyne.
Or if you desire
To spit or fart fire,
I'll teach you the knacks
Of eating of flax,   1130
And out of your noses
Draw ribbons for posies,
As for example
Mine own is as ample
And fruitful a nose   1135
As a wit can suppose;
Yet it shall go hard,
But there will be spared
Each of you a yard,
And worth your regard,   1140
When the color and size
Arrive at your eyes.
And if you incline
To a cup of good wine
When you sup or dine,   1145
If you chance it to lack,
Be it claret or sack,
I'll make this snout
To deal it about,
Or this to run out   1150
As 'twere from a spout.

1132 for] and Ne, F.

1126 EYNE *eyes.*

247

Townshead. Admirable tricks, and he does 'em all *se defendendo*, as if he would not be taken in the trap of authority by a frail fleshly constable.

1155 *Puppy.* Without the aid of a cheese.

Clod. Or help of a flitch of bacon.

Cockerel. Oh, he would chirp in a pair of stocks sumptuously; I'd give anything to see him play loose with his hands when his feet were fast.

1160 *Puppy.* O' my conscience, he fears not that an the marshal himself were here. I protest I admire him.

Patrico.	Is this worth your wonder?
	Nay then you shall under-
	Stand more of my skill.
1165	I can, for I will,
[*Burley*]	Here at Burley o' th' Hill,
	Give you all your fill,
	Each Jack with his Jill,
	And show ye the king,
1170	The prince too, and bring
	The gypsies were here
	Like lords to appear,
	With such their attenders
	As you thought offenders,
1175	Who now become new men,
	You'll know 'em for true men.

[*Burley*]	*Bever*
For he we call chief	The fifth of August
(I'll tell't ye in brief)	Will not let sawdust

1152 SE DEFENDENDO *in self-defense.*
1171 WERE *who were.*
1177b BEVER *Belvoir.*
1178a HE . . . CHIEF *Buckingham.*

Is so far from a thief,
As he gives ye relief,
With his bread, beer and beef,
And 'tis not long syne
Ye drank of his wine,
And it made you fine,
Both claret and sherry;
Then let us be merry,
And help with your call
For a hall, a hall!
Stand up to the wall,
Both good men and tall,
We are one man's all;
Make it a jolly night,
If not a holy night,

Lie in your throats, 1180
Or cobwebs, or oats,
But help to scour ye.
This is no Gowrie
Hath drawn James hither,
But the good man of Bever, 1185
Our Buckingham's father;
Then so much the rather
Make it a jolly night,
For 'tis a holy night,

1190

Spite o' the constable, 1195
Or Mas Dean of Dunstable.

All. A hall! a hall! a hall!

The gypsies changed.

DANCE

Patrico.   Why, now ye behold   1200
                   'Twas truth that I told,

1183a SYNE *since.*
1183b GOWRIE *This was the anniversary of the Gowrie conspiracy, the attempted assassination of King James in 1600.*
1186b FATHER *i.e. father-in-law.*
1189a A . . . HALL *i.e. room to perform in.*
1189b HOLY NIGHT *Sunday.*
1195, 1196 CONSTABLE, DEAN *i.e. civil or ecclesiastical officers.* N.
1196 MAS *master.*
1199 N.

And no device;
They're changed in a trice,
And so will I
1205 Be myself by and by.
I only now
Must study how
To come off with a grace
With my Patrico's place:
1210 Some short kind of blessing,
Itself addressing
Unto my good master,
Which light on him faster
Than wishes can fly;
1215 And you that stand by
Be as jocund as I,
Each man with his voice
Give his heart to rejoice,
Which I'll requite
1220 If my art hit right.
Though late now at night,
Each clown here in sight
Before daylight
Shall prove a good knight,
1225 And your lasses, pages
Worthy their wages,
Where fancy engages
Girls to their ages.

Clod. O, anything for the Patrico; what is't, what is't?
1230 *Patrico.* Nothing but bear the bob of the close;

1209 With] by H.

1202 DEVICE *trick.*
1227 FANCY *love.*
1230 BEAR . . . CLOSE *i.e. join in the chorus.*

It will be no burden you well may suppose,
 But bless the sovereign and his senses,
  And to wish away offences.
Clod. Let us alone; bless the sovereign and his senses.
Patrico. We'll take 'em in order, as they have being;   1235
 And first of seeing.

     1

From a gypsy in the morning,
 Or a pair of squint eyes turning,
From the goblin and the specter,   1240
 Or a drunkard, though with nectar,
From a woman true to no man
 And is ugly besides common,
A smock rampant and that itches
 To be putting on the britches,   1245
Wheresoe'er they ha' their being,
Bless the sovereign and his seeing.

     2

From a fool and serious toys,
 From a lawyer three parts noise,   1250
From impertinence, like a drum
 Beat at dinner in his room,
From a tongue without a file,
 Heaps of phrases and no style,
From a fiddle out of tune   1255
 As the cuckoo is in June,

1231 BURDEN *also means refrain.*
1234 LET US ALONE *i.e. let us do it ourselves.*
1244 SMOCK RAMPANT *bossy woman.*
1249 SERIOUS TOYS *solemn nonsense.*
1253 A FILE *i.e. polish.*

From the candlesticks of Lothbury
  And the loud pure wives of Banbury,
Or a long pretended fit
  Meant for mirth, but is not it,
1260
Only time and ears outwearing,
Bless the sovereign and his hearing.

3

From a strolling tinker's sheet
1265
  Or a pair of carrier's feet,
From a lady that doth breathe
  Worse above than underneath,
From the diet and the knowledge
  Of the students in Bears' College,
1270
From tobacco with the type
  Of the devil's glister-pipe,
Or a stink all stinks excelling,
  A fishmonger's dwelling,
Bless the sovereign and his smelling.

1275
4

From an oyster and fried fish,
  A sow's baby in a dish,
From any portion of a swine,
  From bad venison and worse wine,
1280
Ling, what cook soe'er it boil,
  Though with mustard sauced, and oil,

1259–60 Or . . . it] H *om.*
1265 Or] and H.
1278 From] H *om.*

1257 LOTHBURY *section of London where the foundries were. Jonson is deploring
the noise of metal being turned.*
1258 BANBURY *in Oxfordshire,.a Puritan stronghold.*
1269 STUDENTS . . . COLLEGE *the bears at the beargarden.*

Or what else would keep man fasting,
Bless the sovereign and his tasting.

5

Both from birdlime and from pitch,   1285
   From a doxy and her itch,
From the bristles of a hog,
   Or the ringworm in a dog,
From the courtship of a briar,
   Or Saint Anthony's old fire,   1290
From a needle or a thorn
   I' the bed at ev'n or morn,
Or from any gout's least grutching,
Bless the sovereign and his touching.

Bless him too from all offences   1295
   In his sports, as in his senses;
From a boy to cross his way,
   From a fall or a foul day.

Bless him, O bless him heav'n, and lend him long
  To be the sacred burden of all song,   1300
The acts and years of all our kings t'outgo,
  And while he's mortal, we not think him so.

After which, ascending up, the Jackman sings.

SONG I

The sports are done, yet do not let   1305
Your joys in sudden silence set:
Delight and dumbness never met
   In one self subject yet.

1290 Or] from H.

1290 SAINT ANTHONY'S . . . FIRE *erysipelas.*
1293 GRUTCHING *grating.*

If things opposed must mixed appear,
1310   Then add a boldness to your fear,
        And speak a hymn
          To him,
    Where all your duties do of right belong,
    Which I will sweeten with an undersong.
1315 *Captain.*   Glory of ours, and grace of all the earth,
      How well your figure doth become your birth,
    As if your form and fortune equal stood,
      And only virtue got above your blood.

SONG 2

1320   Virtue! his kingly virtue, which did merit
    This isle entire, and you are to inherit.
4th Gypsy. How right he doth confess him in his face,
      His brow, his eye, and ev'ry mark of state,
    As if he were the issue of each grace,
1325   And bore about him both his fame and fate.

SONG 3

    Look, look, is he not fair,
      And fresh, fragrant too,
    As summer sky or purgèd air?
1330   And looks as lilies do
    That were this morning blown.
4th Gypsy. O more, that more of him were known!
3rd Gypsy. Look how the winds upon the waves grown tame
      Take up land sounds upon their purple wings,
1335   And catching each from other, bear the same
      To ev'ry angle of their sacred springs.

1317 if your] in you H.

1314 UNDERSONG *accompaniment.*
1321 YOU *Prince Charles.*
1331 WERE . . . BLOWN *bloomed.*

So will we take his praise, and hurl his name
    About the globe in thousand airy rings,
If his great virtue be in love with fame,
    For, that contemned, both are neglected things.   1340

SONG 4

    Good princes soar above their fame,
        And in their worth
        Come greater forth
           Than in their name.   1345
    Such, such the father is,
      Whom ev'ry title strives to kiss,
Who on his royal grounds unto himself doth raise
The work to trouble fame and to astonish praise.

4th Gypsy. Indeed, he is not lord alone of all the state,   1350
But of the love of men and of the empire's fate.
The muses' arts, the schools, commerce, our honors, laws,
And virtues hang on him as on their working cause.

2nd Gypsy.   His handmaid Justice is,
3rd Gypsy.   Wisdom his wife;   1355
4th Gypsy.   His mistress, Mercy;
5th Gypsy.   Temperance his life;
2nd Gypsy. His pages Bounty and Grace, which many prove;
3rd Gypsy. His guards are Magnanimity and Love;
4th Gypsy. His ushers Counsel, Truth and Piety,   1360
5th Gypsy. And all that follows him Felicity.

SONG 5

    O that we understood
      Our good!

1350 all . . . state] *so* D², Ne, F; the estate D¹, H.

1358 PROVE *experience.*

1365

There's happiness indeed in blood
And store,
But how much more
When virtue's flood
In the same stream doth hit!

1370   As that grows high with years, so happiness with it.

Captain.

Love, love his fortune then,
And virtues known,
Who is the top of men,
But make the happiness our own;

1375

Since where the prince for goodness is renowned,
The subject with felicity is crowned.

The End.

THE EPILOGUE

At Burley, Bever, and now last at Windsor
1380 (Which shows we are gypsies of no common kind, sir),
You have beheld, and with delight, their change,
And how they came transformed may think it strange,
It being a thing not touched at by our poet;
Good Ben slept there, or else forgot to show it.
1385 But lest it prove like wonder to the sight
To see a gypsy, as an Ethiop, white,
Know that what dyed our faces was an ointment
Made and laid on by Master Wolf's appointment,
The court *lycanthropos*, yet without spells,
1390 By a mere barber, and no magic else.

1374 make] *so* D¹, H, Ne; makes D², F.

1366 STORE *plenty.*
1388 MASTER WOLF *Johann Wolfgang Rumler, the king's apothecary.*
1389 LYCANTHROPOS *wolf-man.*

It was fetched off with water and a ball,
And to our transformation this is all,
Save what the master fashioner calls his;
For to a gypsy's metamorphosis
Who doth disguise his habit and his face,   1395
And takes on a false person by his place,
The power of poetry can never fail her,
Assisted by a barber and a tailor.

Finis

1392 is] was H.
1397 poetry] poesy H.

1391 BALL *of soap.*
1393 FASHIONER *tailor.*
1397 HER *i.e. the metamorphosis.*

Neptune's Triumph
for the Return of Albion

Celebrated in a masque at the court on the Twelfth-night, 1624.

Omnis et ad reducem iam litat ara deum.
Mart. lib. VIII, Epig. XV.

His majesty being set, and the loud music ceasing. All that is discovered of a
scene are two erected pillars dedicated to Neptune, with this inscription
upon the one, NEP. RED.; on the other, SEC. IOV. The Poet entering
on the stage to disperse the argument is called to by the Master-Cook.

Cook. Do you hear, you creature of diligence and business! What is   5
    the affair that you pluck for so under your cloak?
Poet. Nothing but what I color for, I assure you, and may encounter
    with, I hope, if Luck favor me, the gamester's goddess.

3 *Jonson's glosses appear only in Q.*

Title CELEBRATED *in fact, never performed.*
Epigraph OMNIS ... DEUM *Every altar makes fair offerings to greet the returning*
    god. (Adapted from Martial, VIII.xv.2.)
  3 NEP. RED. Neptuno reduci, *to Neptune the guide home.* SEC. IOV. secundo
    Iove, *the second Jupiter.*
  4 DISPERSE ... ARGUMENT *distribute the playbill of the masque.*
  6 PLUCK FOR *a term from primero, a popular card game. So, in the ensuing dialogue,*
    are COLOR FOR (7), ENCOUNTER WITH (7), *and* WHAT WENT YOU UPON?
    (9–10).

Cook. You are a votary of hers, it seems by your language. What
went you upon? May a man ask you?

Poet. Certainties, indeed, sir, and very good ones; the presentation
of a masque. You'll see't anon.

Cook. Sir, this is my room and region too, the Banqueting House!
And in matter of feast and solemnity nothing is to be presented
here but with my acquaintance and allowance to it.

Poet. You are not his majesty's confectioner, are you?

Cook. No, but one that has as good title to the room, his master-
cook. What are you, sir?

Poet. The most unprofitable of his servants, I, sir, the poet. A kind
of a Christmas ingine, one that is used at least once a year for a
trifling instrument of wit, or so.

Cook. Were you ever a cook?

Poet. A cook? No, surely.

Cook. Then you can be no good poet, for a good poet differs nothing
at all from a master-cook. Either's art is the wisdom of the
mind.

Poet. As how, sir?

Cook. Expect. I am by my place to know how to please the palates
of the guests; so, you are to know the palate of the times, study
the several tastes, what every nation, the Spaniard, the Dutch,
the French, the Walloon, the Neapolitan, the Briton, the
Sicilian can expect from you.

Poet. That were a heavy and hard task, to satisfy Expectation, who
is so severe an exactress of duties, ever a tyrannous mistress,
and most times a pressing enemy.

Cook. She is a powerful great lady, sir, at all times, and must be
satisfied. So must her sister, Madam Curiosity, who hath as
dainty a palate as she, and these will expect.

20 INGINE *both engine and wit.*
28 EXPECT *pay attention.*

Poet. But what if they expect more than they understand?

Cook. That's all one, Master Poet, you are bound to satisfy them.   40
For there is a palate of the understanding as well as of the
senses. The taste is taken with good relishes, the sight with fair
objects, the hearing with delicate sounds, the smelling with
pure scents, the feeling with soft and plump bodies, but the
understanding with all these, for all which you must begin at   45
the kitchen. There the art of poetry was learned and found out,
or nowhere, and the same day with the art of cookery.

Poet. I should have given it rather to the cellar, if my suffrage had
been asked.

Cook. O, you are for the oracle of the bottle, I see; Hogshead   50
Trismegistus, he is your Pegasus. Thence flows the spring of
your muses, from that hoof.

 Seducèd poet, I do say to thee,
 A boiler, range and dresser were the fountains
 Of all the knowledge in the universe,   55
 And that's the kitchen, where a master-cook—
 Thou dost not know the man, nor canst thou know him
 Till thou hast served some years in that deep school
 That's both the nurse and mother of the arts,
 And hear'st him read, interpret and demonstrate!   60
 A master-cook! why he is the man of men
 For a professor! He designs, he draws,
 He paints, he carves, he builds, he fortifies,
 Makes citadels of curious fowl and fish;
 Some he dry-ditches, some moats round with broths,   65
 Mounts marrowbones, cuts fifty-angled custards,
 Rears bulwark pies, and for his outer works,

50–1 HOGSHEAD TRISMEGISTUS N.
51–2 PEGASUS . . . HOOF N.
54 DRESSER *kitchen sideboard.*

He raiseth ramparts of immortal crust,
And teacheth all the tactics at one dinner,
70   What ranks, what files to put his dishes in:
The whole art military! Then he knows
The influence of the stars upon his meats,
And all their seasons, tempers, qualities,
And so, to fit his relishes and sauces!
75   He 'as nature in a pot! 'bove all the chemists,
Or bare-breeched brethren of the Rosy Cross!
He is an architect, an inginer,
A soldier, a physician, a philosopher,
A general mathematician!

Poet.   It is granted.
80 *Cook.* And, that you may not doubt him for a poet—
Poet. This fury shows, if there were nothing else.
    And 'tis divine!

Cook.   Then, brother poet—
Poet.   Brother!
Cook. I have a suit.
Poet.   What is it?
Cook.   Your device.
Poet. As you came in upon me, I was then
85   Off'ring the argument, and this it is.
Cook. Silence!
Poet. The mighty Neptune, mighty in his styles,
    And large command of waters and of isles,
    Not as the lord and sovereign of the seas,

---

73 TEMPERS *the proportions in which their qualities are mixed.*

76 BRETHREN . . . CROSS *Rosicrucians, members of a mystical religious brotherhood claiming spiritual and magical powers.*

77 INGINER *engineer.*

83 YOUR DEVICE *i.e. what is your masque about?*

But chief in the art of riding, late did please   90
To send his Albion forth, the most his own—
Upon discovery, to themselves best known—
Through Celtiberia; and to assist his course,
Gave him his powerful Manager of Horse,
With divine Proteus, father of disguise,   95
To wait upon them with his counsels wise
In all extremes. His great commands being done,
And he desirous to review his son,
He doth dispatch a floating isle from hence
Unto the Hesperian shores, to waft him thence   100
Where what the arts were used to make him stay,
And how the sirens wooed him by the way,
What monsters he encountered on the coast,
How near our general joy was to be lost,
Is not our subject now, though all these make   105
The present gladness greater for their sake;
But what the triumphs are, the feast, the sport,
And proud solemnities of Neptune's court
Now he is safe, and Fame's not heard in vain,
But we behold our happy pledge again;   110
That with him loyal Hippius is returned,
Who for it, under so much envy, burned
With his own brightness, till her starved snakes saw
What Neptune did impose to him was law.

90 CHIEF . . . RIDING *Neptune was the creator and tamer of the horse.*
90–7 LATE . . . EXTREMES N.
91 MOST . . . OWN *his dearest possession.*
92 UPON . . . KNOWN *most impressive, too, to the waters and isles when he was revealed to them.*
98 REVIEW *see again.*
100 HESPERIAN *Spanish.*
104 HOW . . . LOST *Charles was nearly drowned on the trip.*
113 HER . . . SNAKES *Envy's; the snakes are emblematic of her.*

Cook. But why not this till now?

115 *Poet.*   It was not time
          To mix this music with the vulgar's chime.
          Stay, till th'abortive and extemporal din
          Of balladry was understood a sin,
          Minerva cried; that what tumultuous verse
120   Or prose could make or steal, they might rehearse,
          And every songster had sung out his fit;
          That all the country and the city wit
          Of bells and bonfires and good cheer was spent,
          And Neptune's guard had drunk all that they meant;
125   That all the tales and stories now were old
          Of the sea monster Archy, or grown cold:
          The muses then might venture undeterred,
          For they love then to sing when they are heard.

Cook. I like it well, 'tis handsome, and I have
130   Something would fit this. How do you present 'em?
          In a fine island, say you?

 *Poet.   Yes, a Delos,
          Such as when fair Latona fell in travail,
          Great Neptune made emergent.

Cook.   I conceive you.
          I would have had your isle brought floating in now
135   In a brave broth and of a sprightly green,
          Just to the color of the sea, and then
          Some twenty sirens singing in the kettle,

115–28 IT WAS NOT TIME . . . HEARD N.

119 MINERVA *goddess of wisdom and inventor of musical instruments.*

123 BELLS, BONFIRES *popular means of celebrating the prince's return.*

126 ARCHY *the court dwarf (hence "monster") Archibald Armstrong, who had accompanied the prince.*

131–33 DELOS . . . EMERGENT N.

With an Arion mounted on the back
Of a grown conger, but in such a posture
As all the world should take him for a dolphin: 140
O, 'twould ha' made such music! Ha' you nothing
But a bare island?

Poet.   Yes, we have a tree too,
Which we do call the tree of harmony,

★ And is the same with what we read the sun
Brought forth in the Indian Musicana first,   145
And thus it grows: the goodly bole being got
To certain cubits height, from every side
The boughs decline, which taking root afresh,
Spring up new boles, and those spring new, and newer,
Till the whole tree become a porticus,   150
Or archèd arbor, able to receive
A numerous troop, such as our Albion
And the companions of his journey are;
And this they sit in.

Cook.   Your prime masquers?
Poet.   Yes.
Cook. But where's your antimasque now, all this while?   155
I hearken after them.

Poet.   Faith, we have none.
Cook. None?
Poet.   None, I assure you, neither do I think them
A worthy part of presentation,
Being things so heterogene to all device,
Mere by-works, and at best outlandish nothings.   160

138 ARION *legendary poet and musician whose singing so charmed a dolphin that it
saved him from drowning and carried him to land.*
139 CONGER *conger-eel.*
142–50 TREE . . . PORTICUS N.
159 HETEROGENE *incongruous.* DEVICE *true invention, inspiration.*
160 BY-WORKS *accessory presentations.*

Cook. O, you are all the heaven awry, sir!
　　　　For blood of poetry running in your veins,
　　　　Make not yourself so ignorantly simple.
　　　　Because, sir, you shall see I am a poet
165　　　No less than cook, and that I find you want
　　　　A special service here, an antimasque,
　　　　I'll fit you with a dish out of the kitchen
　　　　Such as I think will take the present palates,
　　　　A metaphorical dish! And do but mark
170　　　How a good wit may jump with you. Are you ready, child?
　　　　(Had there been masque or no masque, I had made it.)
　　　　Child of the boiling-house!　　　　　　　[*Enter child.*]
Child.　　　　　　　　　　Here, father.
Cook. Bring forth the pot. It is an *olla podrida*,
　　　　But I have persons to present the meats.
175　*Poet.* Persons!
Cook. Such as do relish nothing but *di stato*,
　　　　But in another fashion than you dream of,
　　　　Know all things the wrong way, talk of the affairs,
　　　　The clouds, the curtains and the mysteries
180　　　That are afoot, and from what hands they have 'em—
　　　　The Master of the Elephant or the Camels—
　　　　What correspondences are held, the posts
　　　　That go and come, and know almost their minutes,
　　　　All but their business: therein they are fishes,
185　　　But ha' their garlic, as the proverb says.
　　　　They are our quest of enquiry after news.

173　OLLA PODRIDA *stew.*
176　RELISH . . . STATO *enjoy nothing but gossip about affairs of state.*
178–80　AFFAIRS . . . AFOOT *the preparations for the masque.*
181　MASTER . . . CAMELS *fictitious court functionaries, parodying Buckingham's title Master of the Horse.*
184–85　THEREIN . . . GARLIC *They are as silent as fish about their own business, but their breath fills the air as the smell of garlic does.*
185　PROVERB N.

Poet. Together with their learnèd authors?

Child.   Yes, sir,
     And of the epicoene gender, hes and shes:
     Amphibion Archy is the chief.

Cook.   Good boy!
     The child is learnèd too: note but the kitchen!   190
     Have you put him into the pot for garlic?

Child. One in his coat shall stink as strong as he, sir,
     And his friend Giblets with him.

Cook.   They are two
     That give a part of the seasoning.

Poet.   I conceive
     The way of your gallimaufry.

Cook.   You will like it   195
     When they come pouring out of the pot together.

Child. O, if the pot had been big enough!

Cook.   What then, child?

Child. I had put in the elephant, and one camel
     At least, for beef.

Cook.   But whom ha' you for partridge?

Child. A brace of dwarfs, and delicate plump birds!   200

Cook. And whom for mutton and kid?

Child.   A fine laced mutton
     Or two, and either has her frisking husband
     That reads her the coranto every week.
     Grave Master Ambler, newsmaster of Paul's,
     Supplies your capon, and grown Captain Buz,   205

188 EPICOENE *bisexual.*

189 AMPHIBION ARCHY *Armstrong again (see line 126).*

191 HIM *Archy.*

195 GALLIMAUFRY *hash.*

201 LACED MUTTON *whore.*

203 CORANTO *newspaper.*

204 NEWSMASTER OF PAUL'S *retailer of gossip. Saint Paul's cathedral was notorious for its loungers, "amblers," and gossips.*

His emissary, underwrites for turkey;
A Gentleman of the Forest presents pheasant,
And a plump poult'rer's wife in Grace's Street
Plays hen with eggs i'the belly, or a cony,
Choose which you will.

210 *Cook.*   But where's the bacon, Tom?

Child. Hogrel the butcher and the sow his wife
Are both there.

Cook.   It is well; go dish 'em out.
Are they well boiled?

Child.   Podrida!

Poet.   What's that, rotten?

Cook. O, that they must be. There's one main ingredient
We have forgot, the artichoke.

215 *Child.*   No, sir.
I have a fruiterer with a cold red nose
Like a blue fig performs it.

Cook.   The fruit looks so.
Good child, go pour 'em out, show their concoction.
They must be rotten boiled—the broth's the best on't—
220 And that's the dance: the stage here is the charger.
And brother poet, though the serious part
Be yours, yet envy not the cook his art.

Poet. Not I. *Nam lusus ipse triumphus amat.*

The antimasque is danced by the persons described, coming out of the pot.

225 *Poet.* Well, now expect the scene itself; it opens!

207 GENTLEMAN . . . FOREST *officer in charge of a royal forest.*
208 GRACE'S STREET *for Gracechurch Street, or more popularly Grasse Street.* N.
209 CONY *rabbit, with an obscene pun.*
213 PODRIDA *rotten (Spanish).*
220 CHARGER *serving dish.*
223 NAM . . . AMAT *for even a triumph likes fun. (Martial, VIII.viii.10.)*

The island is discovered, the masquers sitting in their several sieges. The heavens opening; and Apollo, with Mercury, some muses and the goddess Harmony, make the music, the while the island moves forward, Proteus sitting below, and Apollo sings.

SONG 230

*Apollo.	Look forth, the shepherd of the seas,
	And of the ports that keep'st the keys,
	And to your Neptune tell
	His Albion, prince of all his isles,
	For whom the sea and land so smiles,
	Is home returnèd well.

235

Chorus.	And be it thought no common cause
	That to it so much wonder draws,
	And all the heav'ns consent
	With harmony to tune their notes,
	In answer to the public votes
	That for it up were sent.

240

It was no envious stepdame's rage,
Or tyrant's malice of the age
   That did employ him forth;
But such a wisdom that would prove,
By sending him, their hearts and love,
   That else might fear his worth.

245

By this time the island hath joined itself with the shore, and Proteus, Portunus and Saron come forth and go up singing to the state, while the masquers take time to land.

250

226 SIEGES *seats.*
231 SHEPHERD . . . SEAS *Proteus.*
232 THAT . . . KEYS *Portunus, god of ports.*
241 VOTES *prayers.*
250 SARON *god of navigation.* STATE *king's throne.*

SONG

Proteus.   Aye! now the pomp of Neptune's triumph shines!
          And all the glories of his great designs
255   Are read, reflected in his son's return!

Portunus. How all the eyes, the looks, the hearts here burn
          At his arrival!

Saron.   These are the true fires
          Are made of joys!

Proteus.   Of longings!

Portunus.   Of desires!

Saron.   Of hopes!

Proteus.   Of fears!

Portunus.   No intermitted blocks—

260 Saron.   But pure affections, and from odorous stocks!

Chorus.   'Tis incense all, that flames!
          And these materials scarce have names!

Proteus.   My king looks higher, as he scorned the wars
          Of winds, and with his trident touched the stars.
265   There is no wrinkle in his brow, or frown,
          But as his cares he would in nectar drown,
*   And all the silver-footed nymphs were dressed
          To wait upon him to the Ocean's feast.

Portunus. Or here in rows upon the banks were set,
270   And had their several hairs made into net
          To catch the youths in as they come on shore.

Saron.   How! Galatea sighing! O, no more.
          Banish your fears.

Portunus.   And Doris, dry your tears.
          Albion is come—

*Proteus.   And Haliclyon too,

263–66 AS . . . AS *as if . . . as if.*
274 HALICLYON "*renowned at sea*": *Buckingham again, this time allegorized in his office of Lord High Admiral.*

270

	That kept his side, as he was charged to do,	275
	With wonder—	
Saron.	And the sirens have him not—	
Portunus.	Though they no practice nor no arts forgot	
	That might have won him or by charm or song—	
Proteus.	Or laying forth their tresses all along	
	Upon the glassy waves—	
Portunus.	Then diving—	
Proteus.	Then	280
	Up with their heads, as they were mad of men—	
Saron.	And there the highest-going billows crown,	
	Until some lusty sea-god pulled them down.	
Chorus.	See! He is here!	
Proteus.	Great master of the main,	
	Receive thy dear and precious pawn again.	285
Chorus.	Saron, Portunus, Proteus, bring him thus,	
	Safe, as thy subjects' wishes gave him us;	
	And of thy glorious triumph let it be	
	No less a part that thou their loves dost see	
	Than that his sacred head's returned to thee.	290

This sung, the island goes back, whilst the upper Chorus takes it from
them, and the masquers prepare for their figure.

Chorus.	Spring all the graces of the age	
	And all the loves of time;	
	Bring all the pleasures of the stage	295
	And relishes of rhyme;	
	Add all the softnesses of courts,	
	The looks, the laughters and the sports,	
	And mingle all their sweets and salts	

281 OF *for.*
292 FIGURE *dance.*
299 SALTS *with a quibble on* "*leaps.*"

300   That none may say the triumph halts.

Here the masquers dance their entry.

Which done, the first prospective of a maritime palace, or the house of Oceanus, is discovered, with loud music. And the other above is no more seen.

305 *Poet.* Behold the palace of Oceanus!
          Hail, reverend structure! Boast no more to us
          Thy being able all the gods to feast;
          We have seen enough: our Albion was thy guest.

Then follows the main dance, after which the second prospect of the sea is
310   *shown, to the former music.*

 Poet. Now turn and view the wonders of the deep,
          Where Proteus' herds and Neptune's orcs do keep,
          Where all is plowed, yet still the pasture's green,
          The ways are found and yet no paths are seen.

315   *There Proteus, Portunus, Saron go up to the ladies with this song.*

 Proteus. Come, noble nymphs, and do not hide
          The joys for which you so provide.
 Saron. If not to mingle with the men,
          What do you here? Go home again.
320 *Portunus.*   Your dressings do confess
          By what we see, so curious parts
          Of Pallas' and Arachne's arts,
            That you could mean no less.
 Proteus. Why do you wear the silkworm's toils,
325   Or glory in the shellfish spoils,
          Or strive to show the grains of ore

302 PROSPECTIVE *perspective scene.*
322 PALLAS, ARACHNE *both superlative weavers; Arachne became the spider.*

That you have gathered on the shore
    Whereof to make a stock
To graft the greener emerald on,
Or any better-watered stone?   330

Saron.   Or ruby of the rock?
Proteus. Why do you smell of ambergris,
Of which was formèd Neptune's niece,
The queen of love, unless you can,
Like sea-born Venus, love a man?   335

Saron.   Try, put yourselves unto't.
Chorus. Your looks, your smiles and thoughts that meet,
Ambrosian hands and silver feet,
    Do promise you will do't.

The revels follow. Which ended, the fleet is discovered, while the three 340
cornets play.

Poet. 'Tis time your eyes should be refreshed at length
    With something new, a part of Neptune's strength.
    See, yond' his fleet, ready to go or come,
    Or fetch the riches of the ocean home,   345
    So to secure him both in peace and wars,
    Till not one ship alone, but all be stars.

    A shout within follows, after which the cook enters.

Cook. I have another service for you, brother poet, a dish of pickled
    sailors, fine salt sea-boys, shall relish like anchovies or caviar, 350
    to draw down a cup of nectar in the skirts of a night.
Sailors. Come away, boys, the town is ours. Hey for Neptune and
    our young master!
Poet. He knows the compass and the card,
    While Castor sits on the main yard,   355

351 SKIRTS *end.*
354 CARD *map.*
355–56 CASTOR, POLLUX *guardians of travelers at sea.*

273

And Pollux too, to help your hales,
And bright Leucothe fills your sails;
Arion sings, the dolphins swim,
And all the way to gaze on him.

360 *The antimasque of sailors. Then the last song to the whole music: five*
lutes, three cornets and ten voices.

SONG

Proteus.   Although we wish the triumph still might last
For such a prince and his discovery past,
365   Yet now, great lord of waters and of isles,
Give Proteus leave to turn unto his wiles.

Portunus. And whilst young Albion doth thy labors ease,
Dispatch Portunus to thy ports—

Saron.   And Saron to thy seas,
To meet old Nereus with his fifty girls,
370   From agèd Indus laden home with pearls,
And orient gums to burn unto thy name.

Chorus. And may thy subjects' hearts be all one flame,
Whilst thou dost keep the earth in firm estate,
And 'mongst the winds dost suffer no debate.
375   But both at sea and land our powers increase,
With health and all the golden gifts of peace.

The last dance.

The End.

372 one] on Q, F (*cf.* Fortunate Isles, *line 439*).

356 HALES *hauls.*
357 LEUCOTHE *or Ino, sea-goddess who rescued Odysseus when his raft foundered.*
358 ARION *see line 138.*
369 NEREUS *a sea god, father of the fifty Nereids, or sea nymphs.*

The Fortunate Isles, and Their Union

Celebrated in a masque designed for the court
on the Twelfth-night, 1625.

Hic choreae, cantusque vigent.

His majesty being set, entereth in running Johphiel, an airy spirit and
(according to the Magi) the intelligence of Jupiter's sphere, attired in
light silks of several colors, with wings of the same, a bright yellow hair, a
chaplet of flowers, blue silk stockings, and pumps, and gloves, with a silver
fan in his hand. 5

Johphiel. Like a lightning from the sky,
     Or an arrow shot by Love,
Or a bird of his let fly,
     Be't a sparrow or a dove,
With that wingèd haste come I,   10
     Loosèd from the sphere of Jove,
       To wish goodnight
       To your delight.

To him enters a melancholic student in bare and worn clothes, shrouded

Title DESIGNED . . . TWELFTH-NIGHT N.
Epigraph HIC . . . VIGENT *Here dances and songs flourish. (Tibullus, I.iii.59.)*
  2 INTELLIGENCE *the angel who directed the sphere of a heavenly body.*

15 *under an obscure cloak and the eaves of an old hat, fetching a deep sigh,*
his name Master Merefool.

Merefool. Oh, oh!

Johphiel. In Saturn's name, the father of my lord,
What overchargèd piece of melancholy
20 Is this breaks in between my wishes thus
With bombing sighs?

Merefool. No! no intelligence!
Not yet! and all my vows now nine days old!
Blindness of fate! Puppies had seen by this time;
But I see nothing that I should or would see!
25 What mean the brethren of the Rosy Cross
So to desert their votary!

Johphiel. O! 'tis one
Hath vowed himself unto that airy order,
And now is gaping for the fly they promised him.
I'll mix a little with him for my sport.

30 *Merefool.* Have I both in my lodging and my diet,
My clothes, and every other solemn charge,
Observed 'em! made the naked boards my bed!
A faggot for my pillow! hungered sore!

Johphiel. And thirsted after 'em—

Merefool. To look gaunt and lean!

Johphiel. Which will not be.

35 *Merefool.* Who's that?—Yes, and outwatched,
Yea, and outwalked any ghost alive
In solitary circle, worn my boots,

25 BRETHREN ... CROSS *Rosicrucians, a German secret society claiming mystical*
knowledge and power.
28 FLY *familiar spirit.*
33 FAGGOT *bundle of sticks.*
34–5 THIRSTED ... BE *i.e. longed for those who will not appear.*

        Knees, arms and elbows out!

Johphiel.   Ran on the score!

Merefool. That have I—who suggests that?—and for more

        Than I will speak of, to abate this flesh,   40

        And have not gained the sight—

Johphiel.   Nay, scarce the sense—

Merefool. Voice, thou art right—of anything but a cold

        Wind in my stomach—

Johphiel.   And a kind of whimsy—

Merefool. Here in my head, that puts me to the staggers,

        Whether there be that brotherhood or no.   45

Johphiel. Believe, frail man, they be, and thou shalt see.

Merefool. What shall I see?

Johphiel.   Me.

Merefool.   Thee? Where?

Johphiel.   Here. If you

        Be Master Merefool.

Merefool.   Sir, our name is Merryfool,

        But by contraction Merefool.

Johphiel.   Then are you

        The wight I seek; and, sir, my name is Johphiel,   50

        Intelligence to the sphere of Jupiter,

        An airy jocular spirit, employed to you

        From father *Outis*.

Merefool.   *Outis*? Who is he?

Johphiel. Know ye not *Outis*? Then you know nobody:

        The good old hermit that was said to dwell   55

        Here in the forest without trees, that built

        The castle in the air where all the brethren

38 ON . . . SCORE *for that reason.*

43 WHIMSY *dizziness.*

53 OUTIS *literally, "nobody," the name adopted by Odysseus with the Cyclops.*

57–60 CASTLE . . . BLADE N.

Rhodostaurotic live. It flies with wings
And runs on wheels, where Julian de Campis
Holds out the brandished blade.

60 *Merefool.*   Is't possible
They think on me?

Johphiel.   Rise, be not lost in wonder,
But hear me and be faithful. All the brethren
Have heard your vows, salute you, and expect you,
By me, this next return. But the good father
Has been content to die for you.

65 *Merefool.*   For me?

Johphiel. For you. Last New Year's day, which some give out,
Because it was his birthday, and began
The year of jubile, he would rest upon it,
Being his hundred five and twentieth year;
70 But the truth is, having observed your genesis,
He would not live because he might leave all
He had to you.

Merefool.   What had he?

Johphiel.   Had? An office,
Two, three or four.

Merefool.   Where?

Johphiel.   In the upper region,
And that you'll find: the farm of the great customs
75 Through all the ports of the air's intelligences;
Then constable of the Castle Rosy Cross,
Which you must be, and keeper of the keys
Of the whole cabal, with the seals; you shall be.

58 RHODOSTAUROTIC *Rosicrucian* (literally, "*of the rosy cross*").
59 JULIAN DE CAMPIS *pseudonym of Julius Sperber* (*d. 1616*), *Rosicrucian writer.*
68 JUBILE *jubilee.* N.
74–5 FARM *payment.* CUSTOMS . . . INTELLIGENCES *i.e. he was the customs collector of the upper regions.*

Principal secretary to the stars,
Know all their signatures and combinations,   80
The divine rods and consecrated roots—
What not? Would you turn trees up like the wind
To show your strength? march over heads of armies,
Or points of pikes, to show your lightness? force
All doors of arts with the petar of your wit?   85
Read at one view all books? speak all the languages
Of several creatures? master all the learnings
Were, are or shall be? or, to show your wealth,
Open all treasures hid by nature, from
The rock of diamond to the mine of sea-coal?   90
Sir, you shall do it.

Merefool.   But how?

Johphiel.   Why, by his skill
Of which he has left you the inheritance
Here in a pot: this little gallipot
Of tincture, high rose tincture. There's your order;
                    (*He gives him a rose.*)   95
You will ha' your collar sent you ere't be long.

Merefool. I looked, sir, for a halter; I was desperate.

Johphiel. Reach forth your hand.

Merefool.   O sir, a broken sleeve
Keeps the arm back, as 'tis i' the proverb.

Johphiel.   Nay,

95 S.D.] F *om.*

_____

80 SIGNATURES *distinctive marks.*
81 DIVINE RODS *magic wands.*
85 PETAR *petard, explosive engine.*
93 GALLIPOT *ointment pot.*
98 BROKEN *worn at the elbow.*
99 PROVERB N.

100   For that I do commend you; you must be poor
        With all your wealth and learning. When you ha' made
        Your glasses, gardens in the depth of winter,
        Where you will walk invisible to mankind,
        Talked with all birds and beasts in their own language;
105   When you have penetrated hills like air,
        Dived to the bottom of the sea like lead,
        And ris' again like cork, walked in the fire
        As 'twere a salamander, passed through all
        The winding orbs, like an intelligence,
110   Up to the Empyreum; when you have made
        The world your gallery, can dispatch a business
        In some three minutes with the Antipodes,
        And in five more negotiate the globe over,
        You must be poor still.

Merefool.   By my place, I know it.

115 *Johphiel.* Where would you wish to be now, or what to see,
        Without the fortunate purse to bear your charges,
        Or wishing hat? I will but touch your temples,
        The corners of your eyes, and tinct the tip,
        The very tip o' your nose with this collyrium,
120   And you shall see i' the air all the ideas,
        Spirits and atoms, flies that buzz about
        This way and that way, and are rather admirable
        Than any way intelligible.

Merefool.   O come, tinct me,
        Tinct me! I long (save this great belly!), I long!
        But shall I only see?

125 *Johphiel.*   See and command,

116 FORTUNATE PURSE *magic purse that was never empty.*
119 COLLYRIUM *salve.*
122 ADMIRABLE *to be wondered at (not understood).*
124 SAVE . . . BELLY *i.e. my craving is as strong as that of a pregnant woman.*

As they were all your valets or your foot-boys.
But first you must declare—your greatness must,
For that is now your style—what you would see,
Or whom.

Merefool.   Is that my style? My greatness, then,
 Would see King Zoroastres.

Johphiel.   Why, you shall;   130
 Or anyone beside. Think whom you please,
 Your thousand, your ten thousand, to a million;
 All's one to me, if you could name a myriad.

Merefool. I have named him.

Johphiel.   You've reason.

Merefool.   Aye, I have reason;
 Because he's said to be the father of conjurers, 135
 And a cunning man i' the stars.

Johphiel.   Aye, that's it troubles us
 A little for the present; for at this time
 He is confuting a French almanac,
 But he will straight have done. Ha' you but patience;
 Or think but any other in meantime,   140
 Any hard name.

Merefool.   Then Hermes Trismegistus.

---

126 valets] varlets F.

---

126 AS *as if.*
128 STYLE *title.*
130 ZOROASTRES *Zoroaster, or Zarathustra (6th century* B.C.)*, Persian sage, founder of the Magian (or Zoroastrian) religion.*
138 CONFUTING *refuting.*
141 HERMES TRISMEGISTUS *"thrice greatest Hermes," Greek name for Thoth, the Egyptian god of wisdom and supposed author of numerous mystical (hence "hermetic") works.*

Johphiel. O, *ho Trismegistos*? Why, you shall see him;
        A fine hard name. Or him, or whom you will,
        As I said to you afore. Or what do you think
        Of Howleglass instead of him?

145 *Merefool.*   No, him
        I have a mind to.

Johphiel.   O, but Ulen-spiegle
        Were such a name! but you shall have your longing.
        What luck is this, he should be busy too!
        He is weighing water but to fill three hourglasses,
150   And mark the day in penn'orths like a cheese,
        And he has done. 'Tis strange you should name him
        Of all the rest! there being Iamblichus,
        Or Porphyry, or Proclus, any name
        That is not busy.

Merefool.   Let me see Pythagoras.
Johphiel. Good.
Merefool.   Or Plato.

155 *Johphiel.*   Plato is framing some ideas
        Are now bespoken at a groat a dozen,
        Three gross at least; and for Pythagoras,
        He's rashly run himself on an employment
        Of keeping asses from a field of beans,
        And cannot be staved off.

160 *Merefool.*   Then Archimedes.

---

145 HOWLEGLASS *Till Eulenspiegel, medieval German folk-hero.*
150 PENN'ORTHS *pennyworths, small portions.*
152 IAMBLICHUS *4th-century Syrian neo-Platonic philosopher.*
153 PORPHYRY *Porphyrius, 3rd-century neo-Platonist, pupil of Plotinus.* PROCLUS
    5th-century neo-Platonist.
156 GROAT *four pence.*
159 BEANS *Pythagoras is said to have refused to eat beans.*

Johphiel. Yes, Archimedes!

Merefool.   Aye, or Aesop.

Johphiel.   Nay,
            Hold your first man, a good man, Archimedes,
            And worthy to be seen; but he is now
            Inventing a rare mousetrap with owls' wings
            And a cat's foot, to catch the mice alone;   165
            And Aesop, he is filing a fox tongue
            For a new fable he has made of court.
            But you shall see 'em all, stay but your time
            And ask in season; things asked out of season
            A man denies himself. At such a time   170
            As Christmas, when disguising is afoot,
            To ask of the inventions and the men,
            The wits and the engines that move those orbs!
            Methinks you should inquire now after Skelton,
            Or Master Scogan.

Merefool.   Scogan? what was he?   175

Johphiel. O, a fine gentleman and a Master of Arts
            Of Henry the Fourth's times, that made disguises
            For the king's sons, and writ in ballad-royal
            Daintily well.

Merefool.   But wrote he like a gentleman?

Johphiel. In rhyme! fine tinkling rhyme! and flowand verse!   180
            With now and then some sense! and he was paid for it,
            Regarded and rewarded, which few poets
            Are nowadays.

Merefool.   And why?

Johphiel.   'Cause every dabbler

---

166 FILING . . . TONGUE *A filed tongue was the proverbial property of the satirist.*
175 SCOGAN *Henry Scogan (1361?–1407), poet and friend of Chaucer's.* N.
180 FLOWAND *flowing, a fake archaism.*

         In rhyme is thought the same. But you shall see him.
         Hold up your nose.   [*Anoints him.*]

185 *Merefool.*   I had rather see a Brachman,
         Or a Gymnosophist yet.

Johphiel.   You shall see him, sir,
         Is worth them both. And with him Domine Skelton,
         The worshipful Poet Laureate to King Harry,
         And *Tityre tu* of those times. Advance, quick Scogan,
190   And quicker Skelton, show your crafty heads
         Before this heir of arts, this lord of learning,
         This master of all knowledge in reversion!

         Enter Scogan and Skelton, in like habits as they lived.

Scogan. Seemeth we are called of a moral intent,
195   If the words that are spoken as well now be meant.
Johphiel. That, Master Scogan, I dare you ensure.
Scogan. Then, son, our acquaintance is like to endure.
Merefool. A pretty game! like crambo. Master Scogan,
         Give me thy hand. Thou'rt very lean, methinks.
         Is't living by thy wits?
200 *Scogan.*   If it had been that,
         My worshipful son, thou hadst ne'er been so fat.

---

185 BRACHMAN *Brahman.*

186 GYMNOSOPHIST *member of an ancient sect of Indian philosophers.*

187 IS *who is.* SKELTON *John Skelton (1460–1529).*

188 KING HARRY *Henry VIII. Skelton was not in fact the king's laureate, but held the degree of Poet Laureate from Oxford.*

189 TITYRE TU *"One of an association of well-to-do roughs who infested London streets in the 17th c." (OED)* N. QUICK *living.*

190 CRAFTY *clever.*

192 MASTER . . . REVERSION *i.e. master-to-be.*

193 IN . . . HABITS *dressed.*

198 CRAMBO *a rhyming game.*

Johphiel. He tells you true, sir. Here's a gentleman,
       My pair of crafty clerks, of that high caract,
       As hardly hath the age produced his like;
       Who not content with the wit of his own times,   205
       Is curious to know yours, and what hath been—
Merefool. Or is, or shall be.
Johphiel.   Note his latitude!
Skelton.   O, *vir amplissimus,*
         (*Ut scholis dicimus*)
         Et gentilissimus!   210
Johphiel.   The questionissimus
       Is, should he ask a sight now for his life,
       I mean a person he would have restored
       To memory of these times, for a playfellow,
       Whether you would present him with an Hermes   215
       Or with an Howleglass.
Skelton.   An Howleglass
       To come to pass
       On his father's ass;
       There never was   220
       By day nor night
       A finer sight,
       With feathers upright
       In his horned cap,
       And crooked shape,   225
       Much like an ape,
       With owl on fist
       And glass at his wrist.

---

203 CARACT (*1*) *value* (*cf*. carat). (*2*) *character.*
208–10 O . . . GENTILISSIMUS "*O most great* (*as we say in the schools* [*i.e. in Latin*])
    and noble man." Amplissimus *means both very honorable and very fat.*

Scogan. Except the four knaves entertained for the guards

230   Of the kings and the queens that triumph in the cards.

Johphiel. Aye, that were a sight and a half, I confess,

           To see 'em come skipping in, all at a mess!

Skelton.   With Elinor Rumming

           To make up the mumming,

235   That comely Jill

           That dwelt on a hill,

           But she is not grill,

           Her face all bowsy,

           Droopy and drowsy,

240   Scurvy and lousy,

           Comely crinkled,

           Wonderly wrinkled,

           Like a roast pig's ear

           Bristled with hair.

245 *Scogan.* Or what do you say to Ruffian Fitz-Ale?

Johphiel. An excellent sight, if he be not too stale.

           But then we can mix him with modern vapors,

           The child of tobacco, his pipes and his papers.

Merefool. You talked of Elinor Rumming; I had rather

250   See Ellen of Troy.

---

242 Wonderly] *Skelton's original text*; wondersly Q; wondrously F.

---

229 THE . . . KNAVES N. KNAVES *jacks.*

230 TRIUMPH *trump.*

232 MESS *group of four.*

233 ELINOR RUMMING *heroine of Skelton's* The Tunning of Elinour Rumming.

235–44 THAT . . . HAIR *adapted from* The Tunning, *lines 1–6, 15–24.*

237 GRILL *fierce.*

238 BOWSY *boozy.*

245 RUFFIAN FITZ-ALE *Scogan invents a male version of the alewife Elinor.*

246 STALE (1) *old (of people).* (2) *strong (of beer).*

Johphiel.	Her you shall see.
	But credit me
	That Mary Ambree
	(Who marched so free
	To the siege of Gaunt, 255
	And death could not daunt,
	As the ballad doth vaunt)
	Were a braver wight
	And a better sight.
Skelton.	Or Westminster Meg, 260
	With her long leg,
	As long as a crane,
	And feet like a plane;
	With a pair of heels
	As broad as two wheels 265
	To drive down the dew
	As she goes to the stew,
	And turns home merry
	By Lambeth Ferry.
	Or you may have come 270
	In, Thomas Thumb,
	In a pudding fat
	With Doctor Rat.

253 MARY AMBREE *a ballad heroine.*

255 GAUNT *Ghent.*

257 BALLAD *in* Percy's Reliques, *beginning,* "*When captains courageous, whom death could not daunt . . .*"

260 WESTMINSTER MEG *Long Meg of Westminster, a real person and London folk-heroine.*

262–66 AS . . . DEW *adapted from Skelton,* The Tunning, *lines 49–50, 80–4.*

267 STEW *stews.*

269 LAMBETH FERRY N.

273 DOCTOR RAT *a character in* Gammer Gurton's Needle.

Johphiel.	Aye, that! that! that!
275	We'll have 'em all
	To fill the hall!

The antimasque follows, consisting of these twelve persons: Howleglass,
the four knaves, two ruffians (Fitz-Ale and Vapor), Elinor Rumming,
Mary Ambree, Long Meg of Westminster, Tom Thumb and Doctor Rat.
280 *Which done,*

Merefool. What, are they vanished! Where is skipping Skelton?
Or moral Scogan? I do like their show
And would have thanked 'em, being the first grace
The company of the Rosy Cross hath done me.
285 *Johphiel.* The company o' the Rosy Cross, you widgeon!
The company of players! Go, you are
And will be still yourself, a Merefool. In,
And take your pot of honey here, and hog's grease;
See who has gulled you, and make one.
Great king,
290 Your pardon, if desire to please have trespassed.
This fool should have been sent to Anticyra,
The isle of ellebore, there to have purged,
Not hoped a happy seat within your waters.
Hear now the message of the fates and Jove,
295 On whom those fates depend, to you as Neptune,
The great commander of the seas and isles.

285 WIDGEON *wild duck, supposedly a stupid bird; hence, a gull or fool.*
286 COMPANY . . . PLAYERS *i.e. professional actors, as opposed to the courtiers who*
danced in the main masque.
288 HONEY, HOG'S GREASE *used in cooking ducks (or gulls, or widgeons).*
289 MAKE ONE *be one yourself.* GREAT KING *addressed to James.*
291 ANTICYRA *a Greek town (not an island) known for its medicinal Hellebore,*
which was used in treating mental disorders.

That point of revolution being come
When all the Fortunate Islands should be joined,
Macaria, one, and thought a principal,
That hitherto hath floated as uncertain   300
Where she should fix her blessings, is tonight
Instructed to adhere to your Britannia;
That where the happy spirits live, hereafter
Might be no question made by the most curious,
Since the *Macarii* come to do you homage   305
And join their cradle to your continent.

Here the scene opens and the masquers are discovered sitting in their several sieges. The air opens above, and Apollo with Harmony and the spirits of music sing, the while the island moves forward, Proteus sitting below and hearkening.   310

SONG

Look forth the shepherd of the seas,
And of the ports that keep'st the keys,
    And to your Neptune tell,
Macaria, prince of all the isles,   315
Wherein there nothing grows but smiles,
    Doth here put in to dwell.
The winds are sweet and gently blow;
But Zephyrus, no breath they know,
    The father of the flowers;   320

298 FORTUNATE ISLANDS *in classical mythology, islands west of the Pillars of Hercules, where the souls of the blessed were sent after death. English writers often identified them with Britain.* N.
299 MACARIA *blessed (from Greek).*
308 SIEGES *seats.*
309 PROTEUS *"the shepherd of the seas."*
313 THAT . . . KEYS *Portunus, god of ports.*
319 ZEPHYRUS *the west wind.*

> By him the virgin violets live,
> And every plant doth odors give
> As new as are the hours.

Chorus.   Then think it not a common cause
325   That to it so much wonder draws,
> And all the heavens consent
> With harmony to tune their notes,
> In answer to the public votes
> That for it up were sent.

330 *By this time the island having joined itself to the shore, Proteus, Portunus*
and Saron come forth and go up singing to the state, while the masquers
take time to rank themselves.

SONG

Proteus.   Aye, now the heights of Neptune's honors shine,
335   And all the glories of his greater style
> Are read, reflected in this happiest isle.

Portunus. How both the air, the soil, the seat combine
> To speak it blessèd!

Saron.   These are the true groves
> Where joys are born—

Proteus.   Where longings—

Portunus.   And where loves!

Saron.   That live!

Proteus.   That last!

340 Portunus.   No intermitted wind
> Blows here, but what leaves flowers or fruit behind.

Chorus.   'Tis odor all that comes!
> And every tree doth give his gums.

328 VOTES *prayers.*
331 SARON *god of navigation.* STATE *king's throne.*
340 INTERMITTED *intromitted, allowed to enter.*

Proteus.   There is no sickness, nor no old age known
           To man, nor any grief that he dares own.   345
           There is no hunger there, nor envy of state,
           Nor least ambition in the magistrate;
           But all are even-hearted, open, free,
           And what one is, another strives to be.

Portunus. Here all the day they feast, they sport and spring;   350
           Now dance the Graces' hay, now Venus' ring,
           To which the old musicians play and sing.

Saron.   There is Arion, tuning his bold harp
              From flat to sharp.

Portunus.   And light Anacreon,
           He still is one!

Proteus.   Stesichorus there too,   355
           That Linus and old Orpheus doth outdo
           To wonder.

Saron.   And Amphion, he is there.

Portunus. Nor is Apollo dainty to appear
           In such a choir; although the trees be thick,

Proteus.   He will look in and see the airs be quick,   360
           And that the times be true.

Portunus.   Then chanting—

Proteus.   Then,
           Up with their notes they raise the prince of men,

---

351 HAY *a country dance.*
353 ARION *legendary poet and musician associated with the sea.*
354 ANACREON *Greek lyric poet (6th century* B.C.)
355 STESICHORUS *Sicilian lyric poet (7th century* B.C.)
356 LINUS *mythical poet and son of Apollo.*
357 AMPHION *musician and son of Zeus, whose lyre moved stones and built the walls of Thebes.*
358 DAINTY *too fastidious.*
360, 361 AIRS, TIMES *with musical puns.*

Saron. And sing the present prophecy that goes
    Of joining the bright lily and the rose.
Chorus. See! all the flow'rs—
365 Proteus.   That spring the banks along
    Do move their heads unto that under-song.
Chorus. Saron, Portunus, Proteus, help to bring
    Our primrose in, the glory of the spring!
    And tell the daffodil, against that day,
370   That we prepare new garlands fresh as May,
    And interweave the myrtle and the bay.

This sung, the island goes back, whilst the upper chorus takes it from them,
and the masquers prepare for their figure.

Chorus. Spring all the graces of the age,
375   And all the loves of time;
    Bring all the pleasures of the stage,
     And relishes of rhyme;
    Add all the softnesses of courts,
     The looks, the laughters and the sports;
380   And mingle all their sweets and salts,
     That none may say the triumph halts.

The masquers dance their entry or first dance. Which done, the first
prospective, a maritime palace, or the house of Oceanus, is discovered to
loud music. The other above is no more seen.

385 Johphiel. Behold the palace of Oceanus!
    Hail, reverend structure! Boast no more to us

---

364 LILY, ROSE *the projected marriage of Princess Henrietta Maria, daughter of*
 Henri IV of France, and Prince Charles.
369 AGAINST *in anticipation of.*
371 MYRTLE *sacred to Venus, and emblematic of love.* BAY *laurel, the crown of poetry.*
373 FIGURE *dance.*
380 SALTS *with a quibble on "leaps."*
383 PROSPECTIVE *perspective scene.*

Thy being able all the gods to feast;
We saw enough when Albion was thy guest.

The measures.

After which the second prospective, a sea, is shown, to the former music. 390

Johphiel. Now turn and view the wonders of the deep,
Where Proteus' herds and Neptune's orcs do keep,
Where all is plowed, yet still the pasture's green;
New ways are found, and yet no paths are seen.

Here Proteus, Portunus, Saron go up to the ladies with this song. 395

Proteus. Come, noble nymphs, and do not hide
The joys for which you so provide.
Saron. If not to mingle with the men,
What do you here? Go home again.
Portunus. Your dressings do confess 400
By what we see, so curious parts
Of Pallas' and Arachne's arts,
That you could mean no less.
Proteus. Why do you wear the silkworm's toils,
Or glory in the shellfish spoils, 405
Or strive to show the grains of ore
That you have gathered on the shore,
Whereof to make a stock
To graft the greener emerald on,
Or any better-watered stone— 410
Saron. Or ruby of the rock?
Proteus. Why do you smell of ambergris,
Of which was formèd Neptune's niece,

388 ALBION *England, and Jonson's name for Prince Charles in* Neptune's Triumph.
N.
389 MEASURES *slow dances.*
402 PALLAS, ARACHNE *both superlative weavers;* Arachne *became the spider.*

       The queen of love, unless you can,

415   Like sea-born Venus, love a man?

Saron.   Try, put yourselves unto't.

Chorus. Your looks, your smiles and thoughts that meet,

       Ambrosian hands and silver feet,

          Do promise you will do't.

420   *The revels follow.*

Which ended, the fleet is discovered, while the three cornets play.

Johphiel. 'Tis time your eyes should be refreshed at length

       With something new, a part of Neptune's strength;

       See yond' his fleet ready to go or come,

425   Or fetch the riches of the Ocean home,

       So to secure him both in peace and wars,

       Till not one ship alone, but all be stars.

              Then the last song.

Proteus. Although we wish the glory still might last

430   Of such a night, and for the causes past,

       Yet now, great lord of waters and of isles,

       Give Proteus leave to turn unto his wiles.

Portunus. And whilst young Albion doth thy labors ease,

       Dispatch Portunus to thy ports—

435 *Saron.*   And Saron to thy seas,

       To meet old Nereus with his fifty girls,

       From agèd Indus laden home with pearls,

       And orient gums to burn unto thy name.

Chorus. And may thy subjects' hearts be all one flame,

440   Whilst thou dost keep the earth in firm estate,

---

439 one] *so* Q; on F.

---

436 NEREUS *a sea god, father of the fifty Nereids, or sea nymphs.*

And 'mongst the winds dost suffer no debate,
But both at sea and land our powers increase,
With health and all the golden gifts of peace.

After which, their last dance.

The End.

Love's Triumph Through Callipolis

Performed in a masque at court, 1631, by his majesty, with the lords
and gentlemen assisting.
The inventors:
Ben Jonson, Inigo Jones.

Quando magis dignos licuit spectare triumphos?

To Make the Spectators Understanders.

Whereas all representations, especially those of this nature in
court, public spectacles, either have been or ought to be the
mirrors of man's life, whose ends, for the excellence of their
5   exhibitors (as being the donatives of great princes to their people)
ought always to carry a mixture of profit with them no less than
delight; we, the inventors, being commanded from the king to
think on some thing worthy of his majesty's putting in act, with a
selected company of his lords and gentlemen called to the assist-
10   ance, for the honor of his court and the dignity of that heroic love
and regal respect borne by him to his unmatchable lady and
spouse, the queen's majesty, after some debate of cogitation with
ourselves, resolved on the following argument.

Epigraph QUANDO . . . TRIUMPHOS *When could one behold more worthy triumphs?*
    (*Martial, V.xix.3.*)
  5 DONATIVES *gifts.*

First, that a person *boni ominis*, of a good character, as Euphemus, sent down from heaven to Callipolis, which is understood the city 15 of beauty or goodness, should come in; and finding her majesty there enthroned, declare unto her that Love, who was wont to be respected as a special deity in court, and tutelar god of the place, had of late received an advertisement that in the suburbs or skirts of Callipolis were crept in certain sectaries, or depraved lovers, 20 who neither knew the name or nature of Love rightly, yet boasted themselves his followers, when they were fitter to be called his furies, their whole life being a continued vertigo, or rather a torture on the wheel of love, than any motion either of order or measure. When suddenly they leap forth below, a mistress leading 25 them, and with antic gesticulation and action after the manner of the old *pantomimi*, they dance over a distracted comedy of love, expressing their confused affections in the scenical persons and habits of the four prime European nations:

A glorious boasting lover 30
A whining ballading lover
An adventurous romance lover

A fantastic umbrageous lover
A bribing corrupt lover
A froward jealous lover 35

A sordid illiberal lover
A proud scornful lover
An angry quarreling lover

A melancholic despairing lover
An envious unquiet lover 40
A sensual brute lover

14 BONI OMINIS, EUPHEMUS *Both mean literally "of good omen."*
20 SECTARIES *heretics.*
27 PANTOMIMI *Roman mimes.*
28 AFFECTIONS *passions.*
33 UMBRAGEOUS *easily offended.*

All which, in varied, intricate turns and involved mazes expressed,
make the antimasque, and conclude the exit in a circle.

Euphemus descends singing.

45   Joy, joy to mortals, the rejoicing fires
        Of gladness smile in your dilated hearts!
    Whilst Love presents a world of chaste desires,
        Which may produce a harmony of parts.

    Love is the right affection of the mind,
50   The noble appetite of what is best,
    Desire of union with the thing designed,
        But in fruition of it cannot rest.

    The father Plenty is, the mother Want;   *Porus and*
        Plenty the beauty, which it wanteth, draws;   *Penia.*
55   Want yields itself, affording what is scant.
        So both affections are the union's cause.

    But rest not here. For Love hath larger scopes,
        New joys, new pleasures of as fresh a date
    As are his minutes, and in him no hopes
60   Are pure but those he can perpetuate.

    To you that are by excellence a queen,   *He goes up to*
        The top of beauty! but of such an air   *the state.*
    As only by the mind's eye may be seen
        Your interwoven lines of good and fair;

65   Vouchsafe to grace Love's triumph here tonight
        Through all the streets of your Callipolis,
    Which by the splendor of your rays made bright,
        The seat and region of all beauty is.

53 PLENTY, WANT *given in Greek in Jonson's gloss,* Porus *and* Penia. *The explana-*
    tion of the birth of Love alludes to Plato's Symposium *203 b–e, though it*
    does not really follow it.
54 WANTETH *lacks.*
61 In STATE *the queen's throne.*

Love in perfection longeth to appear,
 But prays of favor he be not called on   70
Till all the suburbs and the skirts be clear
 Of perturbations, and th'infection gone.

Then will he flow forth like a rich perfume
 Into your nostrils, or some sweeter sound
Of melting music, that shall not consume   75
 Within the ear, but run the mazes round.

 Here the chorus walk about with their censers.

Chorus. Meantime, we make lustration of the place,
  And with our solemn fires and waters prove
 T' have frighted hence the weak diseasèd race 80
  Of those were tortured on the wheel of love:

 The glorious, whining, the adventurous fool,
  Fantastic, bribing, and the jealous ass,
 The sordid, scornful, and the angry mule,
  The melancholic, dull and envious mass,   85

 With all the rest that in the sensual school
  Of lust for their degree of brute may pass.
   All which are vapored hence; *The prospect of*
              a sea appears.
   No loves, but slaves to sense,
   Mere cattle, and not men.   90
  Sound, sound, and treble all our joys again,
 Who had the power and virtue to remove
 Such monsters from the labyrinth of love.

The triumph is first seen afar off, and led in by Amphitrite, the wife of
Oceanus, with four sea gods attending her: Nereus, Proteus, Glaucus, 95

70 OF FAVOR *by your grace.*
71 SKIRTS *outskirts.*
75 CONSUME *be consumed.*
78 LUSTRATION *purification.*
81 WERE *who were.*
95 OCEANUS *Jonson's error for Neptune.*

Palaemon. It consisteth of fifteen lovers and as many Cupids, who rank themselves seven and seven on a side, with each a Cupid before him with a lighted torch, and the middle person (which is his majesty) placed in the center.

100	1 *The provident*		2 *The judicious*	
	3 *The secret*		4 *The valiant*	
	5 *The witty*		6 *The jovial*	
	7 *The secure*	15 *The heroical*	8 *The substantial*	
	9 *The modest*		10 *The candid*	
105	11 *The courteous*		12 *The elegant*	
	13 *The rational*		14 *The magnificent*	

Amphitrite.	Here stay a while; this, this	
	The temple of all beauty is!	
	Here, perfect lovers, you must pay	
110	First fruits, and on these altars lay	
	(The ladies' breasts) your ample vows	
	Such as Love brings, and beauty best allows.	
Chorus.	For Love without his object soon is gone;	
	Love must have answering love to look upon.	
115 *Amphitrite.*	To you, best judge, then, of perfection!	
Euphemus.	The queen of what is wonder in the place!	
Amphitrite.	Pure object of heroic love alone!	
Euphemus.	The center of proportion—	
Amphitrite.		Sweetness—
Euphemus.		Grace!
Amphitrite.	Deign to receive all lines of love in one.	
120 *Euphemus.*	And by reflecting of them fill this space.	
Chorus.	Till it a circle of those glories prove	
	Fit to be sought in beauty, found by Love.	
Semi-Chorus.	Where love is mutual, still	
	All things in order move;	

96 PALAEMON *the Greek Portunus, god of ports.*

Semi-Chorus.   The circle of the will   125
                      Is the true sphere of Love.
Chorus.   Advance, you gentler Cupids, then, advance,
                    And show your just perfections in your dance.

The Cupids dance their dance, and the masquers their entry. Which done,
Euclia, or a fair glory, appears in the heavens singing an applausive song 130
or paean of the whole, which she takes occasion to ingeminate in the second
chorus, upon the sight of a work of Neptune's, being a hollow rock filling
part of the sea-prospect, whereon the muses sit.

EUCLIA'S HYMN

Euclia.   So Love, emergent out of chaos, brought   135
                The world to light!
     And gently moving on the waters, wrought
                All form to sight!
                Love's appetite
                Did beauty first excite,   140
              And left imprinted in the air
          Those signatures of good and fair,
Chorus.   Which since have flowed, flowed forth upon the sense,
         To wonder first, and then to excellence,
         By virtue of divine intelligence!   145

The Ingemination

            And Neptune too
          Shows what his waves can do,
          To call the muses all to play
        And sing the birth of Venus' day,   150
Chorus. Which from the sea flowed forth upon the sense,
        To wonder first, and next to excellence,
        By virtue of divine intelligence!

131 INGEMINATE *repeat.*
142 SIGNATURES *distinctive marks.*

Here follow the revels.

155 *Which ended, the scene changeth to a garden, and the heavens opening,*
there appear four new persons in form of a constellation sitting, or a new
asterism, expecting Venus, whom they call upon with this song.

JUPITER, JUNO, GENIUS, HYMEN

Jupiter. Haste, daughter Venus, haste and come away.
160 *Juno.* All powers that govern marriage pray
         That you will lend your light
Genius. Unto the constellation of this night.
Hymen. Hymen,
Juno.   And Juno,
Genius.   And the Genius call,
Jupiter. Your father Jupiter,
Chorus.   And all
165   That bless or honor holy nuptial.

Venus here appears in a cloud, and passing through the constellation,
descendeth to the earth, when presently the cloud vanisheth, and she is seen
sitting in a throne.

Venus.   Here, here I present am,
170   Both in my girdle and my flame,
             Wherein are woven all the powers
             The Graces gave me, or the Hours,
             My nurses once, with all the arts
             Of gaining and of holding hearts;
175   And therewith I descend,

---

175 therewith] these with Q, F.

---

157 EXPECTING *awaiting.*
158 GENIUS *tutelary deity of the marriage bed.*
170 GIRDLE *called Ceston; see Jonson's note on* Hymenaei, *line 365.*
173 MY NURSES ONCE *when she rose from the sea, according to the second* Homeric
    Hymn to Aphrodite (*VI, lines 5ff.*).

But to your influences first commend
The vow I go to take
On earth for perfect love and beauty's sake.

Her song ended, and she rising to go up to the queen, the throne disappears;
in place of which there shooteth up a palm tree with an imperial crown on 180
the top, from the root whereof lilies and roses twining together and
embracing the stem flourish through the crown, which she in the song,
with the Chorus, describes.

Beauty and Love, whose story is mysterial,
In yonder palm tree and the crown imperial, 185
Do from the rose and lily so delicious
Promise a shade shall ever be propitious
To both the kingdoms. But to Britain's genius
The snaky rod and serpents of Cyllenius
Bring not more peace than these, who so united be 190
By Love, as with it earth and heaven delighted be.
And who this king and queen would well historify
Need only speak their names; those them will glorify:
Mary and Charles, Charles with his Mary naméd are,
And all the rest of loves or princes faméd are. 195

After this they dance their going out, and end.

The End.

180 PALM TREE *symbolic of triumph.*
181 LILIES AND ROSES *emblems of France and England.*
189 SNAKY ROD *Mercury's caduceus.* CYLLENIUS *Mercury, so called after his*
birthplace on Mount Cyllene in Arcadia.
196 *A list of the masquers' names has been removed to the notes.*

Chloridia
Rites to Chloris and Her Nymphs

Personated in a masque at court by the queen's majesty and her
ladies, at Shrovetide, 1631.
The inventors: Ben Jonson, Inigo Jones.

Unius tellus ante coloris erat.

The king and queen's majesty having given their command for
the invention of a new argument, with the whole change of the
scene, wherein her majesty with the like number of her ladies
purposed a presentation to the king, it was agreed it should be the
5 celebration of some rites done to the goddess Chloris, who in a
general council of the gods was proclaimed goddess of the flowers,
according to that of Ovid in the *Fasti: Arbitrium tu, dea, floris habe.*
And was to be stellified on earth by an absolute decree from
Jupiter, who would have the earth to be adorned with stars, as
10 well as the heaven.

Epigraph UNIUS . . . ERAT *Till then (i.e. till the nymph Chloris was transformed by
Zephyrus into Flora, goddess of flowers) the earth had been of one color. (Ovid,
Fasti V.222.)*

3 LIKE NUMBER *i.e. the same number as in* Love's Triumph, *performed six weeks
earlier.*

7 ARBITRIUM . . . HABE *You, goddess, have dominion over flowers. (V.213.)*

8 STELLIFIED *transformed into a star.*

304

Upon this hinge the whole invention moved.

The ornament which went about the scene was composed of
foliage, or leaves, heightened with gold and interwoven with all
sorts of flowers, and naked children playing and climbing among
the branches, and in the midst, a great garland of flowers in   15
which was written

CHLORIDIA.

The curtain being drawn up, the scene is discovered, consisting of pleasant
hills planted with young trees, and all the lower banks adorned with flowers.
And from some hollow parts of those hills, fountains come gliding down,   20
which, in the far off landscape, seemed all to be converted to a river.

Over all, a serene sky with transparent clouds, giving a great luster to the
whole work, which did imitate the pleasant spring.

When the spectators had enough fed their eyes with the delights of the
scene, in a part of the air a bright cloud begins to break forth, and in it is   25
sitting a plump boy in a changeable garment, richly adorned, representing
the mild Zephyrus. On the other side of the scene in a purplish cloud
appeareth the Spring, a beautiful maid, her upper garment green, under it
a white robe wrought with flowers, a garland on her head.

Here Zephyrus begins his dialogue, calling her forth and making narration   30
of the gods' decree at large, which she obeys, pretending it is come to earth
already and there begun to be executed by the king's favor, who assists with
all bounties that may be either urged as causes or reasons of the spring.

THE FIRST SONG

Zephyrus.   Come forth, come forth, the gentle Spring,   35
            And carry the glad news I bring
            To earth, our common mother:

26 CHANGEABLE *iridescent.*
27 ZEPHYRUS *the west wind.*

It is decreed by all the gods
The heav'n of earth shall have no odds,
40   But one shall love another.

Their glories they shall mutual make,
Earth look on heaven for heaven's sake;
      Their honors shall be even;
All emulation cease, and jars;
45 Jove will have earth to have her stars
      And lights, no less than heaven.

Spring.   It is already done, in flowers
As fresh and new as are the hours,
      By warmth of yonder sun;
50 But will be multiplied on us
If from the breath of Zephyrus
      Like favor we have won.

Zephyrus.   Give all to him: his is the dew,
The heat, the humor—
Spring.   All the true-
55   Belovèd of the Spring!
Zephyrus.   The sun, the wind, the verdure—
Spring.   All
That wisest nature cause can call
Of quick'ning anything.

At which Zephyrus passeth away through the air, and the Spring
60 *descendeth to the earth and is received by the Naiades, or Napaeae, who*
are the nymphs, fountains and servants of the season.

THE SECOND SONG

Fountains.   Fair maid, but are you come to dwell
And tarry with us here?

54 HUMOR *moisture.*
58 QUICK'NING *bringing to life.*

Spring.	Fresh fountains, I am come to tell	65
	A tale in yond' soft ear,	
	Whereof the murmur will do well,	
	If you your parts will bear.	
Fountains.	Our purlings wait upon the Spring.	
Spring.	Go up with me, then; help to sing	70
	The story to the king.	

Here the Spring goes up, singing the argument to the king, and the
fountains follow with the close.

Spring.	Cupid hath ta'en offence of late	
	At all the gods, that of the state	75
	And in their council he was so deserted,	
	Not to be called into their guild,	
	But slightly passed by, as a child.	
Fountains.	Wherein he thinks his honor was perverted.	
Spring.	And though his mother seek to season	80
	And rectify his rage with reason	
	By showing he lives yet under her command,	
	Rebellious, he doth disobey,	
	And she hath forced his arms away—	
Fountains.	To make him feel the justice of her hand.	85
Spring.	Whereat the boy, in fury fell,	
	With all his speed is gone to hell,	
	There to excite and stir up jealousy,	
	To make a party 'gainst the gods,	
	And set heaven, earth and hell at odds—	90
Fountains.	And raise a chaos of calamity.	

The song ended, the nymphs fall into a dance to their voices and instru-
ments, and so return into the scene.

79 PERVERTED *undermined.*
84 FORCED . . . AWAY *taken away his bow and arrows.*

The antimasque.

95 *First entry. A part of the underground opening, out of it enters a dwarf-post*
from hell, riding on a curtal, with cloven feet, and two lackeys; these dance,
and make the first entry of the antimasque. He alights and speaks.

Postilion. Hold my stirrup, my one lackey, and look to my curtal,
the other: walk him well, sirrah, while I expatiate myself here
100 in the report of my office. Oh, the furies! How I am joyed with
the title of it! Postilion of hell! Yet no Mercury, but a mere
cacodemon sent hither with a packet of news. News! never
was hell so furnished of the commodity of news! Love hath
been lately there, and so entertained by Pluto and Proserpine
105 and all the grandees of the place as it is there perpetual holiday,
and a cessation of torment granted and proclaimed forever!
Half famished Tantalus is fallen to his fruit with that appetite
as it threatens to undo the whole company of costard-mongers,
and has a river afore him running excellent wine. Ixion is
110 loosed from his wheel and turned dancer, does nothing but cut
caprioles, fetch friscals, and leads lavoltas with the Lamiae!
Sisyphus has left rolling the stone, and is grown a master
bowler; challenges all the prime gamesters, parsons in hell,

---

95 POST *courier.*

96 CURTAL *small horse.*

101 POSTILION *courier.* MERCURY *courier of the gods.*

102 CACODEMON *evil spirit.*

107 TANTALUS *condemned to suffer from an intense thirst with fruit and water just*
beyond his reach.

108 COSTARD-MONGERS *costermongers, apple sellers.*

109 IXION *punished by being bound on a burning wheel.*

111 CAPRIOLES, FRISCALS *capers.* LAVOLTAS *lively dances.* LAMIAE *demon*
vampires.

112 SISYPHUS . . . STONE *Each time Sisyphus reached the top of the hill, the stone*
rolled back to the bottom.

113 PARSONS *great men.*

and gives them odds; upon Tityus his breast, that, for six of the nine acres, is counted the subtlest bowling ground in all Tartary. All the furies are at a game called nine-pins, or kayles, made of old usurers' bones, and their souls looking on with delight and betting on the game. Never was there such freedom of sport! Danaus' daughters have broke their bottomless tubs and made bonfires of them. All is turned triumph there. Had hell-gates been kept with half that strictness as the entry here has been tonight, Pluto would have had but a cold court and Proserpine a thin presence, though both have a vast territory. We had such a stir to get in, I and my curtal and my two lackeys all ventured through the eye of a Spanish needle; we had never come in else, and that was by the favor of one of the guard who was a woman's tailor and held ope the passage. Cupid by commission hath carried Jealousy from hell, Disdain, Fear, and Dissimulation, with other goblins, to trouble the gods. And I am sent after, post, to raise Tempest, Winds, Lightnings, Thunder, Rain and Snow, for some new exploit they have against the earth and the goddess Chloris, queen of the flowers and mistress of the spring. For joy of which I will return to myself, mount my bidet in a dance, and curvet upon my curtal.

The speech ended, the postilion mounts his curtal, and with his lackeys danceth forth as he came in.

---

114 TITYUS *a giant slain by Artemis and Apollo for attacking their mother Leto. (The game of bowls is being played on his breast.)*

115 SUBTLEST *most difficult.* TARTARY *Tartarus.*

119 DANAUS' DAUGHTERS *Danaus commanded his fifty daughters to murder their husbands on their wedding night. Forty-nine complied, and were punished in hell by having endlessly to fill leaky vats with water.*

125 SPANISH NEEDLE *made of steel, and especially fine.*

134 BIDET *pony.* CURVET *frisk about.*

Second entry. Cupid, Jealousy, Disdain, Fear and Dissimulation dance together.

140 *Third entry. The queen's dwarf, richly apparelled as a prince of hell, attended by six infernal spirits; he first danceth alone, and then the spirits, all expressing their joy for Cupid's coming among them.*

Fourth entry. Here the scene changeth into a horrid storm, out of which enters the nymph Tempest, with four Winds; they dance.

145 *Fifth entry. Lightnings, three in number, their habits glistering, expressing that effect in their motion.*

Sixth entry. Thunder alone, dancing the tunes to a noise mixed and imitating thunder.

Seventh entry. Rain, presented by five persons all swollen and clouded
150 *over, their hair flagging, as if they were wet, and in their hands, balls full of sweet water, which, as they dance, sprinkle all the room.*

Eighth and last entry. Seven with rugged white heads and beards, to express snow, with flakes on their garments mixed with hail. These having danced return into the stormy scene whence they came.

155 *Here, by the providence of Juno, the tempest on an instant ceaseth, and the scene is changed into a delicious place figuring the bower of Chloris, wherein an arbor feigned of goldsmiths' work, the ornament of which was borne up with terms of satyrs beautified with festoons, garlands and all sorts of fragrant flowers. Beyond all this in the sky afar off appeared a*
160 *rainbow. In the most eminent place of the bower sat the goddess Chloris accompanied with fourteen nymphs, their apparel white embroidered with silver, trimmed at the shoulders with great leaves of green embroidered with gold, falling one under the other. And of the same work were their bases,*

---

140 THE . . . DWARF *the famous Jeffrey Hudson.*
151 SWEET WATER *perfumed with cloves, ginger, roses, cinnamon, etc.*
158 TERMS *statues, each consisting of a head and torso on a pedestal.*

their head 'tires of flowers mixed with silver and gold, with some sprigs of
egrets among, and from the top of their dressing, a thin veil hanging down. 165

All which beheld, the nymphs, rivers and fountains, with the Spring, sung
this rejoicing song.

THE THIRD SONG

Rivers, Spring, Run out, all the floods, in joys with your silver feet,
Fountains.   And haste to meet   170
          The enamored Spring,
     For whom the warbling fountains sing
     The story of the flowers
          Preservèd by the Hours
     At Juno's soft command, and Iris' showers,   175
     Sent to quench Jealousy and all those powers
     Of Love's rebellious war;
     Whilst Chloris sits, a shining star
     To crown and grace our jolly song
          Made long   180
     To the notes that we bring
     To glad the Spring.

Which ended, the goddess and her nymphs descend the degrees into the
room and dance the entry of the grand masque.

After this, another song by the same persons as before.   185

THE FOURTH SONG

Rivers, Fountains. Tell a truth, gay Spring, let us know
          What feet they were that so
        Impressed the earth and made such various
                 flowers to grow!

164 'TIRES *attire.*
183 DEGREES *steps.*

190 *Spring.*　　　　　She that led, a queen was at least,
　　　　　　　　　Or a goddess, 'bove the rest,
　　　　　　　　　And all their graces in herself expressed.
Rivers, Fountains. O, 'twere a fame to know her name!
　　　　　　　　　Whether she were the root,
195　　　　　　　　Or they did take th'impression from her foot.

The masquers here dance their second dance. Which done, the farther prospect of the scene changeth into air, with a low landscape in part covered with clouds. And in that instant, the heaven opening, Juno and Iris are seen, and above them many airy spirits, sitting in the clouds.

200　　　　　　　　　　THE FIFTH SONG

Juno.　　　　　Now Juno and the air shall know
　　　　　　　　The truth of what is done below
　　　　　　　　From our discolored bow.
　　　　　　　　　Iris, what news?
205 *Iris.*　　　　The air is clear, your bow can tell,
　　　　　　　　Chloris renowned, spite fled to hell;
　　　　　　　　The business all is well.
　　　　　　　　　And Cupid sues—
Juno.　　　　　For pardon, does he?
Iris.　　　　　　　　　　He sheds tears
210　　　　　　　More than your birds have eyes.
Juno.　　　　　　　　　　The gods have ears.
　　　　　　　　Offences made against the deities
　　　　　　　　Are soon forgot—
Iris.　　　　　　　　If who offends be wise.

Here out of the earth ariseth a hill, and on the top of it, a globe, on which

194 SHE . . . ROOT *i.e. she sowed them.*
203 DISCOLORED BOW *colored rainbow.*
204 IRIS *the rainbow, and messenger of the gods.*
210 YOUR BIRDS *peacocks.*

Fame is seen standing with her trumpet in her hand; and on the hill are   215
seated four persons, presenting Poesy, History, Architecture and Sculpture,
who together with the nymphs, floods and fountains make a full choir; at
which, Fame begins to mount, and moving her wings, flieth singing up to
heaven.

Fame. Rise, golden Fame, and give thy name a birth,   220
Chorus. From great and generous actions done on earth.
Fame. The life of Fame is action.
Chorus.   Understood
   That action must be virtuous, great and good!
Fame. Virtue itself by Fame is oft protected,
  And dies despisèd—
Chorus.   Where the Fame's neglected.   225
Fame. Who hath not heard of Chloris and her bower,
  Fair Iris' act, employed by Juno's power
  To guard the Spring and prosper every flower,
  Whom Jealousy and hell thought to devour?
Chorus. Great actions, oft obscured by time may lie,   230
  Or envy—
Fame.   But they last to memory.
Poesy. We that sustain thee, learnèd Poesy,
History. And I, her sister, severe History,
Architecture. With Architecture, who will raise thee high,
Sculpture. And Sculpture, that can keep thee from to die: 235
Chorus. All help lift thee to eternity.
Juno. And Juno through the air doth make thy way,
Iris. By her serenest messenger of day.
Fame. Thus Fame ascends by all degrees to heaven,
  And leaves a light here brighter than the seven.   240
Chorus.   Let all applaud the sight.
   Air first, that gave the bright
   Reflections, day or night,

> With these supports of Fame,
> That keep alive her name;
> The beauties of the spring,
> Founts, rivers, everything,
> From the height of all
> To the waters' fall,
> Resound and sing
> The honors of his Chloris to the king;
> Chloris the queen of flowers,
> The sweetness of all showers,
> The ornament of bowers,
> The top of paramours!

245
250
255

Fame being hidden in the clouds, the hill sinks, and the heaven closeth.

The masquers dance with the lords.

The End.

258 *A list of the masquers has been removed to the notes.*

Notes

Hymenaei

Performed January 5 (masque) and 6 (barriers), 1606. Editions: Q, F¹, F².

Title MARRIAGE *Of the Earl of Essex and Lady Frances Howard. The match ended in divorce and scandal, and Jonson expunged from the folio text all mention of the occasion and the performers. (The deleted passages are included in the notes.)*

17 SOME . . . OUT *Jonson was under attack for taking the masque so seriously. His most outspoken critic was his rival for the queen's patronage, Samuel Daniel, who had composed the new court's first Christmas masque,* The Vision of the Twelve Goddesses, *in 1604. This was evidently unsuccessful, and Jonson regularly received the yearly commission until the end of the reign; but the sniping continued on both sides. Daniel's attitude is expressed in the prefaces to his two masques,* The Vision, *and* Tethys' Festival *(1610).*

99 EIGHT MEN *The quarto continues:*
   whose names in order as they were then marshalled, by couples, I have heraldry enough to set down.

   1. Lord Willoughby   Sir Thomas Howard
   2. Lord Walden   Sir Thomas Somerset
   3. Sir James Hay   Earl of Arundel
   4. Earl of Montgomery   Sir John Astley

179–92 FIVE . . . RISE *Good hermetic doctrine, expounded by Plutarch (Morals 264A–B) and greatly elaborated in the Renaissance. According to the theory, one is not really a number, but the primal unity from which all numbers come. Five is the marriage of the first two numbers, two and three, and therefore represents the ideal union, with two being conceived as female and three male. An even number, say four or six, leads to discord, since when it separates into its two component twos or threes it does not also contain the great unifying one to hold it together. An even more solemn account than Jonson's is given by Chapman in* Hero and Leander, *V.323–40.*

616 *The quarto continues:*

The design and act of all which, together with the device of their habits, belongs properly to the merit and reputation of Master Inigo Jones, whom I take modest occasion in this fit place to remember, lest his own worth might accuse me of an ignorant neglect from my silence.

And here, that no man's deservings complain of injustice (though I should have done it timelier, I acknowledge) I do for honor's sake and the pledge of our friendship name Master Alfonso Ferrabosco, a man planted by himself in that divine sphere, and mastering all the spirits of music; to whose judicial care and as absolute performance were committed all those difficulties both of song and otherwise. Wherein what his merit made to the soul of our invention would ask to be expressed in tunes no less ravishing than his. Virtuous friend, take well this abrupt testimony, and think whose it is: it cannot be flattery in me, who never did it to great ones; and less than love and truth it is not, where it is done out of knowledge.

The dances were both made and taught by Master Thomas Giles, and cannot be more approved than they did themselves: nor do I want the will, but the skill to commend such subtleties, of which the sphere wherein they were acted is best able to judge.

What was my part, the faults here as well as the virtues must speak. Mutare dominum nec potest liber notus. [*The book, once known, cannot change its master.* (Martial, I.lxvi.9.)]

741 THE . . . WITHERED *An awkward line, emended by both Gifford and the Oxford editors. Nevertheless, the construction is, according to Elizabethan practice, perfectly acceptable, employing a device called* apo koinu, *a grammatical form of the rhetorical figure* zeugma, *whereby a single word*

serves two different functions in one sentence. Here "same" is both the subject of "is" and object of "have desired." The figure is a common one, and Jonson uses it elsewhere. E.g. "Virtue brings forth twelve princes have been bred/ In this rough mountain" (Pleasure Reconciled, lines 181–82). Editors usually explain that in such cases a relative pronoun has been omitted (i.e. "who" should be understood before "have"), and the example from Hymenaei could be treated in the same way, by reading "The same, which when cropped . . . ." But it is surely more correct to say that Jonson tended to use apo koinu where modern English would use a relative pronoun. (For a more startling example that is clearly not an ellipsis, see the note to Neptune's Triumph, line 185.)

779 The quarto continues:

Whose names, as they were given to me both in order and orthography, were these.

Truth	Opinion
Duke of Lennox	Earl of Sussex
Lord Effingham	Lord Willoughby
Lord Walden	Lord Gerrard
Lord Monteagle	Sir Robert Carey
Sir Thomas Somerset	Sir Oliver Cromwell
Sir Charles Howard	Sir William Herbert
Sir John Gray	Sir Robert Drury
Sir Thomas Monson	Sir William Woodhouse
Sir John Leigh	Sir Carew Reynell
Sir Robert Maunsell	Sir Richard Houghton
Sir Edward Howard	Sir William Constable
Sir Henry Goodyere	Sir Thomas Gerrard
Sir Roger Dalison	Sir Robert Killigrew
Sir Francis Howard	Sir Thomas Badger
Sir Lewis Maunsell	Sir Thomas Dutton
Master [Henry] Gunteret	Master [John] Digby

THE MASQUE OF QUEENS

Performed February 2, 1609. Editions: MS, Q, F¹, F².

1 *The following dedication appears only in the quarto:*

To the glory of our own, and grief of other nations, my lord Henry, Prince of Great Britain, etc.

Sir:

When it hath been my happiness (as would it were more frequent) but to see your face, and, as passing by, to consider you, I have, with as much joy as I am now far from flattery in professing it, called to mind that doctrine of some great inquisitors in nature, who hold every royal and heroic form to partake and draw much to it of the heavenly virtue. For whether it be that a divine soul, being come into a body, first chooseth a palace fit for itself, or being come, doth make it so, or that nature be ambitious to have her work equal, I know not; but what is lawful for me to understand and speak, that I dare, which is that both your virtue and your form did deserve your fortune. The one claimed that you should be born a prince, the other makes that you do become it. And when Necessity, excellent lord, the mother of the Fates, hath so provided that your form should not more insinuate you to the eyes of men than your virtue to their minds, it comes near a wonder to think how sweetly that habit flows in you, and with so hourly testimonies, which to all posterity might hold the dignity of examples. Amongst the rest, your favor to letters and these gentler studies that go under the title of Humanity is not the least honor of your wreath. For if once the worthy professors of these learnings shall come (as heretofore they were) to be the care of princes, the crowns their sovereigns wear will not more adorn their temples, nor their stamps live longer in their medals, than in such subject's labors. Poetry, my lord, is not born with every man, nor every day; and in her general right it is now my minute to thank your highness, who not only do honor her with your ear but are curious to examine her with your eye, and inquire into her beauties and strengths. Where, though it hath proved a work of some difficulty to me to retrieve the particular authorities (according to your gracious command and a desire born out of judgment) to those things which I writ out of fullness and memory of my former readings, yet now I have overcome it, the reward that meets me is double to one act: which is, that thereby your excellent understanding will not only justify me to *your own knowledge, but decline the stiffness of others' original ignorance, already armed to censure. For which singular bounty, if my fate (most excellent prince, and only delicacy of mankind) shall reserve me to the age of your actions, whether in the camp or the council chamber, that I may write at nights the deeds of your days, I will then labor to bring forth some work as worthy of your fame as my ambition therein is of your pardon.*

By the most true admirer of your highness' virtues,
And most hearty celebrator of them,
Ben Jonson.

163 FAT *With the fat of murdered children witches were said to be able to transform themselves into other shapes.*

195–200 *For Jonson's classical witches, see the following. Circe:* Homer, Odyssey *X 233–43, 388–96, 515–20. Simatha:* Theocritus, Idylls *ii.10–62. Alphesiboeus:* Virgil, Eclogues *viii.64–106. Dipsas:* Ovid, Amores *I.viii.2–18. Medea:* Ovid, Metamorphoses *VII.192–219. Circe:* Ovid, Metamorphoses *XIV.42–67, 268–86. Saga:* Tibullus, *I.ii.42–52. Canidia:* Horace, Satires *I.viii.24ff.;* Epodes *v.15–24, 48–52. Sagana:* Horace, Satires *I.viii.25ff.;* Epodes *v.25–8. Veia:* Horace, Epodes *v.29–40. Folia:* Horace, Epodes *v.41–6. Medea:* Seneca, Medea *752ff. Nurse:* Seneca, Hercules Oetaeus *452–63. Saga:* Petronius, *not in the* Fragments, *but the witch Oenothea in the* Satyricon *134. Megaera:* Claudian, In Rufinum *I.74–84, 129–63.*

346–50 1 . . . GORGON *Perseus was the child of Zeus and Danae. When he was sent to kill the Gorgon Medusa, Hermes gave him wings for his feet, Pluto a helmet that would make him invisible, and Athena a highly polished shield. To look directly at Medusa was fatal, but Perseus used the shield as a mirror and so defeated her in battle.*

424 ICONOLOGIA . . . RIPA *The Iconology of Ripa (c.1560–c.1625), a standard manual of classical symbolism, was first published in 1593 and frequently reprinted.*

425 ORUS APOLLO *Horapollo Niliacus, Alexandrian commentator of the second or fourth century* A.D. *The Hieroglyphics, an interpretation of hermetic symbolism, was important to Renaissance neo-Platonic theorists.*

449 *Jonson's summary of his sources is relatively economical, but a modern reading of the masque bogs down in it rather badly, hence its (admittedly arbitrary) banishment to the appendix. Some account of its function may be in order. Jonson's problem here was to provide his queens with sufficient solidity to counterbalance the tremendous dramatic force of his witches. This was a problem only in the written text: in production, a contemporary audience's recognition of Queen Anne and her ladies in their heroic roles amply did the work of dramatic action. But since courtiers could not take speaking parts, in the masque-as-poem the action offered Jonson little means of realizing his ideal vision, and he undertook to produce a viable substitute for the reader. He announces that he will describe "the persons they presented"; but in fact his account (unlike that of the scene, immediately following) is not of what the spectator saw, but of what historical roles the ladies took: their reality is established exclusively by means of history and poetry. The 17th century had a strong sense of the relevance of exemplary figures from the past to current political and social realities; still, the success of Jonson's device must have been, even for the Jacobean reader, dubious, and the experiment was not repeated.*

OBERON

Performed January 1, 1611. Editions: F^1, F^2

190–95 THIS ... MAID *The satyrs charge the moon, notorious for inconstancy, with pretending to suffer from the green sickness, an anemic condition most common during puberty, and which was thought to afflict only virgins. The "proper way" to be rid of it (lines 190–91) is therefore to cease to be a virgin.*

222 ARTHUR'S CHAIR *James's court is compared with Arthur's in James's own masque, composed by the 22-year-old king for the wedding of the Earl (later Marquis) of Huntly and Lady Henrietta Stewart in 1588. The marriage was celebrated in Holyrood Palace, at the foot of the hill called Arthur's Seat; hence the allusion had a topographical point in Edinburgh which was lost at Whitehall. See* Poems of James VI of Scotland, *ed. J. Craigie, II (Edinburgh, 1958), p. 140, line 65 and note.*

Love Restored

Performed January 6, 1612. Editions: F¹, F².

47 ENGLAND'S JOY *A famous fraud perpetrated in 1602. It was advertised as a historical extravaganza in which only gentlemen and gentlewomen would act, and attracted a large audience; but at the last moment the producer was found to have decamped with the receipts, and there was no performance.*

80 CASE O' CATSOS *The first folio text reads "ca∫e: v∫es"; the second and fourth (1692) folios end the sentence with "Coryat." The Oxford editors point out that there are two other places in this masque (lines 122 and 164) where what Jonson evidently wrote as o' or i' has been misread by the typesetter as a mark of punctuation. They give warm praise to Gifford's conjecture, "a case of asses," though they do not use it in their text. Sir Walter Greg also feels that "asses" is "not unhappily conjectured," but offers an alternative emendation of his own: "'vses' might of course be a misprint for 'vfes': could this possibly be a form of aufs or oafs, idiots?"* (Review of English Studies, XVIII, 152.)

 But neither conjecture seems to me at all admissible; and it is tempting simply to reprint the corrupt folio text, as Herford and Simpson do. Nevertheless, the folio reading is clearly nonsense, and a modernized edition ought to provide a feasible alternative.

 First, for the arguments against "asses" and "ufes." Both depend on the analogy of lines 122 and 164 to show that the colon represents what Jonson wrote as o'. But both emendations require of, not o', since both asses and ufes begin with vowels. If the o' theory is correct, the following word must begin with a consonant; one would expect a c, considering the heavy alliteration of the rest of the sentence. Moreover, though the sense of "asses" is possible, that of "oafs" is all wrong. Jonson loved Coryat, and contributed an admiring and indulgent character of him to the 1611 edition of the Crudities. *What is needed is a word parallel with "cockscomb"—rogue—which is rude but can also be admiring and indulgent. (Cf. "bastard" in modern slang usage: e.g. "a handsome bastard.") What "asses" and "ufes" have in their favor is their orthographical similarity to "v∫es"—though in the latter case this is more apparent than real: Greg has had to invent the unknown form "ufes."*

But if Jonson's handwriting in the manuscript was so small and crabbed that o' could be taken for a colon or a comma, the argument from orthography will surely support a wider variety of emendations.

I have accepted the suggestion of Christopher Ricks that the phrase should read "a case o' catsos." This seems to me orthographically defensible, and to supply what I take to be the required sense. Catso *is Elizabethan slang; its basic meaning is roughly equivalent to the modern* cock, *but it is also regularly used to mean rogue or scamp, and Jonson elsewhere makes it synonymous with* cockscomb. Every Man Out of His Humor *provides a striking parallel: "He's gone now. I thought he would fly out presently. These be our nimble-spirited catsos, that have their evasions at pleasure. . . ." (II.i.19–21.) Here the catso's facility at getting in and out of difficult places is clearly a significant part of its meaning for Jonson. (See also* The Case Is Altered, *V.vi.1, for a less clear but possibly relevant usage.) For Robin to call Coryat a catso would be rude, but not necessarily pejorative.*

137–39 1 . . . STATES *Puritan attacks on the extravagance of court masques had recently become so serious that James severely limited the cost of this one.*

MERCURY VINDICATED FROM THE ALCHEMISTS AT COURT

Performed twice, January 1 and 6, 1616. Editions: F¹, F².

6 WEAKER NATURE *Evidence for the old age and decay of nature was drawn from both physical and metaphysical sources—for example, Donne in* An Anatomy of the World *cites both the appearance of new stars and the growing interest in skepticism as support for the doctrine, which was strongly debated throughout the age. Jonson's attitude is amply expressed by Nature's opening line (176) in the main masque.*

129–30 PARACELSUS' MAN *The homunculus is described in* De Natura Rerum *(the Latin translation of G. Forberger), in* Opera *(Basel, 1575), pp. 370–71 (A1v-A2r), and the directions for making one are on pp. 377ff. (A[a]5rff.)*

THE GOLDEN AGE RESTORED

Performed twice, January 6 and 8, 1615. This precedes Mercury Vindicated. *Possibly Jonson printed it out of chronological order because the descent of Astraea and closing paean to* King James *made* The Golden Age *a more effective conclusion to the 1616 folio, in which it appears as the final work. Editions: F¹, F².*

186–206 *These stanzas originally followed line 224, and are so printed in some copies of the first folio. Originally, that is, the masque concluded by moving with Pallas from earth to heaven; but Jonson changed his mind while the volume was in the press, and in the revised version Astraea decides to remain on an earth transformed by the excellence of King James. "It is possible," say the Oxford editors, "that the original ending was used at the Court performance and that the revision was an afterthought designed to give a more significant ending to the Folio." (VII.420.)*

The Vision of Delight

Performed twice, January 6 and 19, 1617. Printed after Lovers Made Men in the 1640 folio, presumably by error, since Jonson was not responsible for the arrangement of the volume. I have therefore restored the chronological order. (Herford and Simpson misdate it in their introduction, II.303.) Editions: MS (lines 49–116 only), F³.

49–106 *Fantasy's speech is a verbal antimasque, a treatment of the wordly vices, chiefly gluttony and lechery. It proceeds by a kind of free-associative technique, and through a series of moral emblems in the manner of Brueghel or Bosch presents a vision of society turned upside down. Like the Fool's speeches in* Lear, *which it resembles, it is frequently obscene and full of allusions, slang, and proverbial language, some of which are not recoverable; moreover, its transitions are not always logical. But the general sense is clear, and the speech is not, as all commentators have assumed, either nonsensical or entirely incoherent.*

61–66 *Throughout the speech, people are reduced to attributes, passions, possessions. Here, men and women are seen as items of stylish dress: the women become a farthingale and hood, the courtier (who is the projected audience for Fantasy's first dream) becomes first his plume and then his codpiece.*

64 OSTRICH *See C. Ripa,* Iconologia *(Padua, 1625), pp. 284 and 320 on the ostrich as garrulousness and gluttony, and p. 279 on the bird as justice. Ripa*

also cites Alciati's emblem "In Garrulum et Gulosum" (*Leyden, 1608, no. 95, p. 100*) in an Italian version that translates Alciati's "truo" as "struzzo" (ostrich), though the bird depicted is swimming and resembles a dodo.

67–70. "*The 'pudding' retains its dual nature (serving both lechery and gluttony), even though lechery claims all for itself. What would it be like if creatures did not act according to their natures?*"

71–78 "*If a moral emblem of gluttony and frivolity should frighten you, would you therefore turn yourself topsy-turvy, renounce your nature? Creatures, both glutton (whale) and lecher (mousetrap maker), act according to their natures, as do things (onion and mustard).*" For "*the maker o' the mousetrap,*" cf. Pan's Anniversary, *lines 111–13.*

72 WINDMILL *The figure is used, for example, in Brueghel's engraving* Gluttony. *And an Elizabethan proverb says, "A full stomach is a windmill." (M.P.* Tilley, Dictionary of the Proverbs in England [*Ann Arbor, 1950*], *p. 633.)*

87–95 "*You may take a moralist's position, and say that worldly pleasures (morris-dancing) are merely specious ways of concealing the hard facts of age, disease and decay; but I say that creatures behave as their natures dictate. Though wine may increase the lecher's capacity, it is chiefly the glutton's pleasure (or, people determine how much they will drink not by the goodness of the wine, but by the fullness of their bellies). Common sense will tell you what would happen if you should deny the worldly man (the usurer, who cares solely for worldly wealth) his proper pleasures, and thus overturn the order of society.*"

98 WORLD . . . WHEELS *The image is elucidated by John Taylor the Water Poet, in a pamphlet called* The World Runs on Wheels. *It is illustrated by an emblem showing the globe in a carriage being pulled backward by the devil and a whore, who are harnessed to it by a chain. A caption explains,*

> The devil and the whorish flesh draws still,
> The world on wheels runs after with good will . . .
> The chained ensnarèd world doth follow fast,

Till all into perdition's pit be cast.
The picture topsy-turvy stands kew-waw*:
The world turned upside down, as all men know.
* *kew-waw = upside down*

(*Works, 1630, fol. Aaa4v.*)

102 TAIL . . . KENTISHMAN *Alluding to a belief that the men of Kent had tails; see* OED *under Kentish long-tails. Gluttony was a notorious Kentish vice; again, see Taylor the Water Poet on* The Great Eater of Kent (*Works, 1630, N5vff.*).

104 CRAB, ROPEMAKER *The reference is to two emblems appearing together in Alciati,* Ocni Effigies *and* In Parasitos (*nos. 91 and 92 in Plantin's edition [Leyden, 1608] pp. 96 and 97 [F8v, G1r]). The crab is traditionally associated with gluttony, since Cancer governs the belly, along with the breast and lungs. Alciati's emblem* In Parasitos (*On Toadies*) *shows the toady carrying a platter of crabs (in some editions, only the crab is shown), and the accompanying poem compares the two creatures, explaining that both think only of filling their stomachs.*

The ropemaker is Ocnus, a mythological figure represented as endlessly weaving a rope which is then devoured by an ass standing nearby. Classical commentators explain that the ass is Ocnus' spendthrift wife, and take the scene as a warning against marrying unfrugal women. But Renaissance writers, observing that the name Ocnus (oknos) means sloth, stressed the vicious aspects of misguided industry. Alciati's epigraph explains that the emblem is "about those who give to whores what ought to be converted to good uses," thus allying sloth with lechery, and the accompanying poem characterizes the ass as "foemina, iners animal"—woman, slothful creature. Here it is the woman who embodies sloth, and Ocnus' vice, in supplying hers, is clearly lechery. The close relationship of both sins with gluttony for the Renaissance mind is illustrated by the fact that, despite Alciati's epigraph, many editions print the emblem under the heading Gula (*gluttony*). *Alciati's sixteenth-century commentator Claude Mignault (or Claudius Minos) even managed to reconcile Ocnus' name with his industriousness by explaining that "he is slothful, no matter how much he labors, who misplaces his resources and puts them to wholly unnecessary uses." (*Emblemata [Plantin, Leyden, 1608] p. 346 (Y5v).*)*

PLEASURE RECONCILED TO VIRTUE

Performed January 6, 1618. Editions: MS, F³.

67–68 JOVIAL TINKERS, LUSTY KINDRED *"The Jovial Tinkers" is the title of a popular ballad about drinking, and the Oxford editors therefore assume that the unidentified "Lusty Kindred" is a similar song. But judging from the context, which makes them examples of "any place of quality," they are more likely to be the names of two taverns.*

153–54 SHEEP . . . FRUIT *Diodorus Siculus explains that the golden apples Hercules received for rescuing the daughters of Atlas were metaphorical: "Atlas . . . possessed flocks of sheep which excelled in beauty and were in colour of a golden yellow, this being the reason why poets, in speaking of these sheep as* mela *[sheep], called them golden* mela *[apples]." (The Library of History, tr. C. H. Oldfather [Cambridge, Mass., 1935], II, 429.)*

230–31 WHERE . . . FRIEND *In his youth Hercules came to a crossroad where the goddesses of pleasure and virtue urged him to follow their respective ways. The hero chose the path of virtue, though it was steep and difficult. The story is in Xenophon,* Memorabilia *II.i.21–34.*

321–22 *In fact, the masque was unpopular, and the king interrupted it to complain that the dancing was too short. It was performed again on February 17, with the antimasques of Comus and the pigmies replaced by* For the Honor of *Wales.*

NEWS FROM THE NEW WORLD DISCOVERED IN THE MOON

Performed twice, January 7 and February 29, 1620. Edition: F³.

Title DISCOVERED *By Galileo, and described by him in* Sidereus Nuncius (*The Messenger of the Stars*), *Venice, 1610.*

20 CHRONICLE *The chronicler is compiling a volume of trivia modeled on John Stow's* Survey of London (*1598*), *republished with additions by Anthony Munday in 1618.*

44 SERPENT IN SUSSEX *A real pamphlet, entitled* True and Wonderful: A discourse relating a strange and monstrous serpent (or dragon) lately

discovered and yet living to the great annoyance and divers slaughters both of men and cattle by his strong and violent poison, in Sussex, two miles from Horsam, in a wood called Saint Leonard's Forest, and thirty miles from London, this present month of August, 1614.

85 CORNELIUS AGRIPPA (*1486–1535*) *German soldier, physician, and magician. The Pythagorean moon-writing is described in his* De Occulta Philosophia *I.vi. (Cologne, 1533, fol. a5r. Herford and Simpson's reference is totally incorrect.)*

88–89 CORNELIUS DRIBBLE *"Cornelius Drebbel was a scientific inventor patronized by James I and Rudolph II of Germany. He introduced microscopes, telescopes, and thermometers into England." (Herford and Simpson, X.44.) He also devised a perpetual motion machine, with which King James appears to be credited in lines 319–22.*

148–49 MUST . . . STREAM *If this is an allusion, it is untraced. Jonson also quotes the couplet in* Discoveries, *lines 714–15.*

168, 169 MENIPPUS, EMPEDOCLES *Ancient philosophers, whose flights to the moon are described by Lucian in* Icaromenippus *10 and 13.*

283 PROCRITUS *The Greek title in full is* Prokritos tes Neotetos. *See, e.g.,* Dio *78.17 (or, in the Loeb edition, 79.17; vol. IX, p. 377).*

PAN'S ANNIVERSARY

Performed June 19, 1620. (Misdated 1625 and printed out of place in the folio.) Edition: F[3]*.*

60–61 PAN . . . PEACE *An elaborate compliment to the king. Pan, the prototype of the good shepherd, the arch deity of pastoral, merges with King James; the masque celebrates his birthday, hence the "anniversary rites"; he was an ardent pacifist, hence "the music of his peace."*

132–33 COMPARISON . . . DEITIES *Presumably the antimasque involved parodies of members of the courtly audience.*

THE GYPSIES METAMORPHOSED

Performed three times, August 3 and 5, and sometime in September, 1621.

A note on the text: *Since the masque was performed three times, and changes were made for each performance, the textual problem is unusually complicated. The version Jonson prepared for publication was a revised composite. Unfortunately, the printers of the 1640 folio evidently found the manuscript unclear and confusing, and badly botched the text.*

The masque exists in four significant forms beside the folio:

1. *A duodecimo entitled* Q. Horatius Flaccus: His Art of Poetry. Englished by Ben: Jonson. With other Works of the Author, never Printed before (*London, 1640*). *This contains the first (Burley) version of the masque.*

2. *The same volume, but with certain sheets replaced by others that include some, but not all, of the revisions made for the second and third (Belvoir and Windsor) performances.*

    (With two exceptions [lines 1350 and 1374] only the second of these duodecimos is significant for the purposes of my text.)

3. *A manuscript (now in the Huntington Library) made sometime after the three performances, representing the whole composite version, and attempting to distinguish the texts of the three individual performances. This is called the Heber-Huntington manuscript.*

4. *A manuscript now in the British Museum (MS. Harley 4955, fols. 2–30), which is a copy of Jonson's final revised text, the same text used in the folio, and thus represents a later stage of the masque than does the Heber-Huntington manuscript. It appears to have been made for Jonson's patron the Earl of Newcastle, and is called the Newcastle manuscript.*

A magnificent study of the various states, and an edition of the three texts as performed, has been done by W. W. Greg (Jonson's "Masque of Gipsies," London, 1952), and it is to this, rather than to the Oxford edition, that the interested reader must be referred, especially since the Oxford editors' textual notes for this masque are extraordinarily haphazard, incomplete, and inaccurate. Greg, however, is not primarily concerned with Jonson's final version, but with the original versions from which it grew. The Oxford editors chose to reprint the Heber-Huntington manuscript, because it contains the "best" (i.e. clearest) text of the masque. But this seems to me an error of judgment: the Heber-

Huntington manuscript is an intermediate state of the work, and what one wants is a corrected version of Jonson's final text, that of the folio and the Newcastle manuscript.

My edition, therefore, is prepared from the folio and the Newcastle manuscript, corrected from the Heber–Huntington manuscript and the duodecimo. The following symbols have been used in the textual notes:

D = the second duodecimo, except in two instances, where D^2 has been used to distinguish it from the first duodecimo, called D^1.

H = the Heber–Huntington manuscript.

Ne = the Newcastle manuscript.

F = the 1640 folio.

I have treated H as analogous to the quartos of masques with less vexed histories. Thus, substantial passages which are in H but deleted from F and Ne are either enclosed in brackets or included in the notes. Passages in D and not in H, unless they correct obvious errors of omission, have not been reprinted. Only significant variants have been included in the textual notes, and I have silently normalized Jonson's headings for the dances.

As an aid to sorting out the three versions, I have provided marginal glosses wherever it was possible to do so without confusion. These are necessarily incomplete, however, and detailed information about what sections of the masque were performed where is included in the notes.

A Note on the Identity of the Gypsies

The evidence is given in Herford and Simpson, VII.551. A contemporary manuscript identifies Buckingham, his brother-in-law, Baron Feilding, and the poet Endymion Porter as the first, second, and third gypsies. " The unnamed fourth gypsy," the Oxford editors say, "was probably John, Viscount Purbeck," Buckingham's brother, since the Countess of Buckingham is told that "Two of your sons are gypsies too" (line 490). In volume X.612, however, the Simpsons assert positively that Purbeck "must have been the fourth gypsy." There are advantages to making this assumption, but the evidence really will not support it. In the first place, the fact that two of the Countess' sons are gypsies only means that Purbeck played one of the two remaining gypsies: he need not have been the fourth, but might have been the fifth. The fourth gypsy's is much the larger of the two parts, and we might wish to assume that Buckingham's brother would naturally have taken the better *role. But on the other hand, Purbeck was mentally unstable, and might just as well have been given the simpler part. There is an additional complication in the fact that at line 1186b the Earl of Rutland, Buckingham's father-in-law, is referred to as "our Buckingham's father": perhaps, analogously, the Countess of Buckingham's second son is not Purbeck at all, but her son-in-law Baron Feilding, whom we know to have played the second gypsy. Purbeck's identification as the fourth gypsy is at most a convenient hypothesis, and I have adopted it as such. It is very far from being demonstrable. For the fifth gypsy, see the note to line 94.*

Title THRICE *This was Jonson's most popular masque, the only one performed more than twice.*

52 JACKMAN *"And because no commonwealth can stand without some learning in it, therefore are there some in this school of beggars that practice writing and reading, and those are called jackmen: yea the jackman is so cunning sometimes that he can speak Latin; which learning lifts him up to advancement, for by that means he becomes clerk of their hall, and his office is to make counterfeit licenses, which are called* gybes, *to which he puts seals, and those are termed* jarks.*"* Thomas Dekker, The Bell-man of London, *in* Non-Dramatic Works, *ed. A. B. Grosart (London, 1885), III.103–04.*

74 BENE BOWSE *etc. Jonson's cant terminology is taken from a number of contemporary handbooks, the most important of which are John Awdeley's* The Fraternity of Vagabonds *(1565) and Thomas Harman's* A Caveat or Warning for Common Cursitors Vulgarly Called Vagabonds *(1567).*

94 GERVASE *No plausible candidate for the part of the fifth gypsy has been proposed. My own solution to the mystery is unproved, but not improbable; I can claim at least to have found a gentleman who fulfills all the requirements for having played the role.*

Sir Gervase Clifton, Bart. (1587–1666), of Clifton and Hodsock, was descended from a distinguished family of Nottinghamshire landed gentry. He was made Knight of the Bath at the coronation of James I, and was raised to the baronetage in the first creation of baronets, 1611. He served in parliament for the county 1614–25, 1628–29, 1661–66; for the borough of Nottingham 1626; and for East Retford 1640–44. Though not a courtier, he was well known at court: his first wife was Penelope, daughter of Penelope Rich and

Robert, Lord Rich (later Earl of Warwick); after her death in 1613, he married Lady Frances Clifford, daughter of the Earl of Cumberland. She died in 1627, and he remarried five times thereafter. (See Burke's Landed Gentry, 1952, under *Clifton of Clifton*.)

Clifton seems to have entertained King James on his progress from Edinburgh to his coronation at London in 1603. (See John Nichols, Court Progresses of James I [*London, 1828*], *I.85*.) *His knighthood and baronetcy are evidence enough of James's favor. His association with Charles, both as prince and king, is, however, more significant and better documented. In 1612 he accompanied the prince on a visit to St. John's College, Cambridge, where Clifton was granted an honorary M.A. As king and queen, Charles and Henrietta Maria stayed with him at Clifton.* (See Thoroton's History of Nottinghamshire, *ed. J. Throsby* [*London, 1797*], *I.110*.) *During the Civil War he commanded a royalist troop, and was heavily fined under the Commonwealth for his participation on the king's side.*

He was, according to an account written in 1677, "*generally the most noted person of his time for courtesy; he was very prosperous, and beloved of all. He generously, hospitably, and charitably entertained all, from the king to the poorest beggar. He served eight times in parliament; he was Knight of the Shire* [i.e. parliamentary representative of the county] *in King James's time, and in his present majesty's King Charles II. . . . His port and hospitality exceeded very many of the nobility . . . being . . . of a sound body, and a cheerful facetious spirit.*" (*Thoroton, I.108*.)

Clifton is three miles south of Nottingham, 17 miles from Belvoir, and 25 from Burley. Nottingham was the next stop on James's 1621 progress; he arrived there on August 13, eight days after the Belvoir performance of the masque. Assuming that Viscount Purbeck was the fourth gypsy, if Sir Gervase was the fifth, he was the only one of the five not directly connected with Buckingham. He would presumably have been included as the leading representative of the local gentry.

(*He should not be confused with his older contemporary of the same name, who was Baron Clifton of Leighton, Bromswold, Hunts., the father-in-law of Jonson's patron Esmé Stuart, Lord d'Aubigny, and who committed suicide in the Tower in 1618.*)

95 CHARLES *Jonson evidently intended the part of the Captain for Prince Charles. In fact, it was played by Buckingham, whose name was George.*

122 QUIT . . . PLACES *The change was made because in the Windsor revision of the masque, the gypsies told the fortunes of the lords in the audience, instead of those of the ladies.*

127–30 DRAW . . . HURLEY *Though this passage appears in all texts, the last couplet could have been sung only at Burley, and the whole quatrain, being applicable to women, would presumably have been omitted at Windsor.*

131 PATRICO *"A patrico . . . amongst beggars is their priest, every hedge being his parish, every wandering harlot and rogue his parishioners, the service he says is only the marrying of couples, which he does in a wood under a tree, or in the open field." Dekker,* Bell-man, *in* Non-Dramatic Works, *ed. Grosart, III.104.*

141a–44a THERE'S . . . MEN *According to H, this quatrain was replaced at Belvoir with the alternate couplet, 141b–42b. Thus the Earl of Rutland was praised at Burley, but at Belvoir, where Rutland was host, the compliment was altered to include Buckingham. The same change must also have been made at Windsor.*

149–51 SOME . . . HE *Presumably omitted at Belvoir and Windsor.*

171 PHARAOTES INDUS *The incident is recounted by Philostratus,* Life of Apollonius *II.30. (Herford and Simpson's reference is incorrect.)*

323–40 *The last three stanzas were sung only at Windsor. In D¹, the king's fortune concludes with the following triplet:*

> *This little, from so short a view,*
> *I tell, and as a teller true*
> *Of fortunes, but their maker, sir, are you.*

366 *According to D¹ (in which the stanza concludes with a question mark) the prince's fortune ended here at Burley, as it presumably also did at Belvoir.*

389 CONSTELLATION NEW *On the analogy of Charles's Wain (the Big Dipper), named for Charlemagne.*

391 BURLEY/BELVOIR *These two performances were given by Buckingham and his father-in-law Rutland, and center almost entirely on the favorite. Every one of the ladies was a member of the family, as were, most likely, three of the*

gypsies; a fourth (Endymion Porter) was in Buckingham's service and a member of his household. (See the preliminary note on the identity of the gypsies.) The fifth is presumably the Gervase of line 94, tentatively identified as Sir Gervase Clifton, Bart.

446–47 BOTH . . . COUNTY *This could have been used only at Belvoir, where the countess' husband was Lord Lieutenant of the county (Leicestershire). Burley is in Rutland.*

461 COMING SO LATE *This must have been written at the last minute for the Belvoir performance. It is not included in D¹, which is the text of the masque at Burley. This may account for its being spoken by the Patrico, who would have been played by a professional actor.*

531 WINDSOR *The Windsor version is another matter entirely. Windsor is a royal castle, and here the center of the masque is not only the king, but the whole court as well. So the fortunes of Buckingham's ladies are replaced by those of James's councillors, with their order determined by court protocol; and Buckingham is much less in evidence.*

581 PENSIONS *Greg observes that "Jonson had his pension increased on this occasion." (Jonson's "Gipsies," pp. 36, 215.) This is a frequent error (the DNB is also guilty of it) based on a letter of John Chamberlain's to Sir Dudley Carleton saying that Jonson "hath his pension from 100 marks [£66.13s.4d.] increased to £200 per annum." This would have been an act of enormous generosity on the king's part, but it was evidently mere rumor. In 1629, Jonson wrote asking King Charles to raise his pension, which was still 100 marks, to £100. (See also Herford and Simpson, I.96, for relevant documents.)*

654 TRUTH . . . PAGE *Greg emends "bear" to "be," but this is quite unnecessary. The syntax is only awkward by modern standards.*

705 MOON MEN *OED cites Dekker: "A moon-man signifies in English a madman. . . . By a byname they are called gipsies, they call themselves Egyptians, others in mockery call them moon-men."*

718 POVERTY OF PIPERS *This is a very old joke, though the funniest part of it is probably the OED's and the Oxford editors' solemn discomfort with it. The phrase appears in a section of Dame Julyan Bernes' St. Albans Book (1486), headed "The Companies of Beasts and Fowl." The list includes such classics*

as "*a pride of lions*" and "*a gaggle of geese*," along with "*a disguising of tailors*" (*which also makes the* OED), "*a blush of boys*," "*a skulk of thieves*," "*a superfluity of nuns*," "*a pontificality of prelates*," "*an exalting of larks*," *and about a hundred more* (*fol. f6v*). *This scherzo is included in editions of the book* (*later called* The Boke of Hawkynge, Huntynge, and Fysshynge) *through the middle of the sixteenth century, though it is omitted from Gervase Markham's decorous modernization,* The Gentlemans Academie (*1595*).

719–20 SEE . . . COMES *In Ne and F, this replaces the following passage from H, presumably used at Windsor:*

Clod, will you gather the pipe money?

Clod.   *I'll gather't an you will, but I'll give none.*

Pup.   *Why, well said: claw a churl by the arse and he'll shit in your fist.*

Cock.   *Aye, or whistle to a jade and he'll pay you with a fart.*

Clod.   *Fart? It's an ill wind blows no man to profit! See where the minstrel comes i' the mouth on't.*★

(★ *i' the mouth on't = as we are talking about him.*)

721–35 *Only appropriate to Windsor. The passage it replaced, used at Burley and Belvoir, is essentially an extended version of lines 729–33; it appears only in D.*

776–77 YOU'LL . . . WIFE *In Ne and F, this replaces the following couplet from D and H, presumably used at Burley and Belvoir:*

> *You'll steal yourself drunk, I find it here true;*
> *As you rob the pot, the pot will rob you.*

794 THEY . . . TICKLEFOOT *In Ne and F, this replaces the following passage from D and H, presumably used at all three performances:*

[Townshead.   . . . *Pray God they fit her with a fair fortune*]; *she hangs an arse terribly.*

Patrico.   *She'll have a tailor take measure of her breech,*
        And ever after be troubled with a stitch.

Townshead.   *That's as homely as she.*

Puppy.   *The better! A turd's as good for a sow as a pancake.*

Townshead.   *Hark, now they treat upon Ticklefoot.*

935 OURSELVES *D and H here contain the following passage:*
. . . *for the hobnails are come to me.*

Cockerel.   *Maybe he knew whose shoes lacked clouting.*
Puppy.   *Aye, he knows more than that, or I'll never trust my judgment in*
a gypsy again.

1039–50 AND . . . END *The final three stanzas were sung only at Windsor.*

1052 *At Burley and Belvoir, the text skipped from "in a cage" to line 1157.*

1072–74 TUT . . . THEM *An earlier version of this passage, presumably used at*
Burley and Belvoir, is preserved in H:
     Tut, they have other manner of gifts than telling of fortunes or picking of
pockets.
     Cockerel. *Aye, an if they please to show them, or thought us poor country*
folks worthy of them.

1195, 1196 CONSTABLE, DEAN *The reference to Dunstable, near Windsor, has a*
double point. The borough had strong Puritan sympathies; and gypsies had
been formally expelled from the town in 1552.

1199 *The Burley and Belvoir versions now skip to line 1303.*

NEPTUNE'S TRIUMPH FOR THE RETURN OF ALBION

Prepared for January 6, 1624, but canceled because of a dispute over precedence
between the French and Spanish ambassadors. Editions: Q, F³.

50–51 HOGSHEAD TRISMEGISTUS *A hogshead is a cask of liquor; trismegistus means*
thrice-greatest. The phrase parodies Hermes Trismegistus, the Greek name
for Thoth, Egyptian god of wisdom, to whom a large body of mystical (or
"hermetic") writings was attributed in antiquity. In the gloss in the quarto,
Jonson gives the source of his parody: "the oracle of the bottle" is in Rabelais'
Pantagruel, V.xxxivff.; "la bouteille trimegiste" in V.xlvi.

51–52 PEGASUS . . . HOOF *The winged horse Pegasus, a favorite of the muses, pro-*
duced their sacred spring Hippocrene by striking Mt. Helicon with his hoof,
and was therefore related to poetic inspiration.

90–97 LATE . . . EXTREMES *An allegorical summary of the event the masque is*
celebrating. In 1623 Prince Charles, accompanied by the Duke of Buckingham
and Sir Francis Cottington, the prince's private secretary, had gone to Spain

to attempt to arrange a marriage for Charles with the Infanta Maria, sister of Philip IV. The marriage settlement involved large concessions to the cause of Catholicism in England, and was understandably unpopular with the British public, though it was one of the king's favorite projects. But although Charles agreed to all conditions, the Spanish court correctly felt that he had promised more than he could perform in regard to necessary changes in English law, and the match fell through. The prince's sour homecoming in October was a cause for great public rejoicing. The masque barely touches on the marriage, which would have been a sore point with the court (indeed, no reason at all is given for Albion's trip), but it makes much of the "safe" return of the emissaries. In the poet's allegorization, Neptune is James; Albion, traditional poetic name for England, is Charles; Hippius ("horse tamer") is Buckingham, Master of the King's Horse; Proteus, "father of disguise," is Cottington, an accomplished secret agent; the journey "through Celtiberia" was to Paris and thence, incognito, to Spain.

115–28 IT WAS NOT TIME . . . HEARD *The court had provided no celebration in October for what must have seemed to the king an appalling fiasco. Jonson's allegory here even manages to account for the three-month delay between the prince's landing and the masque.*

131–33 DELOS . . . EMERGENT *Latona, or Leto, was loved by Jupiter and became pregnant by him. She was persecuted by Juno and wandered the earth until Neptune provided the island of Delos for her, where she bore Apollo and Diana.*

142–50 TREE . . . PORTICUS *The tree is the ficus indica, or banyan, and it grows as Jonson says. The story that it was first planted by the sun in Musicanus, on the river Indus, is told by Strabo, Geography, XV.i.21.*

185 PROVERB *The proverb is, "Had I fish was never good with garlic." See M. P. Tilley, Dictionary of the Proverbs in England . . . (Ann Arbor, Michigan, 1950), p. 279. (For the apo koinu, cf. Hymenaei, line 741 and note.)*

208 GRACE'S STREET *According to John Stow in 1598, "poulters of late removed out of the Poultrie, betwixt the Stockes and the great Conduit in Cheape, into Grasse street . . ." Survey of London (London, 1603) p. 82.*

THE FORTUNATE ISLES, AND THEIR UNION

Performed January 9, 1625. Editions: Q, F[3].

Title DESIGNED . . . TWELFTH-NIGHT *In fact, the performance was delayed because of the king's illness.*

57–60 CASTLE . . . BLADE *Jonson is describing an engraving of the Rosicrucian castle in Theophilus Schweighardt's* Speculum Rhodo-stauroticum *(1618). "It has the wheels and wings, the latter projecting from a miniature temple on the top; it is foursquare with corners and turrets, in each of which is a warrior armed with a huge quill pen. The arm of a giant protrudes from a window, and below this is written 'Julian de Campis.'" (Herford and Simpson, X.670) It is also referred to in* News from the New World, *lines 190ff.*

68 JUBILE *The year of jubilee was, according to biblical prescription, every fiftieth year, but Johphiel appears to be following the practice of the Catholic church in making the twenty-fifth year a jubilee.*

99 PROVERB *See M. P. Tilley,* Dictionary of the Proverbs in England . . . *(Ann Arbor, Mich., 1950), p. 611.*

175 SCOGAN *Since Johphiel says Scogan lived in the time of Henry IV (line 177), there is no reason for the Oxford editors to claim, as they do, that Jonson identified Henry Scogan with John Scogan, Edward IV's jester. This was a common confusion, but Jonson is not guilty of it.*

189 TITYRE TU *Tityrus is a reformed rake in Virgil's first Eclogue, of which these are the opening words. The quotation may have been used as a form of greeting by members of the group.*

229 THE . . . KNAVES *The Oxford editors assume this is a reference to the lost play* The Cards, *a satirical drama performed at court in 1582. If this is correct, the allusion must have gone almost unrecognized. The play had been presented once, and over forty years before; it was never printed and, so far as we know, never revived.*

269 LAMBETH FERRY *This ran between Westminster and Lambeth, on the south bank of the Thames, an area notorious for its taverns and stews.*

298 FORTUNATE ISLANDS *For a general discussion of the tradition behind this epithet for England, see J. W. Bennett, "Britain Among the Fortunate Isles," Studies in Philology, LIII, 114–40.*

388 ALBION *Jonson is being careless in adapting material from the last year's masque. Since* Neptune's Triumph *was never produced, "when Albion was thy guest" could have made little sense to a contemporary spectator. It does serve to emphasize, however, the extent to which Jonson was also conceiving his masques as literature: to an audience of readers, it is perfectly appropriate.*

Love's Triumph Through Callipolis

Performed January 9, 1631. Editions: Q, F³.

196   *The folio continues:*

The Masquers' Names

The Marquis Hamilton	Lord Chamberlain [Philip,
Earl of Holland	Earl of Montgomery]
Earl of Newport	Earl of Carnarvon
Lord Strange	Viscount Doncaster
Sir Robert Stanley	Sir William Howard
Master [George] Goring	Sir William Brooke
Master Dymock	Master [Carew] Ralegh
	Master Abercrombie

Chloridia

Performed February 22, 1631. Editions: Q, F³.

258   *The folio continues:*

The Names of the Masquers as They Sat in the Bower

The Queen

Countess of Carlisle	Countess of Oxford
Lady Strange	Countess of Berkshire
Lady Anne Cavendish	Countess of Carnarvon
Countess of Newport	Lady Penelope Egerton
Mistress [Olivia] Porter	Mistress Dorothy Savage
Lady Howard	Mistress Elizabeth Savage
Mistress Anne Weston	Mistress Sophia Cary

Appendix

Note: All quotations are given in translation. Where Jonson wrote his original note in Latin or Greek, the translation has been printed in italics.

HYMENAEI

35–57 IONI . . . SACR. Mystically implying that both it, the place, and all the succeeding ceremonies were sacred to marriage, or union, over which Juno was president, to whom there was the like altar erected at Rome, as she was called *Iuga Iuno* [Juno the yoke], in the street which thence was named Iugarius. See [Sextus Pompeius] Festus, [*De Significatu Verborum*, under *Iugarius*] and at which altar the rite was to join the married pair with bands of silk in sign of future concord

38 FIVE TAPERS Those were the *quinque cerei* which Plutarch in his *Quaestiones Romanae* [ii] [*Morals* 263F–264B], mentions to be used in nuptials.

39 HAIR The dressing of the bridegroom with the ancients was chiefly noted in that *his hair was cut*. Juvenal, *Satires* VI.[26]: "Now your hair is dressed by a master barber." And Lucan, [*Pharsalia*] II.[372], where he makes Cato negligent of the ceremonies in marriage, saith, "He did not remove his terrible long hair from his holy face."

44 MARJORAM See how he is called out by Catullus in *The Marriage of Junia and Manlius* [lxi.6ff.]: "Bind your temples with the blossoms of the sweet-smelling marjoram," etc. PINE TREE For so I preserve the reading there in Catullus [15], "*pineam quate taedam*" [brandish the pine torch], rather than to change it "*spineam*" [thorn], and moved by the authority of Virgil in *Ciris* [439], where he says "Nor does the nuptial pine inflame chaste loves," and Ovid, *Fasti* II.[558], "Let the pine torch anticipate pure days." Though I deny not there was also *the thorn*

torch, which Pliny calls "most auspicious for marriage torches," *Natural History* XVI.[xxx.75], and whereof Sextus Pompeius Festus hath left so particular testimony. For which, see the following note.

46 YOUTH This by the ancients was called *camillus, that is, an acolyte* (for so that signified in the Etrurian tongue), and was one of the three which by Sextus Pompeius Festus were said to be "three boys, having father and mother still living, wearing the bordered toga of youths, who accompany the bride, one who bears the torch of thorn in front, two who support the bride." To which cf. that of Varro, *De Lingua Latina* VII.[34]: "The one who brings the *cumera* in marriage ceremonies is called a *camillus*," as also that of Festus [under *cumeram*]: "The ancients called a certain vessel which they would carry covered in marriage ceremonies, in which were the utensils of the bride, a *cumera*; they also called it a *camillus* for this reason, that they called the ministrant of the ceremonies *kamillon*."

53 AUSPICES *Auspices* were those that hand-fasted the married couple, that wished them good luck, that took care for the dowry, and heard them profess that they came together for the cause of children. Juvenal, *Satires* X.[336]: "The *auspex* will come with the witnesses." And Lucan, [*Pharsalia*] II.[371]: "They were silently and contentedly joined, with Brutus as their *auspex*." They were also styled *pronubi, pronextae, paranymphae*.

55 MUSICIANS The custom of music at nuptials is clear in all antiquity. Terence *Adelphi* V.[905]: "But this is what is delaying me, a flute-player and people to sing the marriage song." And Claudian in *Epithalamium* [i.e. *Fescennine Verses* IV.30]: "Let flutes that play through the night lead the songs," etc.

100 HUMORS . . . AFFECTIONS That they were personated in men hath already come under some grammatical exception. But there is more than grammar to release it. For besides that *humores* and *affectus* are both *masculine in gender*, not one of the specials[2] but in some language is known by a masculine word; again, when their influences are common to both sexes, and more generally impetuous in the male, I see not

2. Specials: particular terms for the individual humors and passions.

why they should not so be more properly presented. And for the allegory, though here it be very clear and such as might well escape a candle, yet because there are some must complain of darkness that have but thick eyes, I am contented to hold them this light. First, as in natural bodies, so likewise in minds, there is no disease or distemperature but is caused either by some abounding humor or perverse affection; after the same manner, in politic bodies (where order, ceremony, state, reverence, devotion are parts of the mind) by the difference or predominant will of what we metaphorically call *humors* and *affections* all things are troubled and confused. These, therefore, were tropically brought in before marriage as disturbers of that mystical body and the rites which were soul unto it, that afterwards, in marriage, being dutifully tempered by her power, they might more fully celebrate the happiness of such as live in that sweet union to the harmonious laws of nature and reason.

112 NUMEROUS FLAME Alluding to that opinion of Pythagoras, who held all reason, all knowledge, all discourse of the soul to be mere number. See Plutarch, *De Placitis Philosophorum* [I.iii] [*Morals* 876E–877C].

123 ORGIES *Orgia* with the Greeks value the same that *ceremoniae* with the Latins, and imply all sorts of rites; however, abusively, they have been made particular to Bacchus. See Servius [commentary] to that of Virgil, *Aeneid* IV.301–02.

126 SPRING . . . END Macrobius, *In Somnium Scipionis* I.[14.14].

149 GENIAL BED Properly, that which was made ready for the new-married bride, and was called *genialis from the generation of children*. Servius on *Aeneid* VI.[603].

155 OMINOUS LIGHT See Ovid, *Fasti* VI.[129–30]: "So saying, he gave her a thorn with which she could drive off all grim harm from the doors; the thorn was white."

157 FIRE . . . WATER Plutarch in *Quaestiones Romanae*, [i] [*Morals* 263E], and Varro, *De Lingua Latina* V.[61].

161 BLUSHING VEIL Pliny, *Natural History* XXI.viii.[11].

Appendix: Hymenaei (pages 53–55)

163 HAIR Pompeius Festus [under *senis crinibus*], [Barnabé] Brisson [*De Ritu Nuptiarum* (Leyden, 1641) p. 46 (B11v)], [Antoine] Hotman [*De Veteri Ritu Nuptiarum* (Leyden, 1641, etc.) chap. xvi], on marriage rites.

167 UTENSILS Varro, *De Lingua Latina* VII.[34], and Festus [under *cumeram*].

169 SNOWY FLEECE Festus [under *in pelle lanata*].

170 ROCK . . . SPINDLE Plutarch in *Quaestiones Romanae* [xxxi] [*Morals* 271F–272A], and in the *Life of Romulus* [xv.3–4].

173 ZONE Pliny, *Natural History* VIII.xlviii. [Incorrect; untraced.]

175 STRONG KNOT That was *nodus Herculeanus* [Hercules' knot], which the husband at night untied in sign of good fortune, that he might be happy in propagation of issue, as Hercules was, who left seventy children. See Festus, under *cingillo*.

179 FIVE . . . NUMBER Plutarch in *Quaestiones Romanae* [ii] [*Morals* 264A–B].

183 MALE . . . NUMBERS See Martianus Capella, *De Nuptiis Mercurii et Philologiae* [VII.735] *on the number five*.

195 JUNO With the Greeks, Juno was interpreted to be the air itself; and so Macrobius, *In Somnium Scipionis* I.17.[15], calls her. Martianus Capella surnames her Aeria, of reigning there [*De Nuptiis Mercurii et Philologiae* II.149].

196 PEACOCKS They were sacred to Juno in respect of their colors and temper, so like the air. Ovid, *De Arte Amandi* [I.627]: "The bird of Juno displays her excellent feathers."[3] And *Metamorphoses*, II.[531–32]: "In her supple chariot Saturnia [=Juno] moves through the yielding air drawn by splendid peacocks." QUEEN She was called *Regina Iuno* with the Latins because she was *sister and wife of Jove, king of gods and men*. WHITE DIADEM Read Apuleius describing her in his *Golden Ass* X.[30].

197 FASCIA After the manner of the antique band, the varied colors implying the several mutations of the air, as showers, dews, serenity, force of

3. Herford and Simpson mysteriously claim that there is no such passage, and that Jonson is fusing two others.

winds, clouds, tempest, snow, hail, lightning, thunder, all which had their noises signified in her timbrel; the faculty of causing these being ascribed to her by Virgil, *Aeneid* IV.[120–22], where he makes her say, "On them . . . I shall pour down from above a black rain mixed with hail, and shake all the sky with thunder."

199 LILIES Lilies were sacred to Juno, as being made white with her milk that fell upon the earth when Jove took Hercules away, whom by stealth he had laid to her breast. The rose was also called *Iunonia*.[4]

200 HIDE . . . LION So was she figured at Argos, as a stepmother insulting on the spoils of her two *stepsons*, Bacchus and Hercules.

206 GOVERNESS See Virgil, *Aeneid* IV.[59]: "Before all, to Juno, guardian of the bonds of marriage"; and in another place [IV.166–67], "Primal Earth and nuptial Juno gave the sign"; and Ovid in *Heroides* II.[41]: "Juno, who as patroness presides over marriage beds."

216 ENSTYLED . . . FACULTIES They were all eight called by particular surnames of Juno, ascribed to her for some peculiar property in marriage, as somewhere after [lines 258ff.] is more fitly declared.

258 CURIS This surname Juno received of the Sabines; from them the Romans gave it her of the spear, which in the Sabine tongue was called *curis*, and was that which they named *hasta caelibaris* [the caelibarian spear], which had stuck in the body of a slain sword-player, and wherewith the bride's head was dressed, whereof Festus under the word *caelibar* gives these reasons: "That just as the spear had been joined with the body of the gladiator, so she herself was joined with the man; or because they are under the protection of the matron Juno-of-the-spear, who was so called from carrying a spear; or because it omened that brave men were to be born; or because in accordance with marriage law the bride is subordinated to the command of her husband, and the spear is the greatest of weapons and implies command," etc. To most of which Plutarch in his *Quaestiones Romanae* [lxxxvii] [*Morals* 285B–D] consents, but adds a better in the *Life of Romulus* [xv.5]: that when they divided the bride's hair with the point of the spear, it noted their first nuptials with the Sabines were contracted by

4. Jonson's error: the lily was called Juno's rose.

force and as with enemies. Howsoever, that it was a custom with them, this of Ovid, *Fasti* II.[560], confirms: "[Nor] let a bent spear adorn the virgin's locks."

259 UNXIA For the surname of Unxia we have Martianus Capella his testimony in *De Nuptiis Mercurii et Philologiae*, II.[149], *because she is in charge of anointings* [*unctiones*]; as also Servius [commentary] on *Aeneid* IV.[459], where they both report it a fashion with the Romans that before the new-married brides entered the houses of their husbands, they adorned the posts of the gates with woolen tawdries, or fillets, and anointed them with oils or the fat of wolves and boars, being superstitiously possessed that such ointments had the virtue of expelling evils from the family; and thence were they called *uxores quasi unxores* [wives as anointers].

260 JUGA She was named Juga *propter iugum* (as Servius says), for the yoke which was imposed in matrimony on those that were married; or (with Sextus Pompeius Festus [under *iuges*]) "because yoked creatures are equals beneath the same yoke, whence also *coniuges* [married people]"; or in respect of the altar (to which I have declared before) sacred to Juno *in Iugarius Street*. [See Jonson's note to lines 35-7.]

261 GAMELIA As she was Gamelia, in sacrificing to her they took away the gall and threw it behind the altar, intimating that after the marriage there should be known no bitterness nor hatred between the joined couple which might divide or separate them. See Plutarch, *Praecepta Coniugalia* [xxvii] [*Morals* 141F]. This rite I have somewhere following touched at [line 294].

262 ITERDUCA The title of Iterduca she had amongst them *because she accompanied brides to the house of the bridegroom*, or was a protectress of their journey. Martianus Capella, *De Nuptiis Philologiae et Mercurii* II.[149].

263 DOMIDUCA The like of Domiduca, *because she led them to the homes they desired*. Martianus, ibid.

264 CINXIA Cinxia the same author gives unto her as the defendress of maids when they had put off their girdle in the bridal chamber; to which, Festus: "The name of Juno Cinxia was held sacred in marriage

because at the beginning of the union there was an untying of the girdle with which the new bride was encircled." And Arnobius [Afer], a man most learned in their ceremonies, [*Disputationes*] *Adversus Gentes* III.[115] saith, "Unxia assists anointings, Cinxia the undoing of girdles."

265 TELIA Telia signifies *Perfecta*, or, as some translate it, *Perfectrix* [she who makes perfect]; with Julius Pollux, *Onomasticon* III, "*Hera teleía*" values "Juno who presides over marriages," who saith the attribute descends of *téleios*, which with the ancients signified marriage, and thence were they called *téleioi* that entered into that estate. Servius interprets it the same with Gamelia, [commentary on] *Aeneid* IV.45, but it implies much more, as including the faculty to mature and perfect; see the Greek scholiast on Pindar, *Nemean Odes* X: "nuptials are therefore called *téleioi* because they bring about the perfection of life," and do note that maturity which should be in matrimony. For before nuptials she is called *Iuno parthénos*, that is, *virgo*; after nuptials, *teleía*, which is *adulta* or *perfecta*.

286 GOLDEN CHAIN Mentioned by Homer, *Iliad* VIII.[19], which many have interpreted diversely: allegorically Plato, in the *Theaetetus* [153c–d], understands it to be the sun, with which, while he circles the world in his course, all things are safe and preserved; others vary it. Macrobius, to whose interpretation I am specially affected in my allusion, considers it thus (*In Somnium Scipionis* I.14.[15]): "Accordingly, since Mind emanates from the Supreme God and Soul from Mind, and Mind, indeed, forms and suffuses all below with life, and since this is the one splendor lighting up everything and visible in all, like a countenance reflected in many mirrors arranged in a row, and since all follow on in continuous succession, degenerating step by step in their downward course, the close observer will find that from the Supreme God even to the bottommost dregs of the universe there is one tie, binding at every link and never broken. This is the golden chain of Homer which, he tells us, God ordered to hang down from the sky to the earth."[5] To which strength and evenness of connection I have not absurdly likened this uniting of humors and affections by the sacred powers of marriage.

5. Translated by W. H. Stall (New York, 1952), p. 145.

Appendix: Hymenaei (pages 59–61)

319 IDALIAN STAR *Stella Veneris* [Venus' star], or Venus, which when it goes before the sun is called Phosphorus, or Lucifer [light-bringer]; when it follows, Hesperus, or Noctifer [night-bringer] (as Catullus translates it [lxii.7]). See Cicero, *De Natura Deorum* II.[xx.53]; Martianus Capella, *De Nuptiis Philologiae et Mercurii* VIII.[883]. The nature of this star Pythagoras first found out, and the present office Claudian expresseth in *Fescennine Verses* [IV.1–2]: "Hesperus, beloved of Venus, rises and shines for the marriage with his Idalian rays."

323 PORCH It was a custom for the man to stand there, expecting the approach of his bride. See [Antoine] Hotman, *De [Veteri] Ritu Nuptiarum* [(Leyden, 1641, etc.) xix].

325–26 MIXED . . . FIRE Alluding to that of Virgil, *Aeneid* IV.[166]: "Primal Earth and nuptial Juno give the sign; fires flashed in heaven, the witness to their marriage," etc.

331 THOUSAND . . . LOVES Statius, *Silvae* I.2.[54]: "About the posts and pillows of her couch swarm a troop of tender loves." And Claudian, *Epithalamium* [*of Palladius and Celerina*, 10–11]: "Here and there, wherever the shade invites them, rest winged boys." Both which prove the ancients feigned many Cupids. Read also Propertius, *Elegies* II.xxix.

335 CYPRIA Venus is so induced by Statius, Claudian and others, to celebrate nuptials.

365 CESTON Venus' girdle, mentioned by Homer, *Iliad* XIV.[214–17], which was feigned to be variously wrought with the needle, and in it woven love, desire, sweetness, soft parley, gracefulness, persuasion and all the powers of Venus.

374 NAME See the words of Aelius Verus, in [Aelius] Spartianus [*Life of Aelius Verus* V.11 (in *Scriptores Historiae Augustae*, Vol. I, Loeb Library)].

376 FLAMING HAIR So Catullus lxi.[77–8] hath it: "Do you see how the torches shake their shining locks?" And by and by after [95], "shake their golden locks."

346

394 EPITHALAMIUM It had the name *from the thalamus, and the nuptial chamber is called thalamos* [Gk.] *because of the original meaning of the word, from "flourishing* [thallein] *together," that is, leading a procreative life together.* [Julius Caesar] Scaliger, in *Poetices*[*Libri Septem ad Sylvium* (Lyons, 1561), III, Chap. 100, "Epithalamion"].

406 'TIS CUPID, ETC. This poem [i.e. the epithalamion] had for the most part *intercalary verses,*[6] or *alternating verses*; yet that not always one, but oftentimes varied, and sometimes neglected in the same song, as in ours you shall find observed.

418 RAP The bride was always feigned to be ravished *from her mother's bosom,* or, if she were wanting, *from the nearest relation,* because that had succeeded well to Romulus, who by force gat wives for him and his from the Sabines. See Festus [under *rapi*], and that of Catullus, [lxi.3–4]: "You who carry off the tender maiden to a husband. . . ."

430 LIKE TO HIM When he is Phosphorus, yet the same star, as I have noted before [line 319].

435 MISTRESS At the entrance of the bride the custom was to give her the keys, to signify that she was absolute mistress of the place, and the whole disposition of the family at her care. Festus [under *clavim*].

437 LIFT . . . FEET This was also another rite, that she might not touch the threshold as she entered, but was lifted over it. Servius saith, because it was sacred to Vesta [commentary on Virgil, *Eclogues* viii.29, 92]. Plutarch in *Quaestiones Romanae* [xxix] [*Morals* 271D], remembers divers causes. But that which I take to come nearest the truth was only the avoiding of sorcerous drugs, used by witches to be buried under that place to the destroying of marriage amity or the power of generation. See Alexander [ab Alexandro], *Dies Geniales* [II.v] [ed. Tiraquell (Lyons, 1586) p. 139 (M4r)], and Constantinus Landus [or Costanzo Landi] upon Catullus [text and commentary, Pavia, 1550, etc. *In Nuptias Iuliae et Manlii,* numbered lxii in Landi, lxi in modern editions, gloss on "Transfer omine . . ." (l. 162).]

6. Intercalary verses: hypermetric lines inserted at intervals.

Appendix: The Masque of Queens (pages 64–81)

451 SNATCH For this, look Festus, on the word *rapi*.

452, 454 SHE, HE "By each of which deeds the other's early death is thought to be desired." Festus, ibid.

483 CYPRIS A frequent surname of Venus, not of the place, as Cypria, but *because she brings about birth* [parere], *the one who causes conception.* Theophilus [i.e. Scholiast · Venetus B on *Iliad* V.458], Phurnutus [i.e. L. Annaeus Cornutus, *De Natura Deorum* xxiv.198n], and the grammarians upon Homer. See them.

493 GENIUS *The god of nature, or of begetting.* And is the same in the male as Juno in the female. Hence *the "genial" bed, which is made at weddings in honor of the Genius.* Festus [under *genium*]: "My Genius, because he begot [*genuit*] me."

496 VENUS She hath this faculty given her by all the ancients. See Homer, *Iliad* V.[429], Lucretius [*De Rerum Natura*] I.[1ff.], Virgil, *Georgics* II.[329], etc.

629 TIME Truth is feigned to be the daughter of Saturn, who indeed with the ancients was no other than Time, and so his name alludes, *Kronos*.[7] Plutarch in *Questiones Romanae* [xii] [*Morals* 266E–F]. To which, cf. the Greek adage, "*Time brings truth to light.*"

646 OPINION Hippocrates in a certain epistle [15 (spurious)] to Philopoemon describeth her: "a woman who does not look evil, but rather bold and vehement." To which Cesare Ripa in his *Iconology* alludeth in these words [on *Opinione*]: "a face neither pretty nor displeasing," etc.

697 EURIPUS A narrow sea, between Aulis, a port of Boeotia, and the isle Euboea. See Pomponius Mela, [*De Situ Orbi*] II.[vii].

THE MASQUE OF QUEENS

24–25 QUAE . . . POSSIT *See Laevinus Torrentius, commentary on Horace* [Antwerp, 1608], *Epodes* v [on line 15].

7. A late classical etymology that identifies *Kronos* with *Chronos*.

36 CEREMONY See the king's majesty's book (our sovereign) [James I] of *Demonology*.[8] [Jean] Bodin [*De la Demonomanie des Sorciers*, Paris, 1580].[9] Remigius [i.e. Nicholas Remy, *Daemonolatria*, Lyons, 1595]. [Martin Antoine] del Rio [*Disquisitiones Magicae*, Louvain, 1599]. *Malleus Maleficarum* [Jacob Sprenger and Henricus Krämer (Henricus Institoris), Nuremburg, 1494, etc.], and a world of others in the general; but let us follow particulars.

40 DAME Amongst our vulgar witches, the honor of Dame (for so I translate it) is given, with a kind of preëminence, to some special one at their meetings. Which del Rio insinuates, *Disquisitiones Magicae* II, question ix [B], quoting that of Apuleius, *The Golden Ass* I.[8], "concerning a certain woman tavern keeper, a queen of sorceresses," and adds, "that you may know that even then some were honored by them with this title." Which title Master Philip Ludwig Elich, *Daemonomagia* [Frankfurt, 1607], question x [p. 140], doth also remember.

43 ANOINT When they are to be transported from place to place they use to anoint themselves, and sometimes the things they ride on. Beside Apuleius' testimony, see these later: Remy, *Daemonolatria* I.xiv. Del Rio, *Disquisitiones Magicae* II, question xvi [C]. Bodin, *Demonomanie* II.iv. Bartolomeo Spina, *Quaestio de Strigibus* [(Rome, 1576, etc.) chapter xviii].[10] Philip Ludwig Elich, [*Daemonomagia*] question x [p. 141]. Paracelsus in *De Magna et Occulta Philosophia*[11] teacheth the confection: "an ointment from the flesh of newborn infants, cooked

8. Jonson is mistaken: James does not discuss witches' dancing.
9. Jonson used the Latin translation, *De Magorum Daemonomania* (Basel, 1581, etc.).
10. Jonson cites the reprint in *Malleorum Quorundam Maleficarum*, part II (Frankfurt, 1588) in his gloss on line 158.
11. Incorrect; Paracelsus discusses witches in a number of places, but the passage quoted appears nowhere among them. Moreover, Jonson has confused the titles of two separate works by Paracelsus, the brief tract *De Occulta Philosophia*, and *Philosophia Magna*, the general title given to a collection of tracts on natural philosophy in the Basel edition of 1570, translated and edited by Gerardus Dorn. Jonson probably copied the error from J. G. Godelmann, *Tractatus De Magis . . .* (Frankfurt, 1591) II.iv, p. 34, who quotes the passage (which he ascribes to "Paracelsus in sua magna Philosophia & occulta Philos."—hence Jonson's confusion about the title), and also cites the Bodin and Porta references (pp. 33, 38).

like a sauce, and with sleep-inducing herbs, such as poppy, nightshade, hemlock," etc. And Giovanni Battista della Porta, *Magia Naturalis* [Naples, 1558, etc.] II.xxvi.[12]

47 FROM THE LAKES These places, in their own nature dire and dismal, are reckoned up as the fittest from whence such persons should come, and were notably observed by that excellent Lucan in the description of his Erictho, [*Pharsalia*] VI.[507ff.]. To which we may add this corollary out of [Heinrich Cornelius] Agrippa [von Nettesheim], *De Occulta Philosophia* [Cologne, 1533, etc.] I.xlviii: "To Saturn correspond any places that are fetid, dark, underground, superstitious or dismal, such as cemetaries, tombs, dwellings deserted by men and ruinous with age, dark and horrible places, lonely caves, caverns, wells. Furthermore, fish-ponds, fens, swamps and the like." And in book III, chapter xlii, speaking of the like; and in book IV [spurious], about the end [last paragraph: in *Opera* ("Lyons,"[13] n.d.) I.453–54 (fol. Ff3r–v)]: "They are the places best suited to the experience of visions, nocturnal incursions, and similar apparitions, such as cemetaries, and places in which the execution of a criminal sentence is usually held, and where in recent years there has been a massacre, or where the corpses of the slain, not yet expiated or duly buried, have in very recent years been uncovered."

57 HORSE Del Rio, *Disquisitiones Magicae* II, question vi[D], has a story out of Triezius of this horse of wood; but that which our witches call so is sometime a broomstaff, sometime a reed, sometime a distaff. See Remy, *Daemonolatria* I.xiv; Bodin, [*Demonomanie*] II.iv, etc.

59 GOAT The goat is the devil himself, upon whom they ride often to their solemnities, as appears by their confessions in Remy and Bodin, ibid. [Jonson's error: the Remy citation should be I.xxiii.] His majesty also

12. The chapter is entitled "*Insomnia Clara . . .*", and appears only in the early editions; it is omitted from the version on which the English translation of 1658 is based. The section on witches' ointments is headed "*Lamiarum Unguenta.*"

13. In fact, a seventeenth-century German edition with a fictitious imprint. The so-called book IV was first printed with *De Occulta Philosophia* around 1600, in an edition with a false Lyons imprint. (The volume was formerly thought to have been published at Paris in 1567; but see the most recent B.M. Catalogue.)

remembers the story of the devil's appearance to those of Calicut, in that form. *Demonology* II.iii. COCK Of the green cock we have no other ground (to confess ingenuously) than a vulgar fable of a witch that with a cock of that color and a bottom of blue thread would transport herself through the air, and so escaped, at the time of her being brought to execution, from the hand of justice. It was a tale when I went to school. And somewhat there is like it in Martin del Rio, *Disquisitiones Magicae* II, question vi(B), of one Zijto, a Bohemian, that, among other his dexterities, "sometimes would follow after a conveyance drawn by carriage horses with dunghill cocks attached to the harness."

72 SPINDLE All this is but a periphrasis of the night in their charm, and their applying themselves to it with their instruments, whereof the spindle in antiquity was the chief, and (beside the testimony of Theocritus in *Pharmaceutria* [*Idylls* II.30], who only used it in amorous affairs) was of special act to the troubling of the moon. To which Martial alludes, IX.xxix.[9]: "Who now will know how to draw down the moon with the Thessalian wheel?" etc. And XII.lvii.[17]: ". . . when the eclipsed moon is being attacked by the Colchian wheel."

75 DITCH This rite also of making a ditch with their nails is frequent with our witches; whereof see Bodin, Remy, del Rio, [Sprenger and Krämer] *Malleus Maleficarum*, [Johann Georg] Godelmann, *De Lamiis* [i.e. *Tractatus De Magis, Veneficis, et Lamiis*, Frankfurt, 1591, etc.] II; as also the antiquity of it most vively expressed by Horace, *Satires* I.viii.[26ff.], where he mentions the pictures, and the blood of a black lamb, all which are yet in use with our modern witchcraft: "Then they (speaking of Canidia and Sagana) began to dig up the earth with their nails, and to tear a black lamb to pieces with their teeth; the blood was all poured into a trench so that from it they might draw forth the spirits, souls that would give them answers. One image there was of wool, and one of wax," etc. And then, by and by [34ff.], "You might see serpents and hell-hounds roaming about, and the blushing moon, that she might not witness such deeds, hiding behind the tall tombs." Of this ditch, Homer makes mention in Circe's speech to Ulysses, *Odyssey* X about the end [516ff.]. And Ovid, *Metamorphoses*

VII.[243–45], in Medea's magic: "Then nearby she dug two ditches in the earth and performed her rites; plunging her knife into the throat of a black sheep, she drenched the open ditches with its blood." And of the waxen images, in Hypsipyle's epistle to Jason [*Heroides* VI.91–2], where he expresseth that mischief also of the needles: "She vows to their doom the absent persons, fashions the waxen image, and into its wretched heart drives the slender needle." Bodin, *Demonomanie* II.viii, hath (beside the known story of King Duff, out of Hector Boethius) much of the witches' later practice in that kind, and reports a relation of a French ambassador's, out of England, of certain pictures of wax found in a dunghill near Islington, of our late queen's; which rumor I myself (being then very young) can yet remember to have been current.

80 MARTIN Their little Martin is he that calls them to their conventicles, which is done in a human voice; but coming forth, they find him in the shape of a great buck-goat, upon whom they ride to their meetings. Del Rio, *Disquisitiones Magicae* II, question xvi[B], and Bodin, *Demonomanie* II.iv, have both the same relation, from Paulus Grillandus, of a witch: "When night and the hour came, she would be summoned by a certain voice, as if human, from the devil himself, whom they do not call the devil, but *Magisterulus* [little master], and others Master Martinet, or Martinel. Having been summoned in this way, she would take up a box of ointment and smear certain parts of her body and limbs. After smearing herself she would leave her house and find her *magisterulus* awaiting her in the form of a he-goat at the door. The woman would ride on him, and she used to take a tight grip on his hair, and immediately the goat would rise up through the air and, after a very short time, set her down again," etc.

87 DAME This Dame I make to bear the person of Ate, or mischief (for so I interpret it) out of Homer's description of her, *Iliad* IX.[505–12], where he makes her swift to hurt mankind, strong, and sound of feet; and *Iliad* XIX.[91–4], walking upon men's heads; in both places using one and the same phrase to signify her power, "harming men." I present her barefooted, and her frock tucked, to make her seem more

expedite, by Horace his authority, *Satires* I.viii.[23–4]: "My own eyes have seen Canidia walk with black robe tucked up, her feet bare, her hair dishevelled . . ." But for her hair, I rather respect another place of his, *Epodes* V.[15–16], where she appears, "Canidia, her locks entwined with short snakes, and her hair dishevelled." And that of Lucan, [*Pharsalia*] VI.[654ff.], speaking of Erictho's attire: "She wore a motley robe such as the furies wear, and revealed her face by throwing back her hair, and wreathed her bristling locks with a garland of vipers." For her torch, see Remy, II.iii.

104 FIRST In the chaining of these vices, I make as if one link produced another, and the Dame were born out of them all; so, as they might say to her, "You alone have as many vices as all of us possess." [Adapted from Claudian, *In Rufinum* I.111.] Nor will it appear much violenced if their series be considered, when the opposition to all virtue begins out of Ignorance. That Ignorance begets Suspicion (for knowledge is ever open and charitable), that Suspicion Credulity, as it is a vice; for being a virtue, and free, it is opposite to it; but such as are jealous of themselves do easily credit anything of others, whom they hate. Out of this Credulity springs Falsehood, which begets Murmur; and that Murmur presently grows Malice, which begets Impudence; that Impudence Slander, that Slander Execration, Execration Bitterness, Bitterness Fury, and Fury Mischief. Now for the personal presentation of them, the authority in poetry is universal. But in the absolute Claudian there is a particular and eminent place where the poet not only produceth such persons, but almost to a like purpose: *In Rufinum* I.[25–34], where Alecto, envious of the times, "summons the hideous council of the infernal sisters to her foul palace gates. Hell's numberless monsters are gathered together, Night's children of ill-omened birth. Discord, nurse of war; imperious Hunger; Age, near neighbor to Death; Disease, whose life is a burden to himself; Envy that brooks not another's prosperity; woeful Sorrow with rent garments; Fear, and foolhardy Rashness with sightless eyes"; with many others fit to disturb the world, as ours the night.

120 JOIN Here again, by way of irritation, I make the Dame pursue the purpose of their coming and discover their natures more largely,

which had been nothing if not done as doing another thing, but "tarrying along the easy and open course" [adapting Horace, *Ars Poetica*, 132]. Than which the poet cannot know a greater vice, he being that kind of artificer to whose work is required so much exactness as indifferency is not tolerable.

134 DISTURB These powers of troubling nature are frequently ascribed to witches, and challenged by themselves wherever they are induced by Homer, Ovid, Tibullus, Petronius Arbiter, Seneca, Lucan, Claudian, to whose authorities I shall refer more anon. For the present, hear Socrates in Apuleius' *The Golden Ass* I.[8] describing Meroë the witch: "Verily, she is a magician, and of divine might, which hath power to bring down the sky, to bear up the earth, to turn the waters into hills and the hills into running waters, to call up the terrestrial spirits into the air, to pull the gods out of the heavens, to extinguish the planets, and to lighten the very darkness of hell." And book II.[5], Byrrhena to Lucius, of Pamphile: "For she is accounted the most chief and principal magician and enchantress of every necromantic spell: who, by breathing out certain words and charms over boughs and stones and other frivolous things, can throw down all the light of the starry heavens into the deep bottom of hell, and reduce them again to the old chaos."[14] As also this later of Remy, in his most elegant arguments before his *Daemonolatria*: "How they may overturn the universe from its very foundations, and mingle the shades below with the gods above, this is their sole concern."[15] And Lucan [*Pharsalia* VI.437]: "they whose art is to do whatever is thought impossible. . . ."

140 BUT FIRST This is also solemn in their witchcraft, to be examined either by the devil or their Dame at their meetings, of what mischief they have done, and what they can confer to a future hurt. See Master Philip Ludwig Elich, *Daemonomagia*, question x [pp. 136–37]. But Remy, in the very form, *Daemonolatria* I.xxii: "Just as masters are accustomed, when they examine the accounts of the managers of their estates, to punish indolence and negligence quite severely, so the devil

14. Translations from Apuleius are those of W. Adlington, 1566.
15. From a verse argument of the book appearing only in the Lyons edition of 1595, p. 9 (B1r).

in his assemblies, at the time which he has set for examining the affairs and the deeds of each, is accustomed to have the lowest opinion of those who present nothing by which they may show themselves baser and more laden with crimes. And it is not safe for anyone if he has not, since the last gathering, committed any new wickedness; rather it always befits him who wishes to be in favor to have done some new misdeed against another." And this doth exceedingly solicit them all at such times, lest they come unprepared. But we apply this examination of ours to the particular use, whereby also we take occasion not alone to express the things (as vapors, liquors, herbs, bones, flesh, blood, fat, and such like, which are called *media magica* [the means of magic]) but the rites of gathering them and from what places, reconciling (as near as we can) the practice of antiquity to the neoteric, and making it familiar with our popular witchcraft.

142 1ST HAG For the gathering pieces of dead flesh, Cornelius Agrippa, *De Occulta Philosophia* III.xlii and IV, last chapter [*Opera* ("Lyons," n.d.) I.452 (Ff2v)], observes that the use was to call up ghosts and spirits with a fumigation made of that (and bones of carcases) which I make my witch here not to cut herself, but to watch the raven, as Lucan's Erictho, [*Pharsalia*] VI.[550ff.]: "Whenever any corpse lies exposed on the ground, she sits by it before beast or bird can come; but she will not mangle the limbs with the knife or her bare hands; she waits for the wolves to tear it, and means to snatch the prey from their unwetted throats," as if that piece were sweeter which the wolf had bitten or the raven had picked, and more effectuous; and to do it at her turning to the south, as with the prediction of a storm. Which, though they be but minutes in ceremony, being observed make the act more dark and full of horror.

146 2ND HAG *The foam of dogs, the hair of a wolf, the hump of a hyena, serpents' eyes, the skin of a snake, an asp's ears* are all mentioned by the ancients in witchcraft. And Lucan particularly, [*Pharsalia*] VI.[670–72]: "With this was blended all that nature inauspiciously conceives and brings forth. The froth of dogs that dread water was not wanting, nor the innards of a lynx, nor the hump of a foul hyena," etc. And Ovid, *Metamorphoses* VII. [264–74] reckons up others. But for the spurging

of the eyes, let us return to Lucan, in the same book, which piece (as all the rest) is written with an admirable height. "But, when the dead are coffined in stone, which drains off the internal moisture, absorbs the corruption of marrow, and makes the corpse rigid, then the witch eagerly vents her rage on all the limbs, thrusting her fingers into the eyes, scooping out gleefully the stiffened eyeballs, and gnawing the yellow nails on the withered hand." [538–43]

150 3RD HAG Pliny, writing of the mandrake, *Natural History* XXV. [xciv.148], and of the digging it up, hath this ceremony: "The diggers avoid facing the wind, first trace round the plant three circles with a sword, and then do their digging while facing the west." But we have later tradition that the forcing of it up is so fatally dangerous as the groan kills, and therefore they do it with dogs, which I think but borrowed from Josephus his report of the root *baaras*, *The Jewish War* VII.[180–84]. Howsoever, it being so principal an ingredient in their magic, it was fit she should boast to be the plucker of it up herself. And that the cock did crow alludes to a prime circumstance in their work; for they all confess that nothing is so cross or baleful to them in their nights as that the cock should crow before they have done. Which makes that their little masters or Martinets, of whom I have mentioned before, use this form in dismissing their conventions: "*Quick! hence away, all of you, for now the cocks begin to crow*"; which I interpret to be because that bird is the messenger of light, and so contrary to their acts of darkness. See Remy, *Daemonolatria* I.xiv, where he quotes that of Apollonius on the shade of Achilles, Philostratus, [*Life· of Apollonius of Tyana*] IV.xvi. And Eusebius [Pamphili] of Caesarea, *Adversus Hieroclem* XXV, on the crowing of cocks.

154 4TH HAG I have touched at this before, in my note upon the first, of the use of gathering flesh, bones, and skulls; to which I now bring that piece of Apuleius, *The Golden Ass* III.[17], of Pamphile: "She gathered together all her accustomed substance for fumigations, she brought forth plates of metal carved with strange characters, she prepared the bones of birds of ill-omen, she made ready the members of dead men brought from their tombs. Here she set out their nostrils and fingers, there the nails with lumps of flesh of such as were hanged, the blood

she had reserved of such as were slain, and skulls snatched away from the jaws and teeth of wild beasts." And for such places, Lucan makes his witch to inhabit them, [*Pharsalia*] VI.[511–12]: "She inhabited deserted tombs, and haunted graves from which the ghosts had been driven."

158 5TH HAG For this rite, see Bartolomeo Spina, *Quaestio de Strigibus* chapter viii, [in] *Malleorum Quorundam Maleficarum*, part II [Frankfurt, 1588], where he disputes at large the transformation of witches to cats, and their sucking both the spirits and the blood, calling them *striges* [screech owls], which Godelmann, *De Magis, Veneficis, et Lamiis* [II,i], would have "from *stridor* [screeching], and from most foul birds of the same name"; which I the rather incline to out of Ovid's authority, *Fasti* VI.[135–38], where the poet ascribes to those birds the same almost that these do to the witches: "They fly by night and attack nurseless children, and defile their bodies, snatched from their cradles. They are said to rend the flesh of sucklings with their beaks, and their throats are full of blood which they have drunk."

162 6TH HAG Their killing of infants is common, both for confection of their ointment (whereto one ingredient is the fat boiled, as I have showed before out of Paracelsus and Porta) as also out of a lust to do murder. Sprenger in *Malleus Maleficarum* [part II, question 1, chapter 13] reports that a witch, a midwife in the diocese of Basel, confessed to have killed above forty infants, ever as they were newborn, with pricking them into the brain with a needle, which she had offered to the devil. See the story of the three witches in Remy, *Daemonolatria* II.iii, about the end of the chapter. And Master Philip Ludwig Elich, [*Daemonomagia*] question vii [pp. 97–8]. And that it is no new rite, read the practice of Canidia, Horace, *Epodes* V, and Lucan, [*Pharsalia*] VI.[554ff.], whose admirable verses I can never be weary to transcribe: "Nor is she slow to take life, if such warm blood is needed as gushes forth at once when the throat is slit, nor does she scorn murder if her rites demand live blood, and if her ghoulish feast demands still palpitating flesh. In the same way she pierces the pregnant womb and delivers the child by an unnatural birth in order to place it on the fiery

357

altar, and whenever she requires the service of a bold, bad spirit, she takes life with her own hand. Every man's death serves her turn."

166 7TH HAG The abuse of dead bodies in their witchcraft both Porphyry and [Michael] Psellus [the younger] are grave authors of. The one, *De Sacrifiis et Diis atque Daemonibus* [Venice, 1497, etc.], [last] chapter, "De Vero Cultu. . . ." The other, *De Daemonibus* [i.e. *De Operatione Daemonum*, Paris, 1577, etc.],[16] which Apuleius toucheth too, *The Golden Ass* II.[21–2]. But Remy, who deals with later persons, and out of their own mouths, *Daemonolatria* II.iii, affirms, "it is the way of evildoers in our time too to do this, especially if the body of someone who has been executed is made an example and raised on a cross. For not only from the corpse do they procure material for their soothsaying, but also from the very instruments of execution, the rope, the stake, the irons, since in the common opinion there is in these things a certain force and efficacy for magical incantations." And to this place I dare not, out of religion to the divine Lucan, but bring his verses from the same book [VI.543–49]: "She breaks with her teeth the fatal noose, and mangles the carcass that dangles on the gallows, and scrapes the cross of the criminal; she tears away the rain-beaten flesh and the bones calcined by exposure to the sun. She purloins the nails that pierced the hands, the clotted filth, and the black humor of corruption that oozes over all the limbs; and when a muscle resists the teeth, she hangs her weight upon it."

170 8TH HAG These are Canidia's furniture in Horace, *Epodes* V.[19–20]: "eggs smeared with the blood of the ugly frog, and the feather of the nocturnal screech-owl." And part of Medea's confection in Ovid, *Metamorphoses* VII.[269]: "the wings of the uncanny screech-owl with the flesh as well." That of the skin (to make a purse for her fly) was meant ridiculous, to mock the keeping of their familiars.

174 9TH HAG *Hemlock, henbane, serpent-tongue, nightshade, martagon* [Jonson's "moonwort"], *doronicum* [Jonson's "libbard's bane"], *wolf's bane* are the common venefical ingredients, remembered by Paracelsus, Porta,

16. In fact, Psellus does not discuss the subject. The error is Remy's; Jonson took both this and the Porphyry and Apuleius references from *Daemonolatria* II.iii.

Agrippa and others; which I make her to have gathered, as about a castle, church, or some such vast building, kept by dogs, among ruins and wild heaps.

178 10TH HAG "Bones snatched from the mouth of a hungry dog" Horace gives Canidia in the place before quoted [*Epodes* V.23]. Which "hungry" I rather change to "gardener's" as imagining such persons to keep mastiffs for the defence of their grounds whither this hag might go also for simples; where meeting with the bones, and not content with them, she would yet do a domestic hurt in getting the cat's brain, which is another special ingredient, and of so much more efficacy by how much blacker the cat is, if you will credit Agrippa, the chapter on fumigations [*De Occulta Philosophia* I.xiv].[17]

182 11TH HAG These also, both by the confessions of witches and testimony of writers, are of principal use in their witchcraft. The toad mentioned in Virgil, *Georgics* I.[184], "and the toad [*bufo*] found in holes." Which by Pliny is called *rubeta*, *Natural History* XXXII.[xviii.48–52], and there celebrated for the force in magic. Juvenal toucheth at it twice within my memory, *Satires* I.[70], and VI.[659]. And of the owl's eyes, see Cornelius Agrippa, *De Occulta Philosophia* I.xv. As of the bat's blood and wings, there, and in chapter xxv; with Baptista Porta, [*Magia Naturalis*] II.xxvi.[18]

186 DAME After all their boasted labors and plenty of materials (as they imagine), I make the Dame not only to add more, but stranger, and out of their means to get (except the first, *horned poppy*, which I have touched at in the confection), as "fig trees dug from burial places, and funereal cypresses," as Horace calls them, where he arms Canidia, *Epodes* V.[17–18]; then "white fungus from the larch tree," of which see Porta, *Magia Naturalis* II, against Pliny [untraced, but the Pliny references are *Natural History* XXV.103, and XXVI *passim*]; and "basilisks [a kind of lizard], which poisoners call the blood of Saturn, and they report that it has such strength," Cornelius Agrippa, *De*

---

17. The chapter does mention black cats and use of cats' brains, but gives no authority for Jonson's point.
18. Only in the early editions; in the section headed "*Lamiarum Unguenta*."

Occulta Philosophia I.xlii; with the viper, remembered by Lucan, [*Pharsalia*] VI.[677–79], and the skins of serpents: "And the viper that is born by the Red Sea and guards the precious pearl shell, or the skin which the horned snake of Libya casts off while living." And Ovid, [*Metamorphoses*] VII.[271–72]: "There also in the pot is the scaly skin of a slender Cinyphian water-snake."

203 FIENDS These invocations are solemn with them, whereof we may see the forms in Ovid, *Metamorphoses* VII.[239–50]; in Seneca's tragedy *Medea*, [740ff.]; in Lucan, [*Pharsalia*] VI.[695ff.], which of all is the boldest and most horrid, beginning "I invoke the furies, the horror of hell, the punishments of the guilty, and Chaos, eager to blend countless worlds in ruins," etc.

205 KNOTS The untying of their knots is when they are going to some fatal business, as Sagana is presented by Horace, [*Epodes* V.25–6], "Lightly clad, sprinkling through all the house water from Lake Avernus, she bristles with streaming hair, like some sea-urchin or a racing boar."

222 THREE-FORMED Hecate, who is called *trivia* and *triformis*, of whom Virgil, *Aeneid* IV.[511]: "threefold Hecate, the three faces of the virgin Diana." She was believed to govern in witchcraft, and is remembered in all their invocations. See Theocritus in *Pharmaceutria* [*Idylls* II.14]: "Hail, frightful Hecate," and Medea in Seneca [*Medea*, 750–51]: "Now, summoned by my sacred rites, do you, orb of the night, put on the most evil face and come, threatening in all your forms." And Erictho in Lucan, [*Pharsalia* VI.700ff.]: "[I cry] to Persephone, and to her, the third incarnation of our patron Hecate," etc.

230 BURY This rite of burying their materials is often confessed in Remy, and described amply in Horace, *Satires* I.viii.[42–3], "how the two stealthily buried in the ground a wolf's beard and the tooth of a spotted snake."

231 FOOT The ceremony also of baring their feet is expressed by Ovid, *Metamorphoses* VII.[182–83], as of their hair: "Medea went forth from her house clad in flowing robes, barefoot, her hair unadorned and streaming down her shoulders." And Horace, [*Satires* I.viii.24], "with bare feet and dishevelled hair." And Seneca, in the tragedy

Medea, [752–53]: "For you, loosing my hair from its bands after the manner of my people, with bare feet have I trod the secret groves."

234 DEEP Here they speak as if they were creating some new feature, which the devil persuades them to be able to do often by the pronouncing of words and pouring out of liquors on the earth. Hear what Agrippa says, *De Occulta Philosophia* IV, near the end [*Opera* ("Lyons," n.d.) I.453 (Ff3r)]: "In the evocation of ghosts we perform fumigations with fresh blood, with the bones of dead men, with the flesh of a sheep, milk, honey, oil, and similar things, which they say are a fit medium for souls for the raising of their bodies." And a little before, "for souls are summoned easily by media akin to those by which they were joined to their bodies, by similar vapors, liquids and fumes." Which doctrine he had from Apuleius, without all doubt or question, who in *The Golden Ass* III.[18] publisheth the same: "Then she said certain charms over entrails still warm and breathing, and dipped them in divers waters, as in well water, cow's milk, mountain honey and mead; which when she had done, she tied and lapped up the hair together, and with many perfumes and smells threw it into a hot fire to burn. Then by the strong force of this sorcery and the invisible violence of the gods so compelled, those bodies, whose hair was burning in the fire, received human breath, and felt, heard and walked, and, smelling the scent of their own hair, came." All which are mere arts of Satan, when either himself will delude them with a false form, or, troubling a dead body, make them imagine these vanities the means; as in the ridiculous circumstances that follow, he doth daily.

249 CAST This throwing up of ashes and sand, with the flintstone, cross-sticks and burying of sage, etc., are all used and believed by them to the raising of storm and tempest. See Remy, *Daemonolatria* I.xxv; [Johann] Nider, *Formicarius . . . de Maleficis* [in *Malleorum Quorundam Maleficarum*, part I, Frankfurt, 1582], chapter iv; Bodin, *Demonomanie* II.viii. And hear Godelmann, [*De Magis, Veneficis, et Lamiis*] II.vi[21]: "For when God gave the devil the power to stir up hail storms, then he taught witches sometimes to cast flintstones over their shoulders toward the west, sometimes to throw sand on the vapor of boiling water, often to dip twigs in water and throw it toward the sky; or,

having made a trench and filled it with urine or water, to move their fingers in it; now and then to boil pigs' bristles in a pot; often to place beams or pieces of wood cross-wise on a river bank; and to do other such nonsensical deeds." And when they see the success, they are more confirmed, as if the event followed their working. The like illusion is of their fantasy, in sailing in egg shells, creeping through augur holes, and such like, so vulgar in their confessions.

268 STAY This stop, or interruption, showed the better by causing that general silence which made all the following noises enforced in the next charm more direful. First imitating that of Lucan [*Pharsalia* VI.725–27]: "Erictho marvelled that fate had power to linger thus. Enraged with death, she lashed the motionless corpse with a live serpent." And then their barking, howling, hissing and confusion of noise, expressed by the same author in the same person [685–93]: "And lastly her voice, more powerful than any drug to bewitch the powers of Lethe, first uttered indistinct sounds, sounds untunable and far different from human speech. The dog's bark and the wolf's howl were in that voice; it resembled the complaint of the restless owl and the night-flying screech-owl, the shrieking and roaring of wild beasts, the serpent's hiss, the beat of waves dashing against rocks, the sound of forests, and the thunder that issues from a rift in the cloud: in that one voice all these things were heard." See Remy too, *Daemonolatria* I.xix.

285 I'LL . . . LIGHT This is one of their common menaces, when their magic receives the least stop. Hear Erictho again [*Pharsalia* VI.742–44]: "And on you, worst of the world's rulers, I shall launch the sun's light, bursting open your den, and the sudden light shall blast you." And a little before, to Proserpina [739–40]: "I shall tell the world the nature of that food which confines you, Proserpina, beneath the huge weight of earth," etc.

289 THAT . . . LEAF That withered straight, as it shot out, which is called "the funereal branch" by some, and "gloomy" by Seneca, *Medea* [804].

290 ACONITE A deadly poisonous herb, feigned by Ovid, *Metamorphoses* VII.[406–19], to spring out of Cerberus his foam. Pliny gives it another beginning of name, *Natural History* XXVII.ii.[10]: "The plant grows on bare crags which are called *aconal*, and for that reason some have given it the name of aconite, there being nothing near, not even dust, to give it nourishment." Howsoever, the juice of it is like that liquor which the devil gives witches to sprinkle abroad and do hurt, in the opinion of all the magic-masters.

292 RUSTY KNIFE A rusty knife I rather give her than any other as fittest for such a devilish ceremony, which Seneca might mean by "sacrificial knife" in the tragedy, where he arms Medea to the like rite (for anything I know) [*Medea* 805–07]: "For you, with breast bared like a maenad, I shall strike my arms with the sacrificial knife; let my blood flow upon the altars."

302 HOO These shouts and clamors, as also the voice "Har, har," are very particular with them, by the testimony of Bodin, Remy, del Rio and Master Philip Ludwig Elich, who, out of them, reports it thus [*Daemonomagia*, question x (pp. 136–37)]: "The whole throng of most wicked rabble sings the most abominable fescennine verses in honor of devils. One sings 'Har, har'; another, 'Devil, devil, dance hither, dance thither'; a third, 'Come frolic here, come frolic there'; still another, 'Sabaath, sabaath,' etc. Nay, rather they rage and rave with shouts, hissing, shrieking and whistling, having received the powders or poisons which they scatter upon men and beasts."

323 MUSIC Nor do they want music, and in strange manner given them by the devil, if we credit their confessions in Remy, *Daemonolatria* I.xix, such as the Syrbenaean choirs were, which Athenaeus remembers out of Clearchus, *Deipnosophists* XV.[697F], where everyone sung what he would without hearkening to his fellow, like the noise of divers oars falling in the water. But be patient of Remy's relation: "They are mixed up and disordered there in marvelous ways, nor can it be sufficiently expressed in any words how they make confused, harsh and discordant noises. Here the devil sings to the flute, or, more exactly, to a pike or a kind of stick which he has found perchance on

the ground and brings to his cheek like a flute. He strikes instead of a lyre the skull of a horse, and rattles it with his fingers. Another beats an oak tree with a staff or a heavier club, whence there is heard a sound or roaring as of drums vigorously struck. The devils sing in between in a disgusting way, with a noise like a trumpet's, and they strike heaven itself with their dull, roaring sound."

328 DANCE The manner also of their dancing is confessed in Bodin, [*Demonomanie*] II.iv, and Remy, [*Daemonolatria*] I.xvii and xviii. The sum of which Master Philip Ludwig Elich relates thus in his *Daemonomagia*, question x [p. 135]: "They participate in the dances sometimes with open and uncovered face, sometimes covered with a mask or linen, bark, a net, a robe or other covering, or enveloped in the chaff of grain." And, a little after: "Everything is done in the most incongruous way and the most alien to the ways of men: they go leaping around, alternately back to back, and with hands joined in a circle, shaking their heads like those who are driven by frenzy." Remy adds [I.xvii], out of the confession of Sybilla Morelia, "The circle proceeds to the left." Which Pliny observes in the priests of Cybele, *Natural History* XXVIII.ii [incorrect, but see XXVIII.v.25; Jonson has confused two references from Remy I.xvii], and to be done with great religion. Bodin adds that they use brooms in their hands [untraced], with which we armed our witches. And so leave them.

346 I . . . WINGS The ancients expressed a brave and masculine virtue in three figures, of Hercules, Perseus and Bellerophon, of which I chose that of Perseus, armed, as I have him described out of Hesiod, *The Shield of Hercules* [221ff.]. See Apollodorus the Grammarian of him, [*The Library*] II.[iv.2].

449 . . . as also of the persons they presented; which, though they were disposed rather by chance than election, yet it is my part to justify them all virtuous; and then the lady that will own her presentation, may.

To follow, therefore, the rule of chronology which we have observed in our verse, the most upward in time was Penthesilea. She was queen of the Amazons, and succeeded Otrera, or (as some will) Orythyia.

She lived and was present at the war of Troy, on their part against the Greeks, where, as Justin (*Epitome of Pompeius Trogus*' [*Historiae Philippicae*] II.[iv.31]) gives her testimony, "among the bravest men great proofs of her valor were conspicuous." She is nowhere mentioned but with the preface of honor and virtue, and is always advanced in the head of the worthiest women. Diodorus Siculus (*Library of History* II. [45.2]) makes her the daughter of Mars. She was honored in her death to have it the act of Achilles. Of which Propertius (*Elegies* III.xi.[12–16]) sings this triumph to her beauty: "to her whose bright beauty conquered the conquering hero, when the golden helmet left her brow bare."

Next follows Camilla, queen of the Volscians, celebrated by Virgil, about the end of the seventh book (*Aeneid* VII.[803ff.]), than whose verses nothing can be imagined more exquisite, or more honoring the person they describe. They are these, where he reckons up those that came on Turnus' part against Aeneas: "Besides these came Camilla of the Volscians, leading a squadron of horse, and troops gorgeously arrayed in brass; a virgin warrior. She had not accustomed her woman's hands to the distaff or the work baskets of Minerva; but, though a maiden, was inured to bear the hardships of war, and in swiftness of foot to outstrip the winds. She could lightly have skimmed over the topmost stalks of standing corn, never once hurting the tender ears in her passage; or upon the sea, suspended on the surging billows, could glide, never dipping her nimble feet in the liquid plain." And afterward, tells her attire and arms, with the admiration that the spectators had of her. All which if the poet created out of himself, without Nature, he did but show how much so divine a soul could exceed her.

The third lived in the age of Cyrus, the great Persian monarch, and made him leave to live: Thomyris, queen of the Scythians, or Massagets, a heroine of a most invincible and unbroken fortitude. Who, when Cyrus had invaded her, and, taking her only son (rather by treachery than war, as she objected), had slain him, not touched with the grief of so great a loss, in the juster comfort she took of a greater revenge, pursued not only the occasion and honor of conquering so potent an enemy, with whom fell two hundred thousand soldiers, but (what was right memorable in her victory) left not a messenger surviving of his side to report the massacre. She is remembered both by Herodotus (in Clio [I.211–14]), and Justin (*Epitome* [I.viii]), to the great renown and glory of her kind, with this elogy: "Because she met the Persian monarch who was mightiest in war, and despoiled him both of his life and of his camp, so that she might duly avenge the most treacherous murder of her son."

The fourth was honored to life in the time of Xerxes, and present at his great expedition into Greece, Artemisia, the queen of Caria, whose virtue Herodotus (in Polymnia [VII.99]), not without some wonder records. That a woman, a queen, without a husband, her son a ward, and she administering the government, occasioned by no necessity, but a mere excellence of spirit, should embark herself for such a war, and there so to behave her as Xerxes, beholding her fight, should say, "Indeed men have shown themselves to me women, yet women have shown themselves men" (Herodotus in Urania [VIII.88]). She is no less renowned for her chastity and love to her husband Mausolus (Valerius Maximus, [*Factorum ac Dictorum Memorabilium*] IV.vi.[5.2], and Aulus Gellius, [*Attic Nights*] X.xviii), whose bones, after he was dead, she preserved in ashes and drunk in wine, making herself his tomb; and yet built to his memory a monument deserving a place among the seven wonders of the world, which could not be done by less than a wonder of women.[19]

The fifth was the fair-haired daughter of Ptolomaeus Philadelphus, by the elder Arsinoë, who (married to her brother Ptolomaeus, surnamed Euergetes) was after queen of Egypt. I find her written both Beronice and Berenice. This lady, upon an expedition of her new-wedded lord into Assyria, vowed to Venus, if he returned safe, and conqueror, the offering of her hair; which vow of hers, exacted by the success, she afterward performed. But her father missing it, and therewith displeased, Conon, a mathematician who was then in household with Ptolemy and knew well to flatter him, persuaded the king that it was ta'en up to heaven and made a constellation, showing him those seven stars *near the tail of Leo*, which are since called *Coma Berenices* [Berenice's hair]. Which story, then presently celebrated by Calli-

19. Jonson has confused two Artemisias. See Herford and Simpson, X.506, line 540n.

machus in a most elegant poem, Catullus more elegantly converted, wherein they call her "the magnanimous, even from [the time she was] a virgin," alluding, as Hyginus (*Astronomy* II, on Leo [xxiv]) saith, to a rescue she made of her father in his flight, and restoring the courage and honor of his army even to a victory. Their words are, "I knew you to be magnanimous even from young girlhood" (Catullus, *On the Lock of Berenice* [lxvi.26]).

The sixth, that famous wife of Mithridates, and queen of Pontus, Hypsicratea, no less an example of virtue than the rest; who so loved her husband as she was assistant to him in all labors and hazards of the war, in a masculine habit. For which causes, as Valerius Maximus ([*Factorum . . . Memorabilium*] IV.vi.[5.3], on conjugal love) observes, she departed with a chief ornament of her beauty: "For she cut her hair and accustomed herself to horses and arms, that she might the more easily share his toils and perils." And afterward, in his flight from Pompey, accompanied his misfortune with a mind and body equally unwearied. She is solemnly registered by that grave author as a notable president of marriage loyalty and love, virtues that might raise a mean person to equality with a queen, but a queen to the state and honor of a deity.

The seventh, that renown of Ethiopia, Candace, from whose excellency the succeeding queens of that nation were ambitious to be called so. A woman of a most haughty spirit against enemies, and a singular affection to her subjects. I find her celebrated by Dion ([i.e. Dio Cassius] *History of Rome* LIV.[v.4–6]) and Pliny (*Natural History* VI.xxxv.[186]), invading Egypt in the time of Augustus; who, though she were enforced to a peace by his lieutenant Petronius, doth not the less worthily hold her place here, when everywhere this elogy remains of her fame: that she was "a woman of the greatest spirit, and of such kindness to her people that all the later queens of the Ethiopians were called by her name."[20] She governed in Meroë.

The eighth, our own honor, Voadicea, or Boodicea; by some, Bunduica, and Bunduca; queen of the Iceni, a people that inhabited that part of our island which was called East Anglia, and compre-

20. The quotation is from C. Estienne (or Stephanus), *Dictionarium Historicum . . .* (Geneva, 1603, etc.), under *Candace.*

hended Suffolk, Norfolk, Cambridge and Huntingdon shires. Since she was born here at home, we will first honor her with a home-born testimony, from the grave and diligent Spenser (*Ruins of Time* [106–11]):

> Bunduca Britoness, . . .
> Bunduca, that victorious conqueress,
> That, lifting up her brave, heroic thought
> 'Bove women's weakness, with the Romans fought;
> Fought, and in field against them thrice prevailed, etc.

To which, see her orations in story made by Tacitus (*Annals* XIV.[xxxi, xxxv–xxxvii]), and Dion ([*Dionis*] *Epitome* [i.e. of Dio Cassius lxii.2–12], [by] Joannes Xiphilinus, on Nero), wherein is expressed all magnitude of a spirit breathing to the liberty and redemption of her country. The later of whom doth honest her beside with a particular description: "Bunduica, a British woman born of royal blood, who not only governed them with great dignity, but also managed the whole war, and whose mind was a man's rather than a woman's." And afterwards, "a woman of most chaste beauty, stern of face," etc. All which doth weigh the more to her true praise in coming from the mouths of Romans and enemies. She lived in the time of Nero.

The ninth in time, but equal in fame and (the cause of it) virtue, was the chaste Zenobia, queen of the Palmyrenes, who after the death of her husband, Odaenathus, had the name to be reckoned among the thirty that usurped the Roman empire from Gallienus. She continued a long and brave war against several chiefs, and was at length triumphed on by Aurelian, but "in such a way that no more splendid display was ever seen by the Roman people." Her chastity was such "that she did not even know her husband, except for the sake of conception." [Trebellius Pollio, *Triginta Tyranni* XXX.] She lived in a most royal manner, and was adored to the custom of the Persians. When she made orations to her soldiers, she had always her casque on. A woman of a most divine spirit, and incredible beauty. In Trebellius Pollio (in *Triginta Tyranni*), read the most noble description of a queen, and her, that can be uttered with the dignity of an historian.

The tenth succeeding was that learned and heroic Amalasunta, queen of the Ostrogoths, daughter to Theodoric, that obtained the principality of Ravenna, and almost all Italy. She drave the Burgundians and Almains out of Liguria, and appeared in her government rather an example than a second. She was the most eloquent of her age, and cunning in all languages of any nation that had commerce with the Roman Empire. (Marco Antonio Coccio Sabellico, out of Cassiodorus [*Rhapsodiae Historiarum ab Orbe Condito*], Enneadis viii.2.) It is recorded of her that "no one saw her without respecting her; to hear her speaking was a marvelous thing. There was in her such severity in judging that those who were convicted of a charge considered that they were suffering nothing harsh if they were merely beaten."

The eleventh was that brave Bohemian queen Valasca, who for her courage had the surname of Bold. That to redeem herself and her sex from the tyranny of men which they lived in under Primislaus, on a night and an hour appointed led on the women to the slaughter of their barbarous husbands and lords; and possessing themselves of their horses, arms, treasure and places of strength, not only ruled the rest, but lived many years after with the liberty and fortitude of Amazons. Celebrated by Raphael Volterranus [i.e. Raphael Maffei of Volterra] (in *Geographia* VII [in *Commentarii Urbani*]), and in an elegant tract of an Italian's (*Forcianae Quaestiones* [Naples, 1536]) in Latin, who names himself *Philalethes, Polytopiensis Civis* ["truth-lover, citizen of many places"; pseudonym of Ortensio Landi], among the most distinguished women.

The twelfth, and worthy sovereign of all, I make Bel-Anna, royal queen of the Ocean, of whose dignity and person the whole scope of the invention doth speak throughout; which to offer you again here might but prove offense to that sacred modesty, which hears any testimony of others iterated with more delight than her own praise. She being placed above the need of such ceremony, and safe in her princely virtue against the good or ill of any witness. The name of Bel-Anna I devised to honor hers proper by, as adding to it, the attribute of *fair*, and is kept by me in all my poems wherein I mention her majesty with any shadow or figure. Of which some may come forth with a longer destiny than this age commonly gives the best births, if but helped to the light by her gracious and ripening favor.

But here I discern a possible objection arising against me, to which I must turn, as, how can I bring persons of so different ages to appear properly together? Or why (which is more unnatural) with Virgil's Mezentius, I join the living with the dead? [*Aeneid* VIII.485–88.] I answer to both these at once, nothing is more proper, nothing more natural; for these all live, and together, in their fame, and so I present them. Besides, if I would fly to the all-daring power of poetry, where could I not take sanctuary? Or in whose poem? For other objections, let the looks and noses of judges hover thick, so they bring the brains, or if they do not, I care not. When I suffered it to go abroad, I departed with my right; and now so secure an interpreter I am of my chance that neither praise nor dispraise shall affect me.

There rests only that we give the description we promised of the scene . . .

OBERON

5 CHROMIS, MNASIL They are the names of two young satyrs I find in Virgil, *Eclogues* VI.[13], that took Silenus sleeping, who is feigned to be the pedagogue of Bacchus, as the satyrs are his collusores, or play-fellows. So doth Diodorus Siculus [IV.4.3, 5.3], Synesius [*Calvitii Encomium* 68], Julian [the Apostate] in *The Caesars* [308C–D] report them.

7 YOU . . . LATE A proverbial speech, when they will tax one the other of drinking or sleepiness; alluding to that former place in Virgil: "The lads Chromis and Mnasyllus saw Silenus lying asleep in a cave, his veins swollen as ever with yesterday's wine." [*Eclogues* VI.13–15.]

15 TANKARD Silenus is everywhere made a lover of wine, as in *The Cyclops* of Euripides [139ff.], and known by that notable ensign, his tankard; out of the same place of Virgil, "And his heavy tankard was hanging by its well-worn handle" [17]. As also out of that famous piece of sculpture in a little gem or piece of jasper observed by Monsieur [Isaac] Casaubon in his tract *De Satyrica* [*Graecorum*] *Poesi* . . . [Paris, 1605, pp. 67–8], from Rascasius Bagarrius; wherein is described the whole manner of the scene and *chori* of Bacchus, with Silenus and the satyrs.

An elegant and curious antiquity, both for the subtlety and labor, where in so small a compass (to use his words), there is "a quite astonishing variety of things, persons and action."[21]

33 SILENUS In the pomps of Dionysus or Bacchus, to every company of satyrs there was still given a silene for their overseer or governor. And in that which is described by Athenaeus in his fifth book, "a pair of silenes is often mentioned who are in charge of a like number of groups of several satyrs. They were their overseers, superintendents and chiefs, on account of their great age." He was also "dressed in a purple cloak, with white shoes, wearing a traveller's hat, and carrying a small gold messenger's staff." See Athenaeus, *Deipnosophists* V.[197E 198A], on the splendor of the Ptolemies.

36 IF . . . TWO The nature of the satyrs the wise Horace expressed well in the word when he called them "laughers and mockers" [*Ars Poetica* 225], as the Greek poets Nonnus [*Dionysiaca* xxxvii.415–17], etc. style them "fond of jeering." *They were conceived and thought of as not only sarcastic but also as prone to love and as incessant dancers. Whence "satiric" dancing, which was called* sikinnis, *and from which the satyrs themselves were called* sikinnists; *or from Sicinus, its inventor; or from the movement, that is, from the satyrs' motion of jumping, which is very violent.*

37 CHASTER LANGUAGE But in the silenes was nothing of this petulance and lightness, but on the contrary, all gravity and profound knowledge of most secret mysteries. Insomuch as the most learned of poets, Virgil, when he would write a poem of the beginnings and hidden nature of things, with other great antiquities, attributed the parts of disputing them to Silenus, rather than any other. [*Eclogues* vi.31–40.] Which whosoever thinks to be easily or by chance done by the most prudent writer, will easily betray his own ignorance or folly. To this see the testimonies of Plato [*Symposium* 215A–C], Synesius [*Epistolae* 154], Herodotus [*History* VII.26, VIII.138], Strabo [*Geography* X.iii.7], Philostratus [*Imagines* I.20], Tertullian [*Adversus Hermogenem* xxvi, *De Pallio* ii], etc.

21. The gem is reproduced in Herford and Simpson, X.526.

48 HE'S . . . RACE Among the ancients, the kind both of the centaurs and satyrs is confounded and common with either. As sometimes the satyrs are said to come of the centaurs, and again the centaurs of them. Either of them are *of double form*, but after a diverse manner. And Galen observes out of *In Hippocratis Epidemiarum* III.[14.38], that both the Athenians and Ionians called the satyrs *féras* or *feréas*, which name the centaurs have with Homer, from whence it were no unlikely conjecture to think our word fairies to come. *Let the critics consider it.*

49 GOD . . . TONGUE Mercury, who for the love of Penelope, while she was keeping her father Icarius' herds on the mountain Taygetus, turned himself into a fair buck-goat, with whose sports and flatteries the nymph being taken, he begat on her Pan, who was born *with horned head and beard, and with goat-like hooves.* As Homer hath it in the *Hymns* [xix.35–6], and Lucian, *The Dialogue of Pan and Mercury* [Jonson's error for *The Double Indictment* ix]. He was called the giver of grace, *bright and white. Cheerful and white,* "the Cyllenian one glistening with his wings." [Virgil, *Aeneid* IV.252.] As Bacchus was called *blooming,* and *Hebe, from her downy and tender age, always flourishing.*

51 WHEN . . . SUNG Apollo is said, after Jupiter had put Saturn to flight, to have sung his father's victory to the harp, *handsome in a purple toga and crowned with laurel, and marvelously to have delighted all the gods who reclined at the banquet.* Which Tibullus in *Elegies* II.[v.7ff.], points to: "Come bright and beautiful, now put on your bright garment, now comb well your long hair; be as men say you were when, after Saturn had been driven from his throne, you sang a paean for victorious Jove."

52 WHEN . . . RUNG He was then lovely, as being not yet stained with blood, and called *chrysopélex Ares* [Ares with a golden helmet], *as having a golden whip, or more properly, a helmet of gold.*

58 GRANDSIRE In Julius Pollux, [*Onomasticon*] V.xix, in that part which he entitles "On Satyric Persons," we read that Silenus is called *páppos,* that is, *grandfather,* to note his great age; as amongst the comic persons, the reverenced for their years were called *páppoi*; and with Julian [the

Apostate] in *The Caesars* [309D], Bacchus, when he speaks him fair, calls him "little grandfather."²²

59 LYAEUS A name of Bacchus, Lyaeus, of freeing men's minds from cares; *from lýo, to loosen, set free.*

91 TABOR *It was the ritual for Bacchus to be carried in a procession of young boys by Silenus and satyrs, with bacchants going before, one of whom was a drummer, one a flute player, etc.* See Athenaeus [*Deipnosophists* V.200D].

162 CYCLOPS *See Euripides'* Cyclops [661ff.], *where the satyrs help Ulysses to burn out the Cyclops' eye.*

NEPTUNE'S TRIUMPH FOR THE RETURN OF ALBION

3 NEP. RED. In the moneys of Vespasian and Hadrian we find this put for *Neptuno Reduci* [to Neptune the guide home], under *Games in Honor of Neptune, Six Holidays Consecrated to Neptune.* SEC. IOV. That is, *Secundo Iovi* for so Neptune is called by Statius in *Achilleis* I.[48–9], "the second Jupiter": "and as for the rest, clinging to the right hand of the second Jupiter ...," as Pluto is called the third Jupiter.

25–26 EITHER'S ... MIND *See Athenaeus,* Deipnosophists I.[7Fff.], *from the comic poet Euphron.*

50 ORACLE ... BOTTLE *See Rabelais* [Pantagruel] V.[xxxiv, xlvi].

94 MANAGER ... HORSE A power of Neptune's by which he is called Hippius [equine] or Damaeus [the tamer], and conferred on a person of special honor, in the allegory, as by office; *vide infra.*

131 DELOS *See Lucian in* The Dialogue of Iris and Neptune [*Dialogues of the Sea Gods* X].

144 SUN *See Strabo,* Geography XV.[21].

231 SHEPHERD ... SEAS *Proteus, the shepherd of the sea.*

232 PORTS ... KEYS *Portunus, who rules over harbors.*

Appendix: Neptune's Triumph (pages 269–270)

250 SARON The god of navigation with Strabo [untraced], [Aelius] Aristides the Rhetor [Oration xlvi, 208 (ed. Dindorff, II, p. 274)], and Pausanias [II.xxx.7], where the proverb grew frequent with the Greeks, "*more nautical than Saron.*"

267 SILVER-FOOTED An epithet frequent in Homer and others, given by them to Thetis, Panope, Doris, etc. "*Silver-footed Thetis.*"

274 HALICLYON *Mari inclytus* (renowned at sea). Another of Neptune's attributes, and given to the same person with Hippius.

A Select Bibliography

I. Texts

Ben Jonson, ed. C. H. Herford, Percy and Evelyn Simpson, 11 vols. (Oxford, 1925–52.) The standard modern edition. Volume II contains the Introduction to the masques, Volume VII the texts, and Volume X the notes.

II. General critical works

a. On the Jonson masques

Barish, Jonas A., *Ben Jonson and the Language of Prose Comedy* (Cambridge, Mass., 1960), especially Chapter VI.

Cunningham, Dolora, "The Jonsonian Masque as a Literary Form," *ELH*, XXII (1955), 108–24.

Furniss, W. Todd, "Ben Jonson's Masques," in *Three Studies in the Renaissance* (New Haven, 1958), pp. 89–179.

Greg, W. W., "Jonson's Masques; Points of Editorial Principle and Practice," *Review of English Studies*, XVIII (1942), 144–66. Review of Herford and Simpson's *Jonson*, Volume VII.

Meagher, John C., *Method and Meaning in Jonson's Masques* (Notre Dame, Ind., 1966).

Orgel, Stephen, *The Jonsonian Masque* (Cambridge, Mass., 1965).

Talbert, Ernest William, "The Interpretation of Jonson's Courtly Spectacles," *PMLA*, LXI (1946), 454–73.

Bibliography

b. On background, history, and production

Chambers, E. K., *The Elizabethan Stage* (Oxford, 1923), especially Volume I, Chapters V and VI.

———, *The Medieval Stage* (Oxford, 1903), especially Volume I, Chapter XVII.

Cutts, John P., "Le Rôle de la Musique dans les Masques de Ben Jonson," in *Les Fêtes de la Renaissance*, ed. Jean Jacquot (Paris, 1956), pp. 285–303.

Evans, H. A., *English Masques* (London, 1897). Excellent Introduction.

Evans, Willa McClung, *Ben Jonson and Elizabethan Music* (Lancaster, Pa., 1929), especially Chapter III.

Gilbert, Allan H., *The Symbolic Persons in the Masques of Ben Jonson* (Durham, N.C., 1948).

Gordon, D. J., "Poet and Architect: The Intellectual Setting of the Quarrel Between Ben Jonson and Inigo Jones," *Journal of the Warburg and Courtauld Institutes*, XII (1949), 152–78.

Nicoll, Allardyce, *Stuart Masques and the Renaissance Stage* (London, 1937).

Palme, Per, *The Triumph of Peace* (London, 1957). A study of Inigo Jones's Whitehall Banqueting House.

Reyher, Paul, *Les Masques Anglais* (Paris, 1909).

Sabol, Andrew J., *Songs and Dances for the Stuart Masque* (Providence, R.I., 1959).

Simpson, P., and Bell, C. F., *Designs by Inigo Jones for Masques and Plays at Court* (Oxford, 1924).

Strong, Roy, *Festival Designs by Inigo Jones* (Washington, 1967). Catalogue of the Chatsworth Exhibition; supplements and corrects Simpson and Bell.

Welsford, Enid, *The Court Masque* (Cambridge, Eng., 1927).

Wheeler, C. F., *Classical Mythology in the Plays, Masques and Poems of Ben Jonson* (Princeton, 1938).

III. Special studies of individual masques

Duncan, Edgar Hill, "The Alchemy in Jonson's *Mercury Vindicated*," *Studies in Philology*, XXXIX (1942), 625–37.

Gordon, D. J., "Ben Jonson's 'Haddington Masque': the Story and the Fable," *Modern Language Review*, XLII (1947), 180–87.

Gordon, D. J., "*Hymenaei:* Ben Jonson's Masque of Union," *Journal of the Warburg and Courtauld Institutes*, VIII (1945), 107–45.

————, "The Imagery of Ben Jonson's *The Masque of Blacknesse* and *The Masque of Beautie*," *Journal of the Warburg and Courtauld Institutes*, VI (1943), 122–41.

Greg, W. W., *Jonson's "Masque of Gipsies"* (London, 1952).

Talbert, Ernest William, "Current Scholarly Works and the 'Erudition' of Jonson's *Masque of Augurs*," *Studies in Philology*, XLIV (1947), 605–24.